CHIPS MOMAN

CHIPS MOMAN

The Record Producer

Whose Genius Changed

American Music

JAMES L. DICKERSON

SARTORIS
LITERARY
GROUP

SARTORIS LITERARY GROUP
Metro-Jackson, Mississippi
www.sartorisliterary.com

CONTENTS

Chapter 1: In the beginning (1937-1958) ... 9

Chapter 2: Launching Stax Records (1959-1962) ... 31

Chapter 3: Creating the American Sound (1963-1965) ... 62

Chapter 4: The Making of a Star (1966-1968) ... 86

Chapter 5: The Steve McQueen of American Music (1969-1972) ... 133

Chapter 6: Triumph in Nashville (1973-1984) ... 171

Chapter 7: Goin' Back to Memphis (1985) ... 234

Chapter 8: Dream Busted (1986-1987) ... 258

Chapter 9: Against the Wall (1988-1994)... 293

Chapter 10: The Final Years (1995-2016) ... 320

Acknowledgments . . . 333

Bibliography / Source Notes... 334

Endnotes ... 340

About the Author ... 345

Toni Wine Moman, left, author James L. Dickerson, Chips Moman
Photo by Dave Darnell, *The Commercial Appeal*

CHIPS MOMAN

"The Steve McQueen of American Music"

Lincoln "Chips" Moman
Photo © Phillip Rauls

CHAPTER 1
In the Beginning . . .

THREE-YEAR-OLD LINCOLN WAYNE MOMAN was ambling along a downtown LaGrange, Georgia, street with his mother, apprehensive about what awaited him around the corner, when he spied a brand new ukulele displayed in a store window. He stopped and pointed.at the enticing instrument. He stood solidly before the violet-tinted glass of the window, his feet planted decisively on the tobacco-stained sidewalk.

Because they were on their way to the dentist to have a tooth pulled, his mother promised he could have the ukulele if he would go to the dentist, allow the dentist to pull the tooth, and not cry about it. It was a tall order for a three year old with an infected tooth.

"Let's go get it right now," he countered, playing the odds as he saw them.

"No," she insisted, knowing full well that if she bought the instrument for him before they went to the dentist, he would act like any child would when his tooth was pulled. She wanted him to act like a little man and make her proud.

"All right then," he agreed.

"Well, let me tell you he got into that chair and had that tooth pulled and there wasn't a cry out of him," Mildred Moman later recalled to me.

He mumbled, gauze packed into his cheek, "Now, let's go get that guitar."

Growing up, Little Lincoln discovered at an early age that he had a talent for music.

"Music was born in him, I reckon," said his father, Abraham Lincoln Moman, a man with angular features and lanky arms common to farm folks in that area. "From the time he could sit up and bang on things, he could make a tune. I don't see how he does it myself. It is amazing to me. It was just born in him. I watch him do it today, but I can't grasp it."

That's not surprising. Abraham Lincoln, who went by the nickname of Dink, didn't have a lick of music in him. As a youth he had hoboed around the country in an effort to find himself. At one point, he thought he had what it took to be a professional baseball pitcher. For about a year he played with the Atlanta Crackers, a minor league baseball team that won more league championships than any other Southern Association team.[1] Because they were a racially segregated team, they made history when they played against Jackie Robinson and the Brooklyn Dodgers in a three-game exhibition series. It was the first time in American history that blacks and whites competed against each other in a professional sports event.

Little Lincoln didn't talk to his father much about his love of music. That was something he shared exclusively with his mother. "My mother played piano and all her sisters played piano, so there was always music in my house." For his part, Abraham Lincoln watched him with bemused interest from a distance the way you would watch an ant carrying something five times its size.

It was Mildred who soon replaced the ukulele with a Gene Autry guitar she purchased from Sears and Roebuck from a mail order catalog. By the early 1940s, when Chips received the guitar, Gene Autry was a star in both the movies and country music and enjoyed a number of hits, including, "You're the Only Star in My Blue Heaven" and "Tears on My Pillow." After World War II, his fame soared even higher with the release of "Here Comes Santa Claus," which quickly sold more than one million and a half records. He followed that up with another hit, "Rudolph the Red-Nosed Reindeer," which sold seven million records.

Slowly, Chips began to realize that there might be fame and money in the music he loved, but because Dink didn't like to hear any more music in the house than he had to, Little Lincoln took the radio into his bedroom at night and listened to it under the covers, with the volume turned real low so his parents would not hear anything that would offend them. Mostly

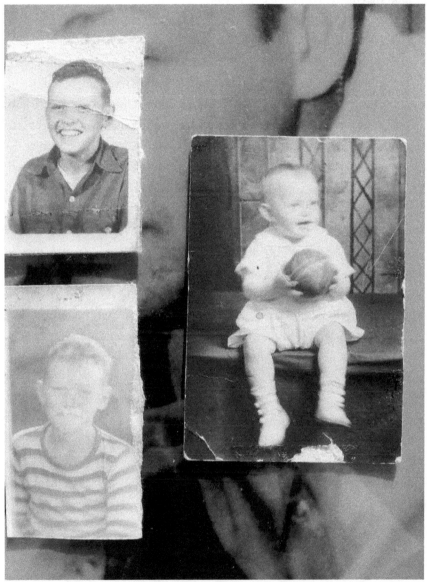

Lincoln "Chips" Moman growing up in LaGrange, Georgia
Photo courtesy Monique Moman

he listened to black gospel programs, of which there was no shortage, but he also was intrigued by the country music he heard on the radio. As Chips was coming of age, the biggest country music stars were Hank Williams and Tex Ritter.

By the end of the 1940s, Williams had assembled an incredible legacy of recordings such as "I'm So Lonesome I Could Cry" and "Cold, Cold Heart." It was music that had a profound impact on Chips. As he grew into maturity he would develop a melancholy approach to male-female relationships, as evidenced in songs he wrote such as the critically acclaimed R&B classic "The Dark End of the Street," recorded by soul singer James Carr, a song Jerry Wexler once described as "eternal," and the Grammy-winning country song "(Hey Won't You Play) Another Somebody Done Somebody Wrong Song."

Also influencing Chips at that time was Tex Ritter, another movie star who also was an important recording artist. His hits included "You Are My Sunshine" and "Have I Told You Lately That I Love You." A regular on the Grand Ole Opry, he had a pop hit in 1952 with a single titled "High Noon," which became the theme song for Gary Cooper's classic movie of the same name. Chips tipped his hat to the singer by naming his dog Tex.

Little Lincoln's sensibilities were indelibly shaped by a Depression Era view of America that held that loneliness, being on the losing end of life, and complicated male-female relationships that hardly ever worked out, were the building blocks of Southern manhood. From the music he listened to and the economic hardships he witnessed firsthand, he developed a deep strain of street smarts, a symbolic distinction made even more poignant by the fact that few of the streets he travelled were actually paved.

The way Little Lincoln later told it he was a pool hustler in his youth, a Huck Finn type of boy who was good at separating his friends from their meager allowances. When asked about his nickname of "Chips," he always said, ""Let's just say Mama didn't name me Chips." Contrary to popular belief later in life, which had it that he was given the nickname "Chips" because of his skill at poker, he actually was given the name "Chips" by his young contemporaries in LaGrange because of his skill with a pool cue, he once explained to me. He carried the name Chips into adulthood, using it to his advantage whenever he needed to call a bluff, either in cards or business. "When you're a kid, the name's all right," he explained to me. "But when you get older (voice trailing off) . . . There have been a million times I wished I didn't have it."

When Lincoln Wayne Moman let out his first cry on June 12, 1937, LaGrange, Georgia was just beginning to emerge from the economic horrors of the decade-long Great Depression. The city of 20,000 residents was half white, half black, and dominated by the strict social restrictions of Jim Crow segregation. When Chips was three, white townspeople lynched a sixteen-year-old black youth.[2] Jobs were in short supply, so men without farmland often lived on the farms where they worked, setting up housekeeping in tenant facilities so that their families would have a place to live. In those days, whether you owned the farm or not, it was a hardscrabble existence for almost everyone except the wealthy.

Not much better were the jobs offered by the numerous cotton textile mills located in LaGrange, a fixture in that community since 1840. Like the farms, the textile mills also provided housing for their workers. That is where Moman's parents worked when he was born. They were happy to have a place to sleep, but the housing was not much better than the internment camps that soon would be built to detain Japanese Americans during World War II. Working conditions at the mills were dangerous and intimidating. The mills were typically hot and noisy, and the lint that continually floated in the air often collected on the hair and skin of workers. Beginning in the 1940s an added threat was the risk of mesothelioma, the result of the mills weaving asbestos into textiles.

After the war, worn down by harsh working conditions for little pay, the Moman family moved to a farm not far from LaGrange. They would still work hard, from sunup to sundown, but at least they would breathe fresh air while doing so, not the polluted air in the mills.

Although Chips was clearly an extraordinarily bright boy, he discovered he had little use for school. Reading, writing and arithmetic seemed like a dead end investment of his time. The hard times experienced by his parents and their friends grated on his still growing sensibilities. Finally, in 1951, the fourteen year old could stand it no longer. Whether it was because of trouble at school or with the law—he never wanted to discuss his reasons—he packed a suitcase, walked out the door wearing farmer's overalls, and made his way to U.S. Highway 22, clutching a well-worn suitcase. Once there he stuck out his thumb and waited for life to snatch him up and carry him away to some exotic location, leaving behind everything he had ever known in life.

"We saw he was never going to be interested in anything much except music," Mildred told me in 1985. Nodding in agreement, Abraham Lincoln mysteriously added, "He had it hard growing up—but he's OK now."

Chips' exodus from LaGrange was a desperate attempt to explore the great unknown. He had never heard of the American Dream, but he was in hot pursuit nonetheless. Three hundred and sixty-nine miles later he arrived in Memphis, Tennessee, a teeming city of 646,000 people who were struggling to deal with the city's decade's old reputation as the "murder capital of America," as the insurance companies labelled the city. Killing was a way of life in the city. Since the turn of the century, it had not been unusual to read about horrific murders on a daily basis. Typical of the headlines was this racially charged one from the city's daily morning newspaper *The Commercial Appeal*: NEGRO DEMON BEATS THE HEAD OF HIS VICTIM INTO AN UNRECOGNIZABLE MASS.

CHIPS MOMAN WAS NOT the only young refuge who arrived in Memphis in the late 1940s and early 1950s. Three years earlier, B.B. King had made his way to Memphis from the Mississippi Delta, as had Elvis Presley, who had left Tupelo, Mississippi, with his mother and father to find a better life in the big city, after his father had served time at Parchman Farm for writing a bad check to purchase a hog to feed his family. Three years after Chips arrived, Johnny Cash settled in Memphis with his wife after being discharged from the U.S. Air Force. Soon Jerry Lee Lewis would move to Memphis from Nashville where it was suggested he switch from piano to guitar, advice he did not take. Carl Perkins and Roy Orbison would soon follow the yellow brick road to Memphis. What they all had in common was a yearning for something in life better than what they had.

Just as music experienced a talent explosion, so did business. Overachievers were a dime a dozen, beginning with Memphian Clarence Saunders who in 1913 founded the nation's first supermarket chain, Piggly Wiggly, a business that grew to 2,600 stores. The year Chips arrived in Memphis, Kemmons Wilson decided the nation needed a chain of moderately priced motels. By 1954 he had established Holiday Inns of America. During that time, a developer named Philip Belz, a Jewish immigrant from Austria-Hungary, bought property on Thomas Street that was formerly used as a harness-horse racetrack to develop into individual businesses, leading to the creation of Belz Enterprises which would acquire the luxury Peabody Hotel and become one of the largest commercial real estate developers in the South.[3] A couple of decades later, a Memphis man named Fred Smith, who had made his way from the Mississippi Delta to Memphis, would create the Federal Express Corporation and forever change the way we receive and send packages, becoming a billionaire in the process.

For half a century, blues had been the dominant music in Memphis, beginning with W. C. Handy's arrival in the city in 1905 by way of Clarksdale, Mississippi, from his hometown of Florence, Alabama. The son of slaves, Handy earned the distinction of becoming the "Father of the Blues," not because he invented the blues, but because he was the first person to merge black folk blues with European-style instrumentation, a distinction that might have evaded history, but for Handy's success in becoming the first person to musically notate the blues. His first copyrighted song was "The Memphis Blues," which spread like a viral epidemic. Very quickly the blues became all the rage in New York City and beyond.

The blues thrived on Memphis's Beale Street for decades, only slowing down in the early 1950s, about the time that Chips Moman, Elvis Presley and all the other refugees from the rural South began arriving in the city. The reason for the slowdown was due to the exodus of black performers to northern cities, where they could make a living by playing music that appealed to white audiences as well as black audiences. Among whites in Memphis at that time the blues was never considered a socially acceptable form of music. It was during this low ebb in the city's music history that Sam Phillips started making his first contributions to American music.

Like W.C. Handy, Sam Phillips was a native of Florence, Alabama. He moved to Memphis in 1945 to work at radio station WREC, which had a predominately white audience. However, it was the music of the city's black station, WDIA, that stirred his soul. WREC featured easygoing pop music and folksy announcers who told corny jokes. WDIA, the first radio station in America with black disk jockeys, exploded across the airwaves with the emotionally raw music of B.B. King, Sonny Boy Williamson 2 and Howlin' Wolf.

By 1950, Phillips was no longer satisfied limiting himself to being a music listener. He leased space in a building at 706 Union Avenue and opened Memphis's first recording studio. He called it Memphis Recording Service. As far as the white residents were concerned, the studio was a place where white people could have vanity recordings done for weddings, birthday greetings, and speeches of various kinds. If you had a song you wanted recorded he would do that, too, without any criticism of the artistic quality of the song. Then he would have the song pressed into vinyl, if you had the money to pay for it. Phillips was selling a vanity service.

What the white residents of Memphis did not know was that Phillips was living a secret life. After the sun went down, he explored the black

16

juke joints in and around Memphis, especially Arkansas and Mississippi, locating talent to bring into his studio. He was convinced he could make blues recordings that could be competitive with the big companies that recorded and distributed the blues to a nationwide audience. Among his discoveries were Walter Horton, Doctor Ross, Joe Hill Louis, Ike Turner, Willie Johnson, and his biggest discovery of all, a man who performed under the name Howlin' Wolf (his friends called him "Big Foot Chester" because of his enormous size and fierce, neck-bulging way of singing). Phillips sold some of his recordings of Howlin' Wolf to Modern/RPM and others to Chess Records. Eventually, Howlin' Wolf ended up betraying Phillips by secretly recording songs for Modern/RPM while Phillips was recording songs for Chess.

Frustrated with his dealings with the major record labels and his disappointing experiences with black blues performers, Phillips decided in 1952 to start his own record label. He named it Sun Records. The first release was "Drivin' Slow" by saxophonist Johnny London. The record failed to get traction, so Phillips closed down Sun Records until he could get a more commercially viable path to success.

After wandering about in a musical desert for an entire year, he discovered a black entertainer, Rufus Thomas, who worked as a disk jockey at WDIA. Thomas, who had a hyperactive personality and a distinctive voice that sounded as if it had been marinated and aged in a jar of gravel, was legendary in the black community. He had left Memphis in 1936, after high school graduation, to join Rabbit's Foot Company, a minstrel show that had been founded in 1900 by an African-American entrepreneur. It provided an important venue for black entertainers over the next sixty years, producing stars such as Ma Rainey, Bessie Smith Big Joe Williams, and Louis Jordan.

"It was truly an experience," Thomas told me. "We traveled the Tri-State area of West Tennessee, Arkansas and Mississippi with three different minstrel shows. They called them minstrel shows, but actually they were musicals. They had high-stepping dancers, comics, singers, they had it all. That was during the days of separation, where the whites sat on one side and blacks on the other side. Man, we had some of the greatest shows ever. Those shows brought out my stage presence. When I returned to Memphis I was already a step ahead of someone who was not a personality."

Because Thomas had something that blues musicians did not have—a media platform from which to sell records—Phillips offered him a recording contract. For their first song they chose a remake of Big Mama Thornton's R&B hit, "Hound Dog." They kept the melody, but wrote new words for it. The new recording was titled "Bear Cat." It proved to be a hit. Phillips followed up with two additional hits—"Just Walking in the Rain" by the Prisonaires and "Feeling Good" by Little Junior Parker.

Phillips's celebration over those hits was short lived. He was sued for copyright infringement of "Hound Dog." That experience soured him on finding new black entertainers and he started looking for white entertainers upon which to build a record label. In 1989, the author asked Rufus Thomas about Phillips' decision and was surprised to hear an undercurrent of bitterness in his voice. Said Thomas: "When I recorded with him his stable was all black. I learned later on that he was looking for a white boy who could sing black music. Sam dropped all the black artists. That is the only thing I dislike about the whole picture—Sam not carrying along the good black artists with the good white artists."

It was during this transition period that guitarist Scotty Moore went by Memphis Recording service to talk to Sam Phillips about the chances of his band, a country group named the Starlight Wranglers, obtaining a recording contract with Sun Records. Phillips wasn't eager to release a country single on the group, but he did so anyway. The session produced a song, "My Kind of Carrying On," that neither sold nor attracted radio airplay.

Moore continued to spend time at the studio, picking Phillips's brain about possible opportunities. Finally, one day Phillips surprised Moore by suggesting he audition a man who had stopped by to record a birthday greeting for his mother. His name was Elvis Presley. If Moore thought he had potential, he would record a side or two with them

The resulting session on July 5, 1954, with Elvis Presley, Scotty Moore and Bill Black, launched a music revolution that forever changed the world. It was an event for which Chips Moman had a front-row seat. Because both the morning and the evening newspapers assigned reporters to cover the music scene—and the city's radio stations had a vested interest in "selling" music to local residents—Chips was able to keep up with it on a daily basis.

BY 1954, CHIPS MOMAN, though still a teenager, had hit pay dirt travelling around the South painting weather-worn service stations with his cousin. Actually, they would paint just about anything if the price was right. Then, as now, good painters were hard to find.

"For a kid my age, I was really successful," he said. "I was making $400 to $500 a week. I did well enough that I could get my dad to move up. We would paint twenty to twenty-five skid tanks in a day [a skid tank is an aboveground tank that rests on a platform.] I painted fridges, post offices, flag poles, anything."

Chips lived in Millington, on the outskirts of Memphis near the U.S. Naval base. Because of his proximity to the base, he got to know a number of the servicemen. They arrived there from all over the country, but all of them had one thing in common—tattoos. Chips was so impressed that he gave himself two tattoos.

Disappointed in their ragged appearance, he went to a tattoo parlor and paid for an additional tattoo, professionally done. Years later he told me the tattoos were the worst mistake he had ever made in his life. He quickly learned that not everyone valued tattoos. As time went by he discovered that the tattoos allowed strangers to pass judgement on him based on the decorations on his forearms. There were even times, he conceded, that his tattoos prevented him from obtaining needed bank loans.

Creating quite a stir in Memphis at that time were Elvis' first releases by Sun Records, "That's All Right Mama" and "Blue Moon of Kentucky." Phillips took the songs to a disk jockey at WHBQ named Dewey Phillips (no relation to Sam Phillips) to play on his *Red Hot and Blue* program. Listeners went wild and demanded more. Dewey Phillips may have been the first "shock jock" in America. He had a manic personality and sometimes played songs he liked over and over again, back to back, with no break for commercials. Sleepy Eyed John, a disk jockey for a country station, played Side B of the record, "Blue Moon of Kentucky," with the same enthusiastic response from listeners.

Jack Clement, who played guitar and sang in a band at a popular night spot, told me that he awoke one morning to hear Sleepy Eyed John introducing the song on his morning show. Said Clement, who later became an engineer and producer at Sun Records: "Sleepy Eyed was saying, 'Here's the record everyone is screaming about.' I said to myself, 'Oh man, that's it. I want to hear that again. It was an instant hit from day one."

Chips Moman was right smack in the middle of the excitement, hearing the records played on radio, and hearing his contemporaries talk about the records. Suddenly, he found he was playing his guitar all the time. He couldn't put it down. He had come to Memphis to escape a "hard" childhood, as so many before him had done, but now he felt the passion of the music and it had a hold on him. His father tried to discourage him with statements such as "a musician isn't supposed to make money. It's nothing but just a waste of your life." But Elvis's high-flying success seemed to prove that advice wrong.

About a year after Elvis's historic Sun Records session, Chips Moman one day found a quiet corner of a local drugstore and made himself comfortable. Then he lifted up a borrowed acoustic guitar and began playing some of the songs he had heard on the radio. He and some of his friends had been playing the songs at teenage parties. Nothing serious. Just having fun to combat late summer apathy.

Shopping in the drugstore that day was Warren Smith, a rockabilly singer five years Chips' senior. Smith was a transplant from the Mississippi Delta who had moved to West Memphis, Arkansas, across the Mississippi River from Memphis. He listened to Chips with great interest, fascinated by his skill at such a young age.

"Would you like a job?" Smith asked.

"Doing what?" asked Chips, always the skeptic.

Smith told him he wanted him to play guitar in his band, which had a booking at an Arkansas nightclub at which both Carl Perkins and Roy Orbison would be performing. Chips jumped at the opportunity. By that time he was beginning to understand that music might offer more financial opportunities than painting service stations.

As word about Warren Smith spread, he landed an audition with Sam Phillips at Sun Records. Phillips liked what he heard and recorded a song titled "Rock 'n' Roll Ruby." The song hit Number 1 in Memphis and went on to outsell the first Elvis Presley releases on Sun. His second release, "Ubangi Stomp," had racist overtones because it told the story of an African chief speaking the way movie Indians spoke. It was his third song, "So Long, I'm Gone," written by Roy Orbison, that was a hit, peaking at Number 74 on *Billboard's* national charts. Feeling he had run out of steam in Memphis, he moved to California and signed a contract with Liberty Records. His first release, "I Don't Believe I'll Fall in Love Today," peaked at Number 5 on *Billboard's* country chart. In 1965, in what could at best be called a weird karma car accident in Chips Moman's hometown of LaGrange, he suffered severe back injuries that took him out of the music scene for nearly a year. Unable to restart his career, he succumbed to addictions to alcohol and pills. That likely contributed to his conviction for robbing a pharmacy, an act that earned him an eighteen-month prison sentence.

CHIPS MOMAN WROTE his first song in 1953, an upbeat, rockabilly tune titled "This Time." He was only sixteen years of age. After polishing the song in 1958, he took it to Fernwood Records, a garage studio owned by Scotty Moore, who had split from Elvis Presley, along with bassist Bill Black. Moore's only recording act was his former paperboy, Thomas Wayne Perkins, the brother of Luther Perkins, the guitarist in the Johnny Cash band. The youngster was still a senior in high school, but Moore felt he had potential. He shortened his singer's name to Thomas Wayne and, using a mono tape recorder, recorded Chips' song and pressed it into a record that was soon picked up by Mercury Records for national distribution. The song generated no interest, but Moore did not give up on his singer.

Soon another song came Moore's way. "Tragedy" was written by Gerald Nelson, a Kentucky disk jockey, but it already had been turned down by Chet Atkins at RCA Records and Sam Phillips at Sun Records. Undeterred by the previous rejections, Moore decided to record Thomas Wayne singing the song. However, instead of using his garage studio, he encouraged Nelson to sing background on a session at Royal Studio in exchange for studio time so Moore would have access to better equipment. The studio, home of Hi Records, a new venture that was owned by Ray Harris, Bill Cantrell, and Quinton Claunch and financed by a group of Memphis investors, including Joe Cuoghi, the owner of Poplar Tunes, one of the largest wholesale and retail record distributors in the South. Hi Records was also the home of the Bill Black Combo.

Scotty and Bill Black were the only musicians on the record. Thomas Wayne brought his girlfriend and two of her friends to sing backup. They recorded three takes and ended up using the first one. On the A-side they used a song titled "Saturday Date" and on the B-side "Tragedy." Radio disk jockeys decided they liked "Tragedy" better and within a short time the song had risen to Number 8 on the national charts, making it a million-seller. "It was like it happened overnight," said Scotty Moore. "We didn't have a dime to promote it."[4]

After Scotty Moore used Chips' song "This Time" on the demo for Thomas Wayne, Chips signed with Tree Publishing in Nashville with the hope they would be able to find another artist to record it. Meanwhile, Chips forged a friendship with brothers Johnny and Dorsey Burnette of Memphis, who had won the Ted Mack Amateur Hour contest in 1956 and were just beginning to record their own high-energy brand of rockabilly. They called themselves the Rock 'n Roll Trio, the third member being guitarist Paul Burlison, who was not related to the brothers. Two years before they appeared on the Ted Mack show, they had toured with Gene Vincent, one of the hottest acts in the country. Vincent's popularity soared two years later with the release of "Be-Bop-A-Lula," a rockabilly tune that peaked at Number 7 on *Billboard's* pop chart. Extending the popularity of the song was Vincent's singing cameo in the Jane Mansfield movie, *The Girl Can't Help It.* It did not hurt his career in the least to be associated with the blonde bombshell in a movie that all his fans were certain to see at the local drive-in movie theater.

Longevity has not always been a common thread in early rock 'n' roll. By 1957, Dorsey Burnette had grown tired of being on the road and maintaining an acrimonious relationship with his brother—they fought like brothers sometimes do, only perhaps with a little more intensity—and he resigned from the group, thus ending a nearly decade-long run of the Rock 'n' Roll Trio. They returned to Memphis and Burlison hung up his guitar at his wife's suggestion, and resumed his career as an electrician. Before long, Dorsey was offered a solo recording contract by a Los Angeles record label. He moved there in January 1958 and landed a night job working as an electrician for Bethlehem Steel. During the day he wrote songs and played them for people in the music business. On his nights off he played in nightclubs.

Johnny decided to join his brother in Los Angeles, but before he left Memphis he asked Chips if he would be interested in going with him. Chips readily said yes because it seemed like the opportunity of a lifetime. But there was a slight problem. He had a brand new wife. As the trajectory of his professional life had begun to change for the better, Chips had begun a relationship with a coffee shop waitress from Mylan, Tennessee, named

Chips Moman, right, with his wife Lorrie
Photo courtesy Monique Moman

Lorrie. They were married in May1958. She was a slender, dark-haired woman who had a passion for writing poetry and rescuing abandoned dogs. Seemingly, every time Chips returned home from work there was a new rescue dog there to greet him.

"She had a fantastic sense of humor," recalled their daughter Monique, who bears a strong resemblance to her attractive mother. "They were broke when they got married, but she hung in there with him."

Lorrie readily agreed to an adventure in Los Angeles, though it would mean leaving the rescue dogs behind. Before long Johnny and Chips (and his wife, Lorrie) joined Dorsey in Los Angeles, where they started playing together again in local nightclubs. At that time, television and recording star Rick Nelson was one of the hottest acts in the country. As one of the stars of the *Ozzie and Harriet Show*, Nelson parlayed his celebrity into an impressive string of hit records. During 1958 and 1959, Nelson had twelve hits on the charts in comparison with Elvis Presley's seven. Among Nelson's hits during that time was "Poor Little Fool." a Number 1 song written by Sharon Sheeley, the girlfriend of rockabilly star Eddie Cochran.

24

She was in a taxi with him in 1960 in London when the car blew a tire and crashed, killing Cochran and badly injuring Shelley.

Dorsey and Johnny set their minds on writing hit songs for Nelson. They was unable to find out where he lived, but they did ferret out the address of his father, Ozzie Nelson, and they sat on his doorstep one day until he returned home. Ozzie told them to bring him some songs the next day and he would take them to his son.

Ricky ended up recording several of their songs, including "It's Late," "Believe What You Say," and "Waiting in School." As a result of that success, they were signed to Imperial Records both as songwriters and artists. This time they were billed as the Burnette Brothers.

Then, as now, being able to make a living in the music business was all about who you knew. Johnny and Dorsey were able to open doors for Chips both as a session player at recording studios and as a guitar player for nightclub and concert engagements. He got a big break when Johnny Meeks, lead guitarist with Gene Vincent and the Blue Caps, left the band and joined the Tune Toppers.[5] Chips was asked to replace Meeks on tour and also in the studio. The experience of touring with Gene Vincent was light years away from his experiences in Memphis. There were no "normal" days on the road with Vincent.

For example, once while performing in Minneapolis, the exhausted band slept in their car before heading out to the next booking. During the night, they were awakened by someone rapping on the window. Policemen with guns drawn dragged them from the car and pushed them against a wall with orders to keep their hands up. After a search of the car, they were handcuffed and driven to headquarters for questioning.

Gradually, it dawned on the band that they were suspected of murdering a service station attendant. Police informed them that a witness had seen Johnny Meeks leaving the station just before the body was discovered by a motorist. Eventually, after an hour of questioning, they convinced the police that they were innocent and they were released. "I was the first guy to ever be arrested for murder in rock 'n' roll who was white," he later boasted, according to Susan Vanhecke in *Race with the Devil*.

Vincent's tours with Jerry Lee Lewis were legendary. Vanhecke also told the story of the time Vincent and Lewis were performing and Vincent decided he had enough and was going home. "We can't, we've got this contract," Jerry protested. "They'll sue us."

Vincent said he didn't care and took the next plane out of town. "Lewis finished the tour by himself, impersonating Gene. Amazingly, no one seemed the wiser."

The part of Chips' California experience that benefited him the most professionally was his opportunity to so session work at Gold Star Studio. Run by two partners, Stan Ross and Dave Gold, Gold Star Studio was located on the corner of Santa Monica Boulevard and Vine Street, with the entrance positioned in an alley that, more often than not, was littered with urban trash. Inside, the rooms were tiny and the carpet had the look and smell of a two dollar a night hotel. It had a bathroom, but according to visitors it was a level or two below the average service station bathroom in cleanliness. It was a place that did a standing-only business. If your reason for visiting the bathroom required more deliberate deliberation, it almost certainly would be undertaken from a squatting position.

Studio A was the main recording space. It was a dark, forbidding place with a low ceiling. First-timers at the studio often compared it to entering a cave. Needless to say, it had a calming effect on musicians, whether by design or not, and stifled the sort of raucous horseplay that has been traditional in recording studios in years past. Behind Studio A was a room with two echo chambers designed by Gold. The chambers allowed the studio to have the rich, resonant sound familiar to musicians who recorded at the studios owned by the major record labels.

Originally opened as a demo studio where songwriters and publishers could get decent renderings of their latest creations at a modest price, it made a giant step forward in 1958 when a group named The Champs recorded an instrumental titled "Tequila." The only lyrics were the words "tequila," which were spoken three times during the recording. The song was used as the B-side for "Train to Nowhere," written by Dave Burgess who did the vocal. The A-side had little success with radio, but a disk jockey in Cleveland flipped the record and started playing "Tequila." The song, which featured high-energy saxophone work by Danny Flores of the Flores Trio, caught fire and by March 1958 the song went to Number 1 on the *Billboard* chart.

All of a sudden Gold Star Studio had a gilded reputation. If there is anything the music industry loves it is a hit record. Get one and everyone comes knocking on your door. The studio's second hit came from rockabilly artist Eddie Cochran who was well known when he went to the studio in March 1958 to record a song he had co-written, "Summertime Blues." Cochran did the vocals and all the guitar parts. The record peaked at Number 8 on the *Billboard* Hot 100 chart and went on to become a rock 'n' roll classic that was covered by the Beach Boys, The Who, Alan Jackson, and others. In 1999 the song was inducted into the Grammy Hall of Fame and subsequently listed on the Rock and Roll Hall of Fame and Museum list of "The Songs That Shaped Rock and Roll." Moviegoers will recognize it on the soundtrack of *Caddyshack*.

Chips Moman likely was not in the studio when "Tequila" was recorded. However, he may have been in the studio when "Summertime Blues" was recorded. He was in and out of the studio doing session work when Phil Spector started recording there. The two men never spoke, Chips told me, but he found Spector to be a memorable character, as did everyone else who encountered him at that time.

The first time Spector walked into the studio, Ross was unimpressed, according to Mick Brown in *Tearing Down the Wall of Sound*: "'He was just this nervous, softy little kid.' He told me he'd just graduated from Fairfax; we're alumni! Then he said he was going to have a hit record' Just like everyone else, thought Ross."

Spector, a Jew who had moved to Los Angeles with his mother from New York after the death of his father, likely had heard "Summertime

Blues" on the radio and put together a random trio he named the Teddy Bears. It consisted of himself and two classmates, Harvey Goldstein and Annette Kleinbard, who later went on to fame as a songwriter, penning the hit "The Night the Lights Went out in Georgia" for Vicki Lawrence. Spector fronted the group and also acted as producer. After borrowing forty dollars from his mother, Spector booked the session at Gold Star. The A side was "Don't You Worry My Little Pet" and the B side was meant to be titled "Wonderful Lovable You," but Spector ended up retitling the song "To Know Him, Is to Love Him." According to author David N. Howard, Spector was obsessed with the suicide of his father and felt that the inscription on his father's tombstone, "To Know Him Was to Love Him," would make a better title.

Studio personnel were annoyed at Spector's seemingly frantic behavior of singing with the group and then running into the control room to hear the playback. If it was not to his satisfaction he would ask the engineer to play the songs back so that the vocal could be redone on top of the previous vocal. In effect, he had the vocals stacked, a novelty at the time. When the record was released the A side received very little traction. More impressed by the B side, disc jockeys flipped the record and began playing "To Know Him, Is to Love Him." In October 1958 it was the Number 1 record in America and sold over one million units. Spector's surprise hit made him a frequent visitor to Gold Star, and before long others were lining up for recording sessions at the studio, including the Beach Boys, Jimi Hendrix, Neil Young, The Who, Joan Jett, the Beatles, Sonny & Cher, Bob Dylan, and many others.

Spector's career accelerated, especially after he perfected his so-called "Wall of Sound" (a sound that did not appeal to Chips; it was in fact the opposite of the musical direction he would follow), and he went on to work with artists such as the Beatles (as a group and with John and George separately), the Ronettes, the Crystals, and the Righteous Brothers.

Gold Star had a gritty feel to it, like the pool halls back in LaGrange. Unlike some people who found the studio threatening, Chips felt oddly at home among the sweaty musicians and studio personnel, learning about echo chambers, stacking vocals, overdubs, and countless other details associated with the studio's custom designed equipment.

As a result, Chips was able to envision a layered approach to music, one in which the vocals, drums, instruments, etc., were recorded with direct lines to the soundboard from microphones placed strategically around the studio to capture a "live" performance, a process that provided a smoother, more vibrant sound that later could be manipulated during the mixing process. By the time he left Gold Star he had the equivalent of a university education in sound engineering. He also learned that when working with bands, it was best to replace the non-vocalists in the band with studio musicians, professionals who were comfortable in the studio and did not waste valuable time on rookie mistakes. In time it would become Chips' trademark, an important reason for his later success.

Gold Star closed its doors in 1984, largely because of new technology that made such studios obsolete. By 1984 artists could make records in their bedrooms if they wanted to. Several months later, the building was destroyed by a fire. In its place, a mall was constructed on land many in the business felt was sacred ground.

Early portrait of Chips Moman
Courtesy of Monique Moman

CHAPTER 2
Launching Stax Records
(1959-1962)

WHILE LIVING IN LOS ANGELES, Chips and his wife Lorrie conceived a child, something they did not know about until they returned to Memphis in mid-1959 and learned that Lorrie was several months pregnant. They named their daughter Monique. She would prove to be their only child. Immediately upon his return, Chips rounded up musicians interested in performing with him in nightclubs. Recalled Chips: "I think I must have had the first integrated band in Memphis, playing rhythm and blues, a little rock 'n' roll. . . in the early 1960s, Booker T. Jones [later of Booker T. and the MGs fame] played organ with me, and a couple of black horn players. That didn't set well with a lot of folks, but others thought it was all right."

In late 1959 he toured with pop singer Gary Stites, who had a Top 40 hit, "Lonely for You." The Denver native had already appeared on Dick Clark's "American Bandstand" and Alan Freed's "Rock 'n' Roll Dance Party" before Chips joined the tour. That association abruptly ended when Chips broke his leg in a car accident and the tour continued without him. Stites released his only LP album in 1960. It produced one song that made the charts, "Lawdy Miss Clawdy."

After he recovered from his broken leg—and in need of money because of his inability to work during his recovery—he went by Sun Records and asked Sam Phillips for a job as a producer, citing his experience at Gold Star Studio in Los Angeles.

"What'd you do at Gold Star?"

"Played sessions."

"You didn't produce any records?"

"No . . . but I learned from watching them do it."

"Boy," Phillips told him, according to Chips' later recollections, "producers are born, not made. You can't just make up your mind to be a record producer. Good Luck."

It was the last conversation he would have with Phillips for more than two decades.

The only sure-fire way to earn money as a musician was to belong to a group that was paid to perform for dances, for entertainment at bars that hired bands to play music that would keep their patrons drinking, or to perform at special events. The economics of it were simple: You perform for four hours, then you get paid before you leave the event. The problem with that economic system was that a musician often could go for weeks without a payday.

Sometimes Chips gathered musicians together for a short-lived band. Other times he played guitar in already established bands such as Donna Rae and the Sunbeams and Ray Scott's rockabilly band. Donna Rae was a local celebrity who worked as a co-host on Wink Martindale's "Teenage Dance Party" on WHBQ-TV (Martindale went on to host a popular game show named *Tic-Tac-Dough*). Ray Scott was a popular rockabilly singer and songwriter who sometimes hired Chips for his performances. It was through Donna Rae and Ray Scott that Chips came to know Jim Stewart, a sometimes fiddle player in the house band at the Eagle's Nest nightclub.

Stewart had minimal skills as a fiddle player and no skills as a songwriter, but he dreamed of owning a recording studio and a record label. Stewart recorded several songs on an inexpensive recorder and took them to Sam Phillips at Sun Records to see if he would be interested. He was not interested and did not sugarcoat the rejection. As luck would have it, Stewart's barber owned some better recording equipment and loaned it to Stewart to use to start up a record label in his wife's uncle's two-car garage. Stewart named the label Satellite Records and started searching for talent.

Jim Stewart's first effort was to write a country song, "Blue Roses." He asked Fred Bylar, a local radio announcer, to sing it. In his mind, Bylar was a celebrity who would be able to get a record deal. Jim had the recording pressed into a record, but it went nowhere.

After the release of another record that tanked, Stewart decided to sign Donna Rae and the Sunbeams to a recording contract. Chips, who played lead guitar with the group, encouraged Stewart to ask Ray Scott to write two songs for them to record. Scott agreed to do so with the understanding that Stewart record his band as well. The deal was a plus for Chips, who learned to network before anyone else knew what networking was, because he played with both groups and was paid to play guitar on the recordings. Scott's two sides were "You Drive Me Crazy" and "Say Anything But Not Goodbye."

Stewart was five years Chips' senior, but he was light years behind Chips in music experience. In Chips he saw someone with the technical expertise to help make his dreams come true. Chips saw their relationship as a way to break into the music business. Stewart's garage studio was pretty crude compared to what Chips had experienced at Gold Star, but he believed that Stewart could be prodded in the right direction. He was also impressed that Stewart had a college education and worked in the bond department of the First National Bank. If push came to shove, he figured Stewart could always borrow money from the bank for their ventures.

Before long Stewart realized the table model recorder they were using was not good enough to give them recordings that could be competitive. He didn't have the funds needed to purchase the sort of equipment used by professionals, so he turned to his older sister, Estelle Axton, for help.

"He said, would you like to get in the music business," she later recalled to me. "I had never thought about something like that. I said, "'Well, I don't have any money.' My husband and I were both working. I was at Union Planters bank. Jim was working at First National Bank, so he wasn't devoting full time to his business. He knew enough that he would have to have a bigger recording machine and a studio. He hadn't had much success with the records he had put out. He said to me, 'I know you don't have any money but you have a house and you have several years paid into it. Maybe you could mortgage it. All we need is $2,500.'"

Estelle discussed Jim's proposal with her husband Everett.

"No way," he said.

"He wasn't into music and wasn't interested in it," explained Estelle. "I had to talk to him for a long time and convince him that it might come out, even though none of us knew anything about the recording business. Finally, I convinced him that we would mortgage the house for $2,500 to buy a console recording machine. My husband always laughed at Jim until Stax became a big company and then he was proud. We didn't pay but $3,800 for the house in 1940 and it was brand new then. Back then that was a lot of money. We sold the house later on and we got $50,000 for it. My monthly payments were $23.63 a month. I will never forget those figures."

Estelle and Everett mortgaged their home for enough money for Jim to purchase the new studio equipment, resolve some existing legal entanglements, and provide operating capital for the new business which they officially named Satellite Records. As Jim and Estelle worked out the details of their new partnership, Chips continued hustling his musical talents, navigating the day to day existence experienced by every other musician in the city.

Once they purchased the one-track recording machine and installed it in their garage studio they realized they needed to have a better location. Another one of Jim's barber friends told him he owned a vacate building previously used as a grocery store in the unincorporated community of Brunswick, located about twenty miles from Memphis.

"The owner and Jim talked about it," recalled Estelle, "and he said he would let us use the building and wouldn't charge us any rent until we saw that we would be able to make it, then we could pay him rent."

But there was one important condition. The store owner had a sixteen-year-old daughter who aspired to become a singer. Would they mind recording her singing a song or two? How could they say no to such a generous barber? Shaking her head, Estelle said, "We recorded something on her, but it never did anything."

Chips never believed they could make a success of a studio twenty miles from Memphis, especially one housed in an empty store with wooden floors that allowed sound to bounce around with wild abandon, but he hung in there with Jim and Estelle, doing what he could to make it a success. However, with his electrical power turned off at his home, and a wife and a daughter to support, Chips frantically organized a recording session at a studio owned by Roland Janes, a former session guitarist for Sun Records. Other people were making money from records, he thought. Why couldn't he?

In an attempt to take advantage of what he had learned at Gold Star, he recorded himself singing and playing guitar on a slow-dance ballad titled "Thank You for Calling." The song had been recorded by Jo Stafford in 1954 and had gone to Number 9 on the *Billboard* chart. This was the first of many hits that Chips would re-record in hopes of finding success. Unlike the original, Chips' version began with a ringing telephone and made use of background singers. One of the singers would later reveal that they were not paid to sing on the recording, but when she notified Chips she could not attend the session unless she received money to pay a babysitter, he borrowed ten dollars to give to her.

Although Chips did a credible job with the vocal, the record never earned his session investment back. The record is of interest today because it signaled Chips' core philosophy toward hit records: Namely, that re-recording a previous hit gives you an advantage in the marketplace and it does not hurt to have a song that reflects on heartbreak over love lost. Those two ingredients became his trademark. To the best of my knowledge, Chips was never again recorded singing solo. He had way too much pride to ever put himself in a position where he could be critiqued on the quality of his singing by anyone with the pocket change to purchase it and a soapbox from which to disparage the purchase.

THE FIRST BLACK group that recorded at Satellite Records was named the Veltones. It consisted of five members, all of whom had been performing at nightclubs in Memphis for years. Chips produced their first record and co-wrote the A-side song, "Fool in Love." Chips also played guitar on the song, joining Jimbo Hale on bass and Jerry "Satch" Arnold on drums. It was an upbeat Doo-Wop song, featuring a lead singer with background singers. The record did surprisingly well and was picked up for national distribution by Mercury Records, which paid several hundred dollars for the honor. It was the first music business money ever earned by Jim and Estelle. Their enthusiasm was short-lived. They dreamed of making millions, but it soon it became apparent that the record was not going to sell enough to bring in any additional income.

Nonplussed, they pushed on with a sixteen-year old boy named Charles Heinz that Chips brought into the fold. They recorded two sides, the A-side written by Chips, a song titled "Destiny." Accompanied by Chips on guitar, Hale on bass and Arnold on drums, Heinz delivered a solid vocal backed by lush background vocals. The record never made a dent in the Memphis market.

Chips argued for the entire year they worked out of the abandoned grocery in Brunswick that they simply had to relocate in Memphis. Two records in twelve months that had minimal sales were not going to make Satellite Records a success. Chips argued that they needed to be in Memphis where all the action was. Finally, Jim and Estelle relented and allowed him to find them a new place to set up shop. He returned with an incredible opportunity.

"We made a deal for the Capitol Theater," said Estelle. "The guy that owned it rented it to us for one hundred dollars a month. Can you imagine a whole movie theater for one hundred dollars? We ripped out all the seats and put a partition down the middle of the theater to compact the sound. The screen was up on the podium. That was where we put the recording machine that I had paid $2,500 for. Our first ten records were recorded on that one-track machine. Sun Records started out that way, too."

Just as important as the cheap rent was the majority black neighborhood that surrounded the new headquarters of Satellite Records. Even if Jim and Estelle did not understand it at that moment, Chips instinctively knew that the future of the record label was in focusing on black recording artists. Sam Phillips had begun as a mostly black recording studio, but then with the success of Elvis, Scotty and Bill, Sam musically retooled into a mostly white recording studio. By design, at least in Chips' musically evolving mind, Satellite Records (later to become Stax Records) would be viewed in the black community as the anti-Sun Records recording studio.

Jim, Estelle, and Chips were unlikely founders of a record label. At age thirty, Jim was a mild-mannered, soft-spoken banker who believed his ability to play a fiddle gave him credibility as a record executive. At forty, Estelle was a former school teacher-turned banker, who was outspoken in her beliefs, a trait some attributed to her flaming red hair. She spoke her mind—and often. At twenty-two, Chips was an eight-grade dropout who possessed an abundance of street smarts, but no business experience other than painting service stations. What he did have was a genius for music, a God-given talent he had nurtured in smoke-filled barrooms under less than ideal conditions and a natural curiosity that allowed him to learn things at Gold Star Studio that no one at the studio was aware he was learning. Perhaps most of all he possessed the savvy to out-bluff his opponents in both poker and business.

Bobby Manual, a former sound engineer and session guitarist at Stax Records, told the author a story told to him about Chips by someone who was there: "We went to a gig, drove up and Chips went inside. There was another band playing. They pulled a gun on him and we all went outside. About thirty minutes later Chips came outside and he had the gun and the booking. He probably never had the booking to begin with."

One of the first problems the threesome had to solve was Estelle's role with the record label. She did not want to become an absentee investor. She wanted to be at the studio on a daily basis to oversee how

37

her money was being spent, but she knew she had no role to play inside the studio. Her solution was to open a record shop with an entrance at the front of the former theater.

"Working at Union Planter's Bank, I took orders for specific records from the people around me," she explained. "They told me what they wanted and I went to Poplar Tunes [a popular record store] and bought the records for sixty-five cents and sold them for one dollar. I took that profit and bought enough records to set up a record shop in space formerly used by a barber shop. In time it became a workshop for writers and musicians."

Once she got the record shop stocked, she went straight there when she got off work at the bank at 4 p.m. Then she opened the doors to the record shop and stayed there until 9 p.m. During the day and early evening Jim and Chips tore up seats and other furnishings inside the theater and re-shaped it into a recording studio. Because none of them had the time to work on the studio during the day, they worked at nights and on weekends to get it finished. They spent several hundred dollars getting the work done, money they didn't really have. They tried to find investors, but no one was interested in financing their venture. To keep the studio going, Estelle mortgaged her home once again to raise four thousand dollars. When Jim first approached her about becoming a partner, little of her time was spent thinking about music. Now that they were deeply into red ink, all she could think about, day and night, was music. It became an obsession from which she never really escaped.

Around the same time, they were getting their studio opened, Sam Phillips closed the doors at Memphis Recording Service, the home of Sun Records, and moved to a new studio at 639 Madison. It was the final step in a slow dance that began when Phillips sold Elvis Presley's contract to RCA Records in 1955 for forty thousand dollars (thirty-five thousand to Sam and a five-thousand-dollar advance to Elvis and his manager Colonel Tom Parker). The month before Phillips sold Elvis's contract, he started up the nation's first all-female radio station. His partner was Holiday Inns founder Kemmons Wilson. The radio studio was set up in a Holiday Inn in downtown Memphis and given the call letters WHER. A sign was hung over the control room that read "Doll Den."

Phillips opened the radio station in a Holiday Inn because Kemmons loaned him $25,000 for the venture on the condition that they would be partners if the station was successful. If the station failed, their agreement was that Phillips would not have to pay back the loan. Apparently, Phillips did not have much choice in the matter. Despite his critical success with Elvis Presley, Johnny Cash, Carl Perkins, Roy Orbison and others, he was rumored to be facing bankruptcy. Understanding that enables one to better understand why Phillips would even consider selling Elvis's contract. As it turned out, Phillips got a good deal on Holiday Inn stocks, an investment that eventually earned him a cool profit of $280,000, more than he ever earned in the music business.

NOW THAT SATELLITE RECORDS had a proper studio, Jim and Chips went into high gear to find talent for their first releases. By that time, Chips had convinced Jim that their best chances for success were with black artists and not with country artists. Once he understood that, Jim backtracked to visit Rufus Thomas, the radio announcer at WDIA whom he had met when he was out and about promoting the Veltones. Because Jim knew that Sam Phillips had recorded Thomas earlier, he encouraged him to make some demo tapes and drop by the recording studio to play them for him.

Meanwhile, Chips was navigating the black music scene in Memphis, getting to know black musicians, and performing with them in various black nightclubs in the city, including the Flamingo Club, located on Hernando Street between Beale and Gayoso. It was a large capacity nightclub with a stage that was raised about three feet from the floor. The only seating was at the various tables that extended far back into the shadows of the room. Because selling liquor was against the law, patrons brought their own bottles. The nightclub offered the set-ups for the drinks.

In the early Sixties, black nightclubs did not hire white bands, but they allowed white musicians to perform with black musicians. I am well acquainted with the Flamingo Club because my all-white band from Ole Miss performed there in 1965 and backed rhythm and blues singer Tommy Tucker ("Hi-Heel Sneakers"). The band didn't know it at the time, but it apparently was the first all-white band to perform at a black nightclub in Memphis. I played the Hammond B 3 organ that dominated the left side of the stage, totally ignorant of the fact that Booker T. Jones had played the same organ before the melody of my favorite song, "Green Onions," took shape in Booker T.'s mind. In 1965 segregation was still rigorously enforced by Memphis police. The Ole Miss band had no idea race was an issue because black performers from Memphis, including Rufus Thomas, performed regularly without incident at the all-white fraternities at the university.

Skirting the race laws, Chips worked at the Flamingo Club whenever he could. It was where he eventually befriended Booker T. Jones and other black musicians he later recruited to play sessions at Satellite Records. Blacks found him to be an enigma. When he was in his everyday frame of mind, he looked, talked and walked like a Georgia cracker, something that always gave blacks pause. But when he was playing music he was something else entirely. His speech loosened, his eyes glistened, and his rhythm of walking changed. The belief in the South, for at least the last two hundred years, is that blacks know more about white folks than they know about themselves. Certainly, Memphis blacks got Chips' number right away, a major reason they came to trust him more than they did the taciturn, better educated banker Jim Stewart.

Taking Jim's advice, Rufus Thomas recorded some demo tapes of himself and his teenage daughter Carla. Jim listened to the tapes with great interest and set up a session to record two songs—"Cause I Love You" and "Deep Down Inside." With Jim engineering, Booker T. Jones on baritone sax (he was given a phony pass to get him excused from high school), Rufus's son Marvell on piano and Wilbur Steinberg on bass, they

Rufus and Carla Thomas
Photo courtesy Mississippi Valley Collection
University of Memphis Libraries

laid down the tracks and Jim wasted no time getting the songs pressed into a record. It was the first for the new studio.

To everyone's surprise, the record sold more than five thousand copies in the Memphis area and another five thousand copies in Nashville and Atlanta. Jim, Estelle and Chips released a collective sigh of relief. Their backs had been against the wall. Estelle had run out of money to loan to Satellite Records. The record label's only income for months had come from the record store. Both Jim and Estelle had day jobs, but Chips' day job was actually a night job, namely playing his guitar at nightclubs. He stuck with Satellite Records because he understood he had a one-third sweat-equity interest in the company and he believed it would all someday be worth his while.

"Musicians have never had much security in their life," Chips later explained. "That's why we worked so hard. We lived like that for years. We had no idea what I was all about. None of us thought we would be professionals. I still have those feelings. I've been doing it all these years and I still feel the same way about it—that it could be over at any time."

Giving another take on the perils of playing in a band, Chips' father told me a story that made Chips cringe (he was sitting close by listening to his father speak). Said Abraham Lincoln: "He got into a band in Memphis and went off on a trip and liked to have got killed. His legs were cut in two places. There was five of them and one of the guys got his nose cut off his face. When he came out of that, he went back to the studio where he was working like nothing had ever happened."

Soon after "Cause I Love You" was released, Jerry Wexler at Atlantic Records, was tipped off by a pressing plant operator that the record was a hit. Hearing that, Wexler offered Jim and Estelle one thousand dollars for the master, plus a royalty of twelve to eighteen percent on retail sales, with no deductions. That was not a bad deal for a production company, but not such a good deal for a record label. Nonetheless they signed on the dotted line and did not discover until much later it was not a leasing and distribution deal, but an outright sale of all rights to the record. It took a while for them to discover the truth, but for the time being they were on top of the world. *They had released a hit record!*

Jerry Wexler flew to Memphis from New York to pick up the master tapes. Jim, Estelle and Chips could not believe their good fortune. Wexler was a big deal in the music business. They never dreamed that a record executive of Wexler's reputation would consider coming to them. He was eager to meet Rufus and Carla, so he invited them to dinner. Because of segregation, he was afraid to take them out to dinner at a public place. Instead, he invited them to have a private dinner in his hotel room.

Wexler and Jim picked up Rufus and Carla at the radio station and, on the advice of Jim, parked the car and walked them around a garbage alley to the freight elevator, thereby avoiding the lobby where they would be seen by hotel guests. Not happy with that development was Rufus, who muttered, according to Wexler, "Nothing changes. Down in the alley with the garbage. Same ol' same ol' shit." It was a comment that made Wexler feel like shit.

"That night, after they'd gone and I was asleep, I thought I was dreaming," he wrote in his memoir, *A Life in Rhythm & the Blues*. "But the pounding at the door was a different kind of nightmare."

"'Vice squad! They shouted. 'You got a woman in there? Open up!'"

"Like hell I would. I met them in public, down in the lobby. Meanwhile, I dashed off a note to Amet [the record label head], telling him what was happening, and dropped it in a mailbox just in case. I had visions of these guys throwing me in the trunk of a car and dumping me somewhere in Arkansas. Apparently someone had seen black people leaving my room, and this was their response.

"I got the cops' superior on the phone, some redneck lieutenant, and unburdened myself. 'Lovely fucking greeting card you send me!' I said.

Rufus and Carla, freaked out by the incident, took the studio more songs after Wexler was safely airborne, but none of them sounded like hits to Jim. Sometime later Jim, Estelle and Carla were sitting in the studio, tossing out ideas. Things were going nowhere in particular when Carla abruptly blurted out, "I've got a song called 'Gee Whiz.'"

"As soon as Jim and I heard that song we knew it was a hit," recalled Estelle. "It's funny. When you hear a song, you know if it's got something in it that will sell."

Jim asked Chips to produce the session. The more they discussed it— Jim wanted to add strings and that meant paying union scale to violinists— the more they realized the song needed to be recorded in a better studio. They knew "Gee Whiz" could be a big hit and they wanted to do everything they could to help it along. Surprisingly, they turned to a competitor. Royal Recording Studio, which was located in a black neighborhood not far from Stax Records. Factoring into Jim's decision was the success of the Bill Black Combo, an instrumental trio made up of Elvis Presley's former bass player Bill Black, co-founder and guitarist Reggie Young, drummer Jerry Arnold, Joe Lewis Hall on piano, and Martin Willis on saxophone. Willis was sometimes replaced by Ace Cannon and Hall was sometimes replaced by Bobby Emmons. In later years, Reggie Young and Bobby Emmons would become lifelong recording partners of Chips Moman.

At the time Chips booked recording time at Royal Recording Studio, the Bill Black Combo was one of the most successful recording groups in the nation, much less Memphis. Their first hit had come in 1960 with "Smokie, Parts 1 & 2." Over the next ten years they scored eighteen additional hits. Much of the success of their music was due to the popularity of the music on juke boxes. People could dance to it.

One of the traits that all music executives, producers, and musicians share is a superstitious belief in success. If someone gets a hit in a certain city or recording studio, or with a certain brand of instrument, hit-hungry musicians fall over each other to duplicate that success. That played a role in Jim's decision to record at Royal. The Bill Black Combo had a sound that translated into financial success. What did Stax have to lose giving it a try?

As it turned out, they had everything to lose. Chips took Carla to Royal Recording Studio and laid down a track. When he returned to Stax Records with the tape and they listened to it they were disappointed in the way it sounded. The tempo was too fast, and it was flat, lifeless. Jim decided it needed to be re-cut at the Stax studio. Chips agreed. He didn't like the tape he brought back from Royal, either.

For the Stax session, Jim hired a string section and Chips recorded the session "live" as Carla sang and the musicians played and the background singers sang, everything picked up by a solitary microphone because there was only one input into the recorder. To everyone's surprise, they obtained a recording that did not have to be re-recorded. "Gee Whiz" was released in November 1960 to a lukewarm reception, but the Stax family stood by their artist and within three months the record was Number 10 on *Billboard's* pop chart, selling in excess of 500,000 units. Initially, Jim, Estelle and Chips thought the income from the record belonged to Stax, but then they were informed that the contract they had signed with Atlantic for the Rufus and Carla recording was specific to that record. That was not the case. According to the contract, Atlantic Records, had the right to distribute anything recorded by Carla Thomas. So instead of receiving the net profits from the record's sale, they only received a royalty based on the sales. Despite this disappointment, Jim later agreed to give Atlantic first refusal on all future releases by Stax.

"It took a while to see the significance of what I was getting into," said Carla in an interview for *Goin' Back to Memphis*. "What I thought was fun was a business. Being young, black, and it being in the Sixties, it was a thrill to just record."

With the success of "Gee Whiz," Atlantic expressed interest in an entire album. Up until that time, the popular music business focused entirely on singles, especially 45s, but that started changing with the success of Elvis Presley and the appetite of his fans for albums, the demise of jukeboxes, which exclusively used 45s, and with the increased popularity of FM radio, which delivered a technically superior sound that favored albums.

Because Carla Thomas had been graduated from high school and entered college in Nashville, it was decided to record her album in that city. The album included her first recordings with Satellite, plus original songs by Chips, Carla and Rufus Thomas, and covers of records already released by the Drifters and others.

After the release of "Gee Whiz," Chips began work on a new project. Acutely aware of the success the Bill Black Combo was having with instrumentals, he tried to figure out a groove for an instrumental for Satellite Records. It was one of those things that he heard in his head, but could not translate with his guitar. He was aware of a high school band, the Royal Spades, in which Estelle Axton's son, "Packy," played saxophone. There was a popular saying in Memphis at the time that was used to refer to African Americans —"black as the ace of spades." Because the band had no black players someone thought it would be clever to use the term in the band's name. The group consisted of Steve Cropper on guitar, Donald "Duck" Dunn on bass, Don Nix on baritone sax, Wayne Jackson on trumpet, Packy Axton on tenor sax, and Terry Johnson on drums. Whenever they needed a vocalist they brought in Ronnie Stoots, who performed under the name Ronnie Angel.

During an intermission at a local nightclub Chips asked keyboard player Smoochie Smith to help him transfer to a piano the groove he heard in his head, but could not make come alive on guitar. Chips was aware of the national success that the Bill Black Combo was having with its guitar-driven instrumentals. A big part of that success was the popularity of the group's music on juke boxes across the country. Their formula for success was simple: Play music people can dance to. In this case it was a popular new dance named the Twist. According to the liner notes on the group's 1961 album *Movin': The Untouchable Sound,* they had enjoyed "phenomenal success with eight straight million-selling records."

**The Mar-Keys: Top row-Don Nix, Terry Johnson, Duck Dunn
Bottom row- Steve Cropper, Packy Axton, Wayne Jackson
Photo courtesy Don Nix**

The next day at the Satellite Records studio Chips continued to work on the song, adding members of the Royal Spades and several black musicians he had been working with. They continued to experiment with the dance groove he had concocted, debating when to add the keyboard and horn parts until they patched together a completed song. The one thing Chips did not want on the record was the sound of a guitar because that would be too derivative of the Bill Black Combo. Interestingly, on the finished product it was a piano that played on the first verse between the horn accents. Subsequently, it changed to a B-3 organ. That perhaps suggests separate recording sessions and a splice between the first and subsequent verses.

Once Chips heard the sound that was rolling around inside his head during rehearsals, he turned on the recorder to get it on tape. Then he played it back and no one except Estelle and himself liked it. She had an acetate made of the recording and played it in her record store for customers to hear. Meanwhile, Chips took the tape with him to Nashville and played it for people in the music business there, but no one was encouraging. Disappointed, Chips returned, thinking it had been a waste of his time.

"I thought it was a hit," said Estelle. She talked Jim into taking a tape of the song to WLOK, a radio station that targeted a black audience. The first time they played it they received a dozen calls. That confirmed Estelle's instincts about the song. "I kept bugging Jim. Then I started in on Chips. I said, 'Look this is a hit record.' They said, 'Forget it.' Finally, I got them to agree to it. They said for Packy to get the tape mastered and take it down to the pressing plant. That's when we discovered sixteen or eighteen bars had been wiped out."

"We did that song fifty times," Jim responded. "Get Packy to find another front end, same tempo, and let him splice it on the front."

"That's what Packy did. Whenever I hear that song, I can still hear the splice. There's about a half note difference."

When he heard the final product, Jim Stewart agreed to release it,

48

although with great reluctance. He told Chips they needed a song for the B side. He called them into the studio a few days later and they recorded "The Night Before."

There was still unfinished business.

Estelle insisted that they drop the name The Royal Spades.

Don Nix, who wanted to keep the "royal" connection (a competing band in Memphis was named the Counts), suggested they adopt the name the Marquis, but his bandmates pointed out that few people in the city could read French, nor would they be able to pronounce it. Nix, who had a knack with words, suggested they use a phonetic rendition of the word and call themselves the Mar-Keys.

Then because Smoochie Smith played on the record, Estelle insisted he become a member of the band. There were so many takes on "Last Night" it seems likely that Packy, Don Nix, and Wayne Jackson were the only members of the original Royal Spades to perform on the record. Steve Cropper contributed to the development of the song but did not play guitar. Lewis Steinberg, not Duck Dunn, played bass. Chips Moman and Smoochie Smith were both given songwriter credits on the record. It would be Chips' first hit record as a songwriter.

Satellite Records released "Last Night" in July 1961. To the surprise of both Jim and Chips, the record went to Number 2 on the pop charts. It was the hottest selling record in Memphis history, outshining any of the early releases of Elvis Presley. They immediately organized a touring band to support the record. They were quickly booked on Dick Clark's "American Bandstand." In those days there was no higher honor for a new band out of the chute.

"'Last Night' was going to be a big record and everyone knew it," said Nix. "At last we were going on the road and we were going to be rich and famous. Our wildest dreams were coming true. But if we had known what lay ahead we probably would have gotten day jobs and stayed at home."[6]

Going out on the road with the group was Estelle, who saw herself as a mother figure for the boys, all the more so since her son was in the band. "I travelled with the Mar-Keys quite a bit," she explained. "I remember going all the way to Canada with them. We had a vehicle that could comfortably hold six people and we piled in about nine or ten, along with all the instruments and the clothes. The musicians were all just like a family. If one didn't show up, I'd check and make sure they weren't sick. I think that family feeling had a lot to do with the way the music was put together."

IN 1961, AS "LAST NIGHT" was soaring, Chips received word, probably from Tree Publishing, that a twenty-two-year-old singer from Fort Wayne, Indiana, named Troy Shondell, had recorded his song, "This Time." The song was released in June 1961 by Goldcrest Records. It sold 10,000 copies the first week and went on to sell more than three million copies the first year, making Shondell a legend among other rock bands. He had begun his career as a teenager with songs such as "My Hero" and "Kissin' in the Drive-In." At one point he was the opening act for headliners such as Chuck Berry and Frankie Avalon. Tommy James, who had the hits "Hanky Panky" and "Mony, Mony," gave him a tip of the hat by naming his band the Shondells.[7]

Chips Moman was thrilled as a songwriter because it gave him two hit songs, "This Time" and "Last Night," that were played on the radio in 1961. His mechanical royalties (paid for record sales) for "This Time" amounted to two cents per record, which would have totaled $60,000 for the first year, with $30,000 going to Chips and $30,000 going to the publisher. To understand what a windfall that was, consider that in 1960 the average cost of a new car was $2,700 and the cost of a new house in the Mid-South averaged $7,900. He was able to buy a house for his wife and daughter in Frayser, just north of Memphis, and purchase a British Leyland Triumph. Later, he would move to Steele Street in Frayser and purchase Cadillacs for both himself and his wife. By the end of the 1960s he had earned enough to move to Woodstock-Cuba Drive, a rural area on the outskirts of the Shelby Forest. There he lived on a farm he named Shelby Downs (because of the illegal horse racetrack he built on the farm).

The experience would forever affect his philosophy of making records. Today, a record producer can earn anywhere from $26,000 to $75,000 per album, with top producers setting their own price and perhaps receiving royalty points on album sales, especially if they are a staff producer for a record label. In the 1960s, when single records were the norm, a producer might earn anywhere from $100 to $1000 for supervising production of two sides of a record. Once his royalties started rolling in for "This Time," Chips realized that the real money in the record business went to the people who wrote the songs, not the producers or even the artists in many instances. For the remainder of his career his goal was to have one or two songs of his own on every album he produced. That did not always work out for him, but mostly it did.

"Last Night" had not been out long when Jim and Estelle received a letter from another record company named Satellite Records. "They wrote us and indicated that they'd be willing to sell the name to us for a lot of money," Jim Stewart told Rob Bowman. "I didn't bother to respond. Satellite Records was always a name that I never really liked, but it was the only one we [could come up with] at the time."

Fortunately, Jim and Estelle already had discussed a name change for the company. The "cease and desist—or pay up" letter they received was all they needed to motivate them to get moving on the name change. They chose Stax Records, a name formed by combining the first two letters of their last names. They made the change immediately, which meant that some of the Mar-Key records in the pipeline had a Satellite Records label and others had the new Stax label. By the time the Mar-Keys recorded an entire album, it was released on the Atlantic Records label, with no mention of Satellite or Stax. However, getting to that point was a rocky road.

"When we first let Atlantic have 'Last Night,' we had already proved it was a hit," said Estelle. "But when Jerry Wexler got it he wouldn't do anything with it. He didn't promote it like he did 'Gee Whiz.' I thought maybe the reason why he didn't do that is that they had transferred 'Gee Whiz' to the Atlantic label and they distributed 'Last Night' on Stax. He didn't believe in it. But I knew from experience it was a hit. I was arguing with Jim about it. He told me to get on the phone and talk to Wexler about it. I did, and I told him that it had been a hit in Memphis and a record that could be a hit in Memphis could be a hit anywhere. Well, he didn't like my attitude at all. He called Jim back and said, 'Don't let your sister get on the phone anymore to me. I don't want to talk to her.' Well, I proved him wrong. I did not want to lose that record. I knew it was a hit."

By the time they got around to recording an album, the single was Number 2 in the nation. The only individual name on the album was that of Jim Stewart, who was identified as being the album supervisor. There was no mention of Chips Moman on the album, neither as the producer nor the co-writer of the big hit "Last Night." Four of the twelve songs on the album were identified as being written by "The Mar-Keys." There was no mention of the members of the band anywhere on the album cover or inside the sleeve.

The education of Chips Moman in the music industry had begun in earnest. Already he had learned that instrumentals could be a fast-track to success. He had learned that songwriters earn more from an album than the artist who records it. And he had learned that music had a utilitarian feature that was greatly underrated by those individuals committed to a more artistic approach to music, namely that there was money in records that could get people onto the dancefloor, whether it was to do the Twist, the Bop, or a slow dance. Later, he would learn the benefits of building artistry into a recording, but for now he had a wife and a daughter to support.

Chips Moman made next to nothing working for Stax Records, even though with Jim still working days at the bank and Estelle spending her time at the bank where she worked and in the record store, Chips pretty much had the studio to himself. His primary income at this point was still the money he earned playing in nightclubs. But there were other benefits as well. Being a musician allowed him to network with other musicians and learn who had talent and who did not. He would invite those with talent into the studio to see what they could do.

Chips named his nightclub band the Triumphs because he drove a British Leyland Triumph. Individual players in the band varied from night to night. What set his group apart from the Mar-Keys, the Counts, and others was his willingness to have an interracial mix of musicians. He especially relied on black horn players, usually sax and trumpet, along with black drummers and keyboard players. He was always the only guitarist.

The success of the Mar-Keys encouraged him to write another instrumental, this one titled "Burnt Biscuits." To record it, he invited some of the rotating members of The Triumphs into the Stax studio. The result was a raunchy, three-chord dance tune that was driven by a B 3 organ, horn accents and a high profile drum beat. It was also distinguished by a harmonica solo that is remarkably similar to one the Beatles used in "Little Child" a couple of years later. For the flip side, Chips wrote a song titled "Raw Dough." It was different in that it showcased Chips' guitar work and featured a bass bridge. By that time, Jim and Estelle decided they needed a subsidiary label as a marketing technique. They named the new label Volt. Over the years, the Stax/Volt sound became a Memphis music trademark. "Burnt Biscuits" only sold about 30,000 copies, according to Rob Bowman, which meant there would be no encore by The Triumphs.

There is little doubt Chips Moman deserves credit as the hardest working man in the Memphis music industry, namely because he was so relentless in his pursuit of success. No sooner had "Burnt Biscuits" been scorched by the record buying public than Chips moved on to a new project.

Neither Jim nor Estelle spent much time with musicians outside the studio and record store, but Chips did because those were his people. Most of them were like him. They had street smarts, but not much academic education. It was rare to find a musician who had attended college. Few musicians had high school educations. All shared a passion for music. It was what made their worlds go around. They knew the same songs, shared the same dreams.

The first musician Chips recruited for Stax was a black singer/songwriter by the name of William Bell. Their paths crossed frequently in the nightclub circuit in and around Memphis, despite rigidly enforced racial segregation. Once Chips learned that Bell had written his first song at the age of ten, he encouraged him to write something for Stax. Bell, who was twenty-two at the time, wrote a song he thought Jim and Chips would like and took it by the studio to play for them. The song, "You Don't Miss Your Water (Till Your Well Runs Dry)," was so impressive that Jim signed Bell as a songwriter and Chips recorded the song as a demo.

"We just went in to do a demo, but they liked it so well they said, 'Let's finish it up.'" Bell explained to Peter Guralnick. "We had had just a three-piece rhythm section on it, bass, drums, and organ, I believe, plus the horns."[8]

Playing the studio's M-3 organ (a smaller organ than the B-3) was Booker T. Jones. He later recalled that the song was recorded on one take. They played the song while the tape recorder spun. Then they went into the control room to listen to the playback to see what they needed to do differently. To everyone's amazement the song was perfect.

Shortly after the song was released it became a smash hit in the South and made the national pop charts. Chips was amazed at how quickly a song could transition from just being an idea in a songwriter's head to being released on vinyl to becoming a royalty making machine. They had big plans for Bell, but he was drafted into the armed forces not long after the song was released. He would not return to Stax until after his two years of service had ended, but his smooth, soulful voice and excellent songwriting played a major role in defining the Stax sound.

54

"You Don't Miss Your Water" set the template for all future Stax releases and ended up changing the direction of American music. When his hitch with the U.S. Army ended, he returned to Stax to discover that his position at the record label had been assumed by the more dynamic Otis Redding, but he continued to write songs and perform for the record label. However, it was not until after Stax folded that he had a smash hit with Mercury Records, a song titled "Trying to Love Two." Bell ended up becoming one of the most beloved figures to ever record for Stax. Co-workers typically described him as "brilliant."

IN THE SPRING OF 1962, Chips and Booker T. Jones were alone in the studio, when Chips picked up his guitar and encouraged Booker T. to improvise on the M-3 organ. The studio was dimly lit and the room had a laidback vibe to it, a feel that empty classrooms have if you enter and sit alone at one of the desks. As Booker T. doodled on the keyboard, Chips followed him on guitar, sometimes following him, other times venturing into counter point. He was trying to help Booker T. learn how to find the "hook" in his composition, that twist in the melody that is memorable, especially if a lyric is found to accent it. Good hooks are addictive to the listening public, acting like a drug to hold their attention. Booker T. wrote about a similar moment in his memoir, *Time is Tight*:

> *"Play something for me," Chips said. I played "Slumpety Slump," a tune I'd learned onstage with Ben Branch at Currie's Club Tropicana. On the organ, I played the same guitar line that Ben's guitarist Clarence, used to get everyone on their feet for our first song every night. Chips watched me from the corner of his eye, his lit-cigarette hanging loosely from his lip. He played a few choice licks on his guitar, a cross between rockabilly and blues—clean, sharp toned, the notes of an experienced master. Real southern riverboat guitar. Chips was one of those people who moved up in the world, by hook or by crook—mostly the latter. He wasn't lacking in talent or style. Something about him said there was a derringer in his bag.[9]*

Chips was in an especially good frame of mind. For the past three quarters he had received royalty checks from his music publisher. He had done the heavy lifting at Stax, locating a movie theater they could rent for $100 a month, ripping up the seats and designing the interior, and designing the layout, making it look as much as possible like Gold Star Recording Studio in Los Angeles—all while Jim and Estelle attended their day jobs at the bank. Then because neither Jim nor Estelle knew anything about the music business he put his heart and soul into finding talent for them and then producing it so it would meet professional standards.

Chips had a charismatic personality, but he presented a rough exterior that sometimes worked to his disadvantage in most places outside a pool hall, despite his obvious good looks that women found very appealing. He was aware of his country ways and the way his tattoos negatively affected people. He once said to me: "You are a writer and you look the part. You can go into a bank and walk out with a loan. I've written hit songs that have earned millions, but because of the way I look and talk banks will not give me a loan, and that's not right."

In addition to a sense of inferiority toward those who wore business suits and spoke "over his head" on serious economic topics, Chips experienced wide mood swings. Because the author was once a mental health professional, he concluded after knowing Chips a short while that he was probably bipolar. He went through periods of both depression and manic mood swings. He self-medicated, first with alcohol and then latter with cocaine. Medication would have helped him greatly, then again it might have dulled his creative edge. The end result of his mood swings was an inability to maintain relationships for long periods of time. People who knew him and loved him took that into account and found ways of avoiding him when he was in an emotional spiral.

For most of 1962 Chips was in an extended high because of his music successes. There were storm clouds on the horizon, but his protective mechanisms prevented him from picking up on the subtle signs. He never developed a close friendship with Jim or Estelle. They never invited him over for holiday gatherings. More telling, Jim never slapped him on the back and presented him with a big check in appreciation of his efforts. Estelle never joked around with him the way she did with the musicians, most of whom were her son's age. As far as the money was concerned, Chips figured earnings had not reached the point where he could be paid a percentage share of the company. Chips did the heavy lifting at the studio with an understanding that he was a partner in the venture, an understanding that was never put in writing.

For much of 1962, Chips worked on two albums. The first was the eagerly awaited Mar-Keys album that was titled *Last Night*. They already had "Last Night" and the B-side "Night Before," so that required them to come up with ten additional songs to complete the album. As a group they wrote two additional songs and covered the remaining ones: "Morning After" by Earl Forest and Robert Talley, "Diana" by Paul Anka, "Alright, OK You Win" by Sid Wyche and Mamie Watts, "Sticks and Stones" by T. Turner, "Misty" by Erroll Garner, "Sack O Woe" by Julian Adderley, "Hold It" by Clifford Scott and Billy Butler, and "Ebb Tide" by Robert Maxwell and Carl Sigma.

The second album Chips worked on was Carla Thomas's first LP release, *Gee Whiz (Look at His Eyes*.) Carla and Rufus Thomas had four songs on the album and Chips had one, "Promises." The remainder were covers, including "Fools Fall in Love" and "Dance with Me." Most of the album was recorded in Nashville in March 1962, but additional work was done on the album in Memphis in May.

That same month a Sunday session was set up at Stax to record a jingle for a local business. Jim Stewart was there to engineer (Chips never had any interest in recording jingles), along with Booker T. Jones on organ, Steve Cropper on guitar, Lewie Steinberg on bass, and newcomer Al Jackson on drums. It was a racially diverse group. Jones and Jackson were black, while Cropper and Steinberg were white, with Steinberg having the added distinction of being a Jew. Two years later, Duck Dunn would replace Steinberg.

When the singer did not show up for the session, Jim asked Booker T. to play a song he had heard him do in a local nightclub. Booker T. explained the song to the others and started playing it, with them falling in behind him. When Jim felt they had a tight groove, he turned on the tape recorder. After the playback they knew they had a song. Jim played it for Estelle and she named it "Behave Yourself," according to Booker T.[10]

"Jim Stewart didn't want to release it without a B side so he said, 'Why don't you guys record something for the B side and we'll have a record.' Steve [Cropper] and I started messing again with this idea, and it became 'Green Onions.'"[11]

The next step was to come up with a name for the group. They considered several names, but not until someone pointed out that because Chips had a group named the Triumphs, so named because he drove a British Leyland Triumph, they should name their group after another British Leyland sports car, the MG. Thus they became Booker T. and the MGs. Later, in an effort to avoid legal problems with British Leyland over their trademark for the MG, they announced that MG stood for Memphis Group. Subsequent records used both "MGs" and MG's" in an effort to make the spelling make sense. Stax released the single and then began work on the album, with a target release date of September 1962.

Chips continued to perform in local nightclubs, as much for the fun of it as the money. With the arrival of summer, he spent less time at the studio and more time with his wife, Lorrie, and his daughter, Monique, taking them fishing whenever he could. There was a pattern to the way he lived his life. When he was depressed and feeling down, he stayed away from the studio because it dampened his creative process. To be an effective record producer he needed to be somewhere within the manic phase of his personality. He needed to be "up" and excited about what he was doing. Accompanying a manic high were usually periods of irritability or being "touchy" over criticism of his studio efforts, however well-meaning the criticism. Anyone who worked with him or maintained a friendship with him learned to accept his mood swings, mainly because he was essentially a soft-hearted, generous individual who would do anything for his friends and co-workers when he wasn't in his manic phase.

Chips never talked much about Booker T. and the MGs, but it is likely his feelings were hurt that they had excluded him from the project. That they proceeded without him for the impromptu session after the jingle booking fell apart, was understandable, but why would they begin work on the album cuts without him when he had been the staff producer almost from the beginning? That made no sense at all to him. He had built Stax from the ground up while Jim and Estelle spent their days at the bank. Why would they do an important album without him unless they planned to ease him out of the company?

Late in the summer of 1962, Chips went into the studio to talk to Jim about the company's finances. Jim told him he had no money coming to him. Chips asked about his percentage. "Jim Stewart stood there and just said to my face, 'I'm fucking you out of it.'" Moman told Peter Guralnick. "We had made over a million dollars at that point; I'm supposed to have a 25 percent share. And I got nothing." Wayne Jackson, who was stretched out on a couch outside the office told Rob Bowman he heard the whole thing, adding that Jim told Chips, "I fucked you and if you can prove it fine and if you can't . . . I'm the bookkeeper and I've got the money."

Chips stormed out of the office and never returned.

What Estelle told me about the breakup made me wonder if Jim had told her the entire story. "Chips was trying to take over the place," she said. "I think their agreement was that if Chips would come back in a couple of weeks and agree to go along with Jim, then he would accept him back. Well, Chips didn't want to do that, so he didn't come back. That's when others took over and helped Jim out."

Asked in 1995 how long it took for the hard feelings to fade away, Estelle said, "I don't think they ever did. I think Chips was going to prove that he could do it, and he did. There's no doubt he was talented. But Chips wanted half the company. I was left out and I was the one who put all the money up for it. So everybody got more out of it than me. I took me several years before I ever got anything back. I didn't resent it. I kept working with the kids. They looked at me as their mama. They had someone they could talk to. Jim wasn't that type of person. They couldn't talk to him. They needed someone to talk to about their personal feelings."

Years later, when Rob Bowman asked Jim about the confrontation with Chips he said that so many years had passed he could no longer remember what happened. There seems little doubt Chips was promised a percentage. Whether that percentage was 25, 30 or 50 percent probably will never be resolved.

STAX WAS BEGINNING to unravel in 1967 as Jim Stewart's lack of savvy in the music business began to catch up with him. They were already having management problems when they learned in October 1967 that Atlantic Records was being acquired by Warner Brothers. Jerry Wexler told Jim not to worry because he was staying on at Atlantic and nothing between them would change. In fact, *everything* was about to change. The troubles began when Jim was informed he would have to renegotiate Stax's distribution agreement with Atlantic because of the merger. When they couldn't agree, Jim took the deal to Gulf & Western.

"Then came the shocker—to him as well as to me: Atlantic owned every one of his masters," said Wexler. "In no uncertain terms, the ownership was in the original contract drawn up by Atlantic's lawyer, Paul Marshall. I hadn't known, hadn't read the fine print, and neither had Jim. I felt lousy, certain that Stax was entitled to retain those enduring records produced in their own studio; but the contract specified otherwise . . . I argued with the corporate bosses on Jim's behalf; the new owners, however, had absolutely no reason to return valuable properly which was incontestably a key part of the overall Atlantic assets. There was no righting this wrong. Jim was screwed, and I feel bad about it to this day."[12]

Chips Moman
Photo courtesy Mississippi Valley Collection
University of Memphis Libraries

CHAPTER 3
Creating the American Sound
(1963-1965)

CHIPS MOMAN'S LIFE FELL APART after his blowup with Stax Records. He sank into a deep depression and stayed drunk for almost a year. As a result, he lost his house on Mink Street, his car, everything he had except his daughter and wife, Lorrie, who stuck by him despite the hard times. He found work as a producer at Royal Studio, owned by Hi Records, but he was often drinking during the sessions, the joke at the studio being that you didn't have to pay him money, just provide him with a bottle of whiskey and he would do anything you asked of him. Words could not come close to describing the dark night of his tortured soul during that turbulent year. Emotionally he was lost at sea with land nowhere in sight.

Chips found a lawyer, Seymour Rosenberg, who was willing to sue Jim Stewart, if necessary, over what happened to Chips at Stax, at least he told Chips he would. If he ever filed any documents no one has ever found them. What he did was talk to Jim about the incident and return to Chips with a three thousand dollar settlement which Chips accepted because he didn't know any better. He subsequently told one interviewer in jest that he didn't even know how to spell lawyer at the time. As it turned out Rosenberg also represented Stax, according to Peter Guralnick, and wanted to get in the music business and suggested Chips partner up with him.[13]

With cash in his pocket and feeling more than a little desperate, Chips readily agreed to the arrangement. For their studio they chose a vacant grocery at the corner of Thomas and Chelsea, down the street from Rosenberg's law office. They purchased some used studio equipment and Chips tried to breathe life into the rickety building. They named the studio

American Sound Studio. No one kept good records then, but one group that Chips recorded during that time (1961) was a rock group named Tommy Burk and the Counts. He either recorded them at the newly opened American Sound Studio or at Royal Studio, where he also did freelance sessions and production work. The band was very popular in Memphis at the time and on fraternity row at the University of Mississippi, where they frequently were booked for weekend parties. One of the things that made them stand out, other than a tight band, were their background singers, two twin brothers. Usually bands had female background singers. Twin males singing into the same microphone was an unusual twist.

The group was represented by Rosenberg, who also represented other music acts such as Charlie Rich. Chips took a 1933-penned song recorded by Billie Holiday in 1952, "Stormy Weather," a song he likely heard on the radio in Memphis the year after he arrived, and he gave it a modern up-tempo beat for Tommy Burk and the Counts. It was the first known instance of a recording philosophy that would bring him great success later in his career. As far as songs were concerned, his thought process had it that "once a hit, always a threat." He understood that record buyers chose records released by artists they liked, but if the artist was an unknown, the next best thing was to record a song that was familiar to the record buyer. They might buy the record simply because they liked the song. "Stormy Weather" was released on Nat Records, but did not do well. Not long after that Chips sold his share of the studio back to Rosenberg, who was unable to make a go of it and eventually sold the studio to an Arkansas farmer named Don Crews, who was interested in the studio because he had a nephew who wanted to get into the music business. Crews and his nephew became partners in the venture.

Only Chips and Lorrie know precisely when he pulled himself out of his alcoholic hell—and neither are with us now to give testimony—but it was probably in early 1964, most likely around the time Chips tiptoed into Don Nix's darkened one-bedroom apartment in the dead of night looking for him. The apartment was located on Poplar Avenue across the street

63

from Overton Park, which was home to the Memphis Zoo, the Memphis Art Academy, and an impressive expanse of greenery. Because many of the students at the academy were what were called Beatniks, the forerunner to the hippie generation, many sought apartments in Nix's building, where rent averaged only fifty dollars a month.

It was the perfect place for a member of the Mar-Keys to hang out when he was not on the road. Because the apartments were so cheap, he rented two units and furnished both, leaving one vacant so he would not be bothered by nosey or noisy neighbors. His apartment concealed a secret that he only shared with a couple of people, for obvious reasons. There was a door in the kitchen that appeared to be a back door. It wasn't. It opened into a closed-off hallway that had a second door that led to a stairway that went upstairs to a secret space with two bedrooms. Nix fashioned one of them into his bedroom. He slept there every night, hidden away from the world, to escape the traffic noises on Poplar, confident no one would ever be able to find him. He kept the door to the bedroom locked. The only way to get in when he was asleep was to pick the lock.

One night Nix awakened to feel someone shaking him.

Unable to get him fully awake, they shook harder.

The room was dark, so he couldn't see who it was.

From the black void he heard a voice he immediately recognized.

"Chips?"

The producer was down on his knees at the edge of Nix's bed.

"What are you doing in here?" Nix asked.

"I need to go to Nashville. Can you take me?"

"What time is it?"

"I don't know," Chips said. "We can make it."

"So I got up and took him. I always loved Chips. There was no one like him I ever met. He could talk you into anything. And he could talk you out of being mad at him. That's why I didn't argue with him."

Chips needed to go to Nashville to find work now that he was sober. He didn't expect to be there very long, so he left his family in Memphis and rented a three-bedroom, second floor apartment in a Nashville complex that was a favorite hangout for musicians. Four doors down from him lived Ed Bruce, a singer/songwriter/actor who would later achieve fame for writing the 1975 hit, "Mamma Don't let your Babies Grow Up to Be Cowboys" and for co-starring with James Garner in the television series "Bret Maverick." A frequent guest at Chips' apartment was Charlie Freeman, a highly regarded guitarist who had been with the Mar-Keys when they were the Royal Spades, but had left before they recorded their hit record, only to rejoin the group later to replace Steve Cropper when he grew tired of being on the road.

"One Sunday morning Charlie Freeman came out of a bedroom with this stark-naked stripper he had picked up on Printers' Alley the night before," recalled Nix, who was a guest at the apartment at the time. "They sat on the couch in front of the door, and I'm sitting in a chair on another side of the couch and Chips is sitting in a chair reading the newspaper. No one locked their doors in those days, so when Ed Bruce walked in without knocking and saw everyone it startled him. He just stood there a moment. No one said anything to him, so finally he said, 'Well, I guess there's nothing happening around here,' and left."

While in Nashville Chips worked for Tree Publishing recording demos of country songs. Tree was owned by producer Buddy Killen, who thought Chips would be a good person to work with a black rhythm and blues singer he recently had signed named Joe Tex. Killen had so much faith in Tex he established a record label, Dial, specifically for him. For some reason the collaboration with Chips did not work out in Nashville. Killen ended up taking Tex to Muscle Shoals in late 1964 to record what would become his biggest hit, "Hold Onto What You've Got."[14] Although Killen had decided he wanted to produce the session, he invited Chips to go as a session player and perhaps to advise him because Killen had not made a name for himself as a rhythm and blues producer.[15] It was at this session that Chips probably first met a young woman named Sandy Posey, who was there as a backup singer with the Hershel Wigginton Singers.

65

Later, she would play a pivotal role in Chips' development as a pop record producer.

One afternoon Chips told Nix, "Let's go to Memphis."

"What time do you want to leave?"

"One a.m.," he said. "We're going to fly. I've got the tickets."

"We got a DC-7 that was coming down from New York," said Nix. "The lights were out inside. Everyone was sleeping. It was real cozy. We got back to Memphis and he bought a Thunderbird."

Clear-eyed and optimistic, Chips called Don Crews once he returned to Memphis and asked him if they could be partners. By that time Crews had bought out his nephew and was then full owner of a recording studio that had no one on staff with music expertise. It was an awkward position for a farmer to be in. Crews was delighted to partner with Chips.

After his return to Memphis, Chips wasted no time getting his new house in order. One of the first groups he recorded was a high school rock band named the Gentrys. They were very much into the so-called "British Invasion" that had occurred in 1964, most notably with the release of the Beatles' first album in the United States, featuring the Number One single, "I Want to Hold Your Hand." Other British groups that followed were the Dave Clark Five, Gerry and the Pacemakers, the Rolling Stones and Manfred Man. Among the characteristics the British Invasion groups shared were tendencies to dress in matching or proper suits, a willingness to make fun of their elders with a wink of the eye, upbeat music that was driven by drums and guitars, and clever, avant-garde song lyrics that did not focus on story-telling, as was the style in country and rhythm and blues. The band chose the name Gentrys for two reasons: because it sounded British and because that was the name of a popular brand of condoms in the 1960s.[16] As it turned out, all those things that the Gentrys loved about the British groups, Chips disliked and that made for an interesting partnership.

Lead vocalist and guitarist of the original group was Larry Raspberry. Other vocalists included Bruce Bowles and Jimmy Hart; the horns were

66

composed of Jimmy Johnson on trumpet and Bobby Fisher on saxophone; Larry Butler on keyboards; and Larry Wall on drums, subsequently replaced by Rob Straube, who was later replaced by Mike Gardner. Juniors and seniors at Treadwell High School in Memphis, they all had better academic educations than their producer.

The Gentrys' first recording was "Sometimes" released on Chips' label, Youngstown Records. He had created the label back in 1963 during the dark night of his soul. Probably recorded at Royal Studios, the first release featured Jeb Stuart singing "All for Love." Stuart was a black rhythm and blues singer who already had recorded numerous releases for Sam Phillips' various labels. He sang lead in a doo-wop style, backed by several male background singers. The record didn't go anywhere and Youngstown lay dormant until Chips returned to Memphis. The Gentrys' followed up "Sometimes" with an upbeat dance tune, "Keep on Dancing," which also was released on Youngstown Records.

"Sometimes I Cry," didn't attract much attention, but the band did by winning a state fair talent show that resulted in an appearance on the Ted Mack Amateur Hour, at that time the major television talent show in the United States. By the time the band returned from New York, "Keep on Dancing" was doing well in Memphis, so well that MGM Records picked up distribution of the record. By October 1965, the record was Number 4 in the nation, which put the band ahead of their British idols such as the Rolling Stones ("Get Off My Cloud") and Herman's Hermits ("Just a Little Bit Better").

No one was more surprised than Chips Moman, who once confided to me that he hated the record so much he mixed it with the sound turned off, using only the meters to balance the volume levels. Lead singer Raspberry once alluded to that in an interview: "Chips really understood rhythm and blues and country, because he helped put Stax Records together. He didn't understand much about this wild British garage stuff

ion>

NAN by James L. Dickerson

**Larry Raspberry, lead singer of The Gentrys, left,
Don Nix of the Mar-Keys
Photo courtesy Larry Raspberry, Don Nix**

68

we played. He didn't appreciate it and he didn't like it. I don't say that to make him sound like a villain. He wasn't. He was just a guy who couldn't understand it."[17]

Years later, interviewed for *Nine-O-One Network* magazine, Raspberry, said, "It made me grow up pretty fast. I think even now it gave me an overview of the recording industry. It taught me to never say never. It taught me how to compromise." Raspberry subsequently moved to Los Angeles, where he still lives, to write songs for artists such as Carly Simon, the Everly Brothers and Jimmy Buffet.

AS CHIPS RE-ESTABLISHED himself in Memphis with American Sound Studio, a future competitor who would end up having a big influence on music recording in the city, was just getting started in the music business. John Fry became interested in music while still in high school. With the help of two high school classmates, John King and Fred Smith, he cleaned out a room in his parents' garage that had once been used as a sewing room by his grandmother and converted it into a very rough facsimile of a recording studio.

Don Nix tells the story of meeting Fry in 1964 and hanging out at the garage studio with friends, including girls who liked to swim in the family's pool. "John would go to bed, but we would stay all night. I don't know that I have ever met anyone who loved recording as much as John Fry. That studio was his life. He could have been anything in life he wanted to be, but he loved recording so much."

At that time what Fry had in mind was not selling time in his studio but creating a record label—he named it Ardent—and making recordings that could be pressed into records. One of his first groups to record was the Ole Miss Down Beats, who wrote and recorded songs such as "Geraldine" and "Hucklebuck" that were pressed into 45s and sent to radio stations for airplay. Fry seldom got airplay or sales, but he did gain valuable experience. By 1966 he had opened a studio on National Street in Memphis. His partners, John King and Fred Smith, did not stick with him past high school. King got into the radio business and later worked in promotions for Ardent. Smith, who was born in Marks, Mississippi, went off to college at Yale and returned to found a mammoth overnight delivery company named Federal Express.

Because Fry had no ambitions to become a star in the music business, he set out to build one of the most technically advanced recording studios in the South. Ardent had the best recording equipment that money could buy. As a result, record companies began to send their artists to Ardent because of the quality of the sound captured in the studio. Among the acts that recorded at the studio over the next couple of decades were the Fabulous Thunderbirds, ZZ Top (most of their albums were recorded at Ardent, not in Texas), Joe Cocker, to name a few. Both John Fry and his former partner Fred Smith subsequently would become central figures in Chips Moman's 1985 high-profile return to Memphis to breathe new life into the city's music industry.

BY THE TIME CHIPS recorded his first hit after returning to Memphis, he had perfected his philosophy of record production and cleared a path for his genius to take root and flourish in the protective environment of a recording studio. Working with the high-energy Gentrys was, in many respects, a nightmare for Chips. The band's definition of rock was not his definition, which had been forged from rockabilly. The Gentrys were avant garde, experimental, and light years away from rockabilly.

While working with the Gentrys, Chips realized rock was not his forte. His strength was rhythm and blues, pop, and country music. Secondly, as the individual who had put together the Stax house band, he knew he had to put together an American Sound Studio band that would be able to record rhythm and blues, pop, and country music. The Gentrys were a terrific live performance band, but as a studio band they were only as good as their weakest link. Instrumentally, Chips' experience in the studio was limited to the guitar, an instrument he played with great expertise. He was neither an accomplished vocalist, drummer, bassist, keyboard player, nor horn player. As a result, he had to use words, not demonstration, to explain what he wanted from a particular instrument, with the exception of the guitar. With some musical problems in the studio, words failed him and he ended up melting down in frustration.

For the next couple of years he set out to create a house band that had no weak links. He wanted every member to be the best musician possible for each individual instrument. The first musician to show up on Chips' radar was **Tommy Cogbill** (1932-1982), a Tennessee-born bassist and jazz guitarist Chips probably first encountered at Royal Studio where he and Cogbill often were booked for sessions. As far as live performances were concerned, Cogbill focused almost entirely on jazz clubs, but since there was little demand for jazz guitarists for studio sessions he relied more on his skills as a bassist and rhythm guitar player to earn a living. In the early days of American Sound Studio, Cogbill was a key player in Chip's ambitious plans for the studio. As time went by, Cogbill gravitated more toward production work.

The second person Chips recruited for his house band was **Mike Leach** (1941-2017), a native Memphian who had attended but not graduated from Memphis State, where he majored in music with a focus on the trumpet. After he left college he learned that it was easier to earn a living playing bass than it was with a trumpet, so he switched instruments.

"I used to see Chips playing in the clubs," he told me. "We'd run into each other on the same gig together. He was always talking about opening a studio one of these days. I said, 'Man count me in.' One day he called. He said, 'I have a little place now and would love for you to come work with me. I did this off and on for about a year. Then one day I said, 'I don't want to do this anymore.'"

"OK, I won't call you anymore," Chips said, without argument.

"Next thing I knew Tommy Cogbill was working for him and they were cutting all these records. I was extremely jealous. Finally, Chips called me. The first session was with Sandy Posey. Ever since then I was part of the group. Tommy and I took turns playing bass. When Tommy started producing, I started playing bass full time."

It is difficult to know, more than sixty years after the fact, the exact timeline for the acquisition of the remaining members of the house band, later to be identified as the 827 Thomas Street Band, but all were in place by 1968. Four years earlier, several of the soon-to-be American Sound Studio team—Mike Leach, Gene Chrisman, **Bobby Wood** (1941-present), and even Chips himself—did a session at Sam Phillips' studio under Stan Kesler's supervision to record an album featuring Bobby Wood as the artist and pianist. Originally from New Albany, Mississippi, Bobby already had recorded several successful singles for Joy Records, including "This Time," written by Chips and "If I'm a Fool for Loving You," written by Stan Kesler. Influenced by Jerry Lee Lewis's piano work, his singing style was more akin to Bobby Vee. He was out on the road promoting the record when he was involved in a car accident. "He lost an eye and split his head wide open," said Chips. "He was in the hospital for months. They said he was not going to live. He pulled through and never wanted to go on the road again because it hurt so badly. That's when he came over to work for me. He's no lightweight." For two years, Wood worked part-time for Chips, not becoming a full-time member of the band until 1968.

"There's a street down in Southaven that says Bobby Wood Boulevard," said Chips. "He's always been a religious boy. He built his church a big driveway and a big cover over it so that the old folks wouldn't get wet getting out of their cars."

In 1958, Chips' band was booked for a performance in Corinth, Mississippi. Chips asked around town if anyone there could play piano. **Bobby Emmons'** (1943-2015) name came up, so he called him and asked him to play with the band. He was fifteen years old at the time. Chips was impressed with his piano work. "He played piano like Chet Atkins played guitar." Subsequently, Bobby played organ with the Bill Black Combo. He joined Chips' house band shortly after Mike Leach did and became an integral member of the group. They soon discovered they had similar interest in music and became songwriting partners, a relationship that last more than half a century and produced many hit records. As far as the house band was concerned, Bobby mainly focused on playing the B-3 organ. When a piano part was needed, Chips called in Bobby Wood. If you were to spend a lot of time listening to records produced by Chips Moman, you would learn that all of his productions utilized a B 3 organ, a fact that sometimes caused conflicts with artists who did not like the sound of a B 3 organ on their record. If that ever became a source of conflict—and it did—Chips had only one answer: "I don't make records without a B 3." The use of the organ was not negotiable.

Drummer **Gene Chrisman** (1941-present) started playing drums in a high school band. "I picked it up off records," he explained to Jody Flans, a writer for *Modern Drummer* magazine. "I beat my cardboard boxes and pots and pans, while I listened to Fats Domino, Little Richard, and all that stuff . . . I hated country. When a country record came on, it turned me off . . . Now I enjoy country. Of course 'country' is not as it was before. You can do things in country now that you couldn't do back when I was growing up. That kind of makes a difference." In 1958 Chrisman played on his first recording session in a studio at the Chisca Hotel in Memphis. The artist was rockabilly singer Jody Chastain, who often performed with a more experienced rockabilly artist named Charlie Feathers. A single was released as a result of that first session, "My, My" and "Jody's Beat." After that Gene mostly worked in nightclubs in and around Memphis. One night in 1960 he was performing at the Five Gables Congress Club when Jerry Lee Lewis visited the club and let it be known he was looking for a new drummer. He listened to Chrisman play for a while, then sat in with the band and played a couple of his songs. Shortly after that he asked Chrisman to join his band. After that he played the nightclub circuit and did session work for Stan Kesler at Phillips Recording Studio. Chips played a session or two with him and asked him to join his house band at American Sound Studio. While describing Chrisman to me, Chips once said, "He does a little preaching on the side. A very religious guy."

Undoubtedly, the "star" of the American Sound Studio house band was guitarist **Reggie Young** (1936-2019), who immigrated to Memphis from Osceola, Arkansas, with his family at the age of fourteen. Packed among his belongings was a guitar. A quick learner, he was playing professionally at the age of fifteen. Soon he would join rockabilly singer Eddie Bond's band. His first recording session was on Bond's hit record "Rockin' Daddy." Not long after that country star Johnny Horton asked him to play in his band. By the late 1950s, he had found a home as the house guitarist at Royal Studios in Memphis. Also playing on sessions at the studio was Elvis Presley's former bassist Bill Black. As a result of that association, Young and Black decided to create a band.

Undecided about whether to call the band the Bill Black Combo or the Reggie Young Combo, they decided on the former. In late 1959 they released a single—"Smokie, Part1" was the A side; "Smokie, part 2" was the B side. An instrumental, it quickly went to Number 1on the rhythm and blues chart and entered the Top 20 on the pop chart. The song was very popular on juke boxes as a dance tune, making the Bill Black Combo one of the top bands in the nation.

Unfortunately, within months Young was drafted by the U.S. Army. After two years of service—during which the Bill Black Combo continued to flourish—he returned to Memphis to resume work as a session player at Royal Studios. He continued to play guitar on recordings made by the Bill Black Combo, but allowed guitarist Bob Tucker to replace him in the touring band.

When the Beatles requested that the Bill Black Combo be their opening act on their first American tour in 1964, Reggie rejoined the group and Tucker moved over to bass. At that time Bill Black was ill with a brain tumor and was no longer performing. Black died in 1965.

After the Beatles' tour, Young showed little interest in continuing as a road band guitarist. He preferred studio work and remained at Royal Studios until Chips was able to entice him into joining the American Sound Studio house band. "Up until then I was the guitar player at the studio, but I got busy producing and got Reggie to take my place," said Chips. "He was so great I couldn't ever go back. I'm a pretty good musician, but every one of those boys in the band are better than me. I'm not in their league."

At that point Chips had a house band in which each player was an expert with his own instrument. With time he would develop a top notch horn section and Mike Leach would become proficient in string arrangements. What he didn't have—and wouldn't have until 1970—was someone who was a vocals expert, someone who could advise singers on what they could do to improve their vocals. Until that time came, Chips remained the expert on vocals, making decisions based on what sounded right to him. His guide was whether a vocal melded with the sound track in such a way as to sound like a hit. When it came to hits, Chips was a stone-cold genius at recognizing one when he heard one. No American producer was ever better.

Chips did not put his super group together overnight. It took several years to get everyone in place. Throughout the early years of American Sound Studio, Tommy Cogbill alternated with Mike Leach on bass, sometimes played rhythm guitar, often was booked on sessions in Muscle Shoals, and remained a member of the house band until everyone moved to Nashville in 1972. Cogbill died in 1982. During their years in Memphis and for numerous years in Nashville, the house band was always identified as the 827 Thomas Street Band. As time went by Nashville pickers referred to them as "those Memphis boys." By the late 1990s, the band was answering to the name "Memphis Boys." They remained a cohesive unit for almost half a century, until Bobby Emmons passed away in 2015, Mike Leach in 2017, and Reggie Young in 2019.

Not only did they stick together all those years as musicians, they also remained close friends, often referring to each other as brothers. Chips Moman felt the same bond to them. "Once I got busted on an income tax thing," Chips once told me. "They were fixin' to take what I had to pay the tax. Bobby Emmons was the first one down there. 'I just heard about it,' Emmons said. 'The bank told me they would let me have $80,000 and I'll have it for you by this afternoon.' Then Reggie came along and said, 'Hey man, I'm gonna borrow some money on my farm. I can let you have $100,000.' Bobby Wood called. They all came to bail my ass out. I said, 'I don't want you to do that. Let me see if I can't take care of it myself.' And I did take care of it myself. But do you know what kind of an honor it is to have your friends offer to do that for you? They are special people. Whatever I got is theirs if they want it. That's the kind of relationship we got."

WHEN PEOPLE REFER TO MUSCLE SHOALS, Alabama, as a music center, they are talking about three small cities that are interconnected: Muscle Shoals (pop. 9,611), Florence (pop. 36, 426), and Sheffield (pop. 10,380). What they most have in common is the Tennessee River that flows through the northeast corner of Alabama. As a community, residents are closer to the Natchez Trace (20 minute drive) than to an interstate highway (one hour drive).

Two historically prominent figures from this community are W.C. Handy, father of the blues, and Sam Phillips of Sun Records fame. In the late 1950s and early 1960s there were several abortive attempts to establish recording studios in the community, but not until 1962 was anyone successful. Rick Hall opened a studio that year that he named Fame Studio. It was located in a twenty-by-seventy-foot cinderblock building that resembled a quick-change oil business more so than it did a hatchery for legendary music. Of course, appearances can be deceptive, especially in the South, where nothing is ever exactly what it appears to be.

Fame's first hit was a rhythm and blues song, "Steal Away," recorded in 1964 by a rubber factory employee named Jimmy Hughes. It attracted attention, but none of the recording studios in Memphis—Stax, Royal Studio, Phillips Recording—considered the upstart Alabama studio much of a threat. The next hit out of Fame, "Hold Onto What You've Got," by Joe Tex also created waves among rhythm and blues fans. But it was not until a local hospital orderly named Percy Sledge recorded what became a major hit, "When a Man Loves a Woman," that the world realized that something great was taking place in Muscle Shoals. The recording was done at a small studio put together by Quin Ivy, a popular local deejay. He named his studio Quinivy. The session was engineered by Rick Hall's assistant, Jimmy Johnson, who sometimes moonlighted at Quinivy.

When they had it down on tape, Ivy played it for Rick Hall, who volunteered to send it to Jerry Wexler at Atlantic because he already had a relationship with him and Ivy did not. Ivy was grateful for the referral. Wexler was ecstatic when he listened to the recording, calling his partner Ahmet Ertegun, who was in Europe at the time, to tell him he'd found a single that was "going to pay for our whole summer." And it did, too.

Rick Hall received a finder's fee for the referral, but the real benefit was that it elevated the recording industry as a whole in Muscle Shoals. Hall's house band at that time consisted of Dan Penn, a sixteen-year-old singer/songwriter/guitarist, piano player Spooner Oldham, bassist Norbert Putnam, and drummer Donnie Fritts. They were all white rednecks in social transition, but the music they played was sleight-of-hand soul that sounded as if it was done by hard-core, seasoned black musicians.

In time Dan Penn and Spooner Oldham left Fame to go to Memphis. They were replaced by Jimmy Johnson on guitar, David Hood on bass, Roger Hawkins on drums, and Barry Beckett on keyboards. Eventually, the house band lineup at Fame fractured yet again, with Hood, Johnson, and Roger leaving Fame to open a studio of their own. They named it Muscle Shoals Sound Studio. Their first major artist was Cher, who recorded an album titled *3614 Jackson Highway*, the studio's mailing address. She was followed by the Rolling Stones, Paul Simon, Bob Segar, Rod Stewart, Bobbie Gentry, and many others.

Muscle Shoals' loss was Chips Moman's gain. Dan Penn and Spooner Oldham both relocated to Memphis. Chips and Dan were so similar, people often concluded they were brothers. Both spoke in the same irreverent Southern dialect that alternated between haughty sarcasm and tactless confrontation. They even resembled each other in their facial features and posture, and they walked with the same shuffling cockiness. They could almost finish each other's sentences, so much so that when they spoke on serious issues it revealed they possessed the same worldview. Chips greatly valued Penn's songwriting skills and his ability to sing in a black voice that was so soulful that you would swear the song was being sung by an African American if you closed your eyes. Two considerations kept Chips from recording Penn as a vocalist, the first being his rough edges and his don't-give-a-damn attitude, neither of which were consistent with being an entertainer, and the second being the low demand in the marketplace for white singers who could sound black.

Spooner Oldham did none of the above, but he fit nicely into the mix. Skinny as a rail in the early days, he vacillated between sporting a goatee and mustache, or a full beard. Like Penn, his roots were in Alabama. Throughout high school he played piano in various bands. After graduation, he enrolled at the University of North Alabama, a public university in Florence, where he attended classes until he dropped out to work at Fame Studio. Like most of the people Chips worked with, he was an academic dropout, but unlike all the others, with the exception of Mike Leach, he had university credits. It was not that Chips had a phobia about working with educated people; it was just that he felt more comfortable working with individuals who had similar life experiences and education.

What he saw in Oldham was someone who had above average talents as a songwriter and keyboard player. After having a rewarding career with Chips at American Sound Studio for a time, Oldham would move to Nashville and then on to Los Angles where he performed with Joe Cocker, Jackson Browne, Linda Ronstadt, and others, and then formed close associations with Bob Dylan and Neil Young during the glory years of rock and folk music.

From the mid-1960s through the early 1970s, Memphis and Muscle Shoals had an open relationship. Personnel and ideas were exchanged with

Chips Moman, center, Spooner Oldham, left, Dan Penn
Photo © Phillip Rauls

great frequency. In many ways they were dependent upon each other for their individual successes. As Muscle Shoal Sounds churned out hit after hit, Rick Hall remained competitive at Fame, the main difference being that he found more and more of his clients doing records for country music labels. In practical terms that meant that beginning in the mid-1970s, when the Memphis music industry was imploding, Muscle Shoals studios looked northward to Nashville for continued commercial success.

DAN PENN CO-WROTE SOME SONGS with Oldham—"Cry Like a Baby" and "I'm Your Puppet"—but mostly he wrote with Chips. The results were often spectacular. One night they were playing poker with a group of radio people at a disk jockey convention in Memphis, when they decided to take a break to try to write a song or two. Quinton Claunch, a co-founder of Hi Records, told them they could use his room if they would write him a song for James Carr, a black rhythm and blues artist he planned to record in Royal Studio for his Goldwax label. Thirty minutes later they gave him a song titled, "The Dark End of the Street."[18]

As a singer, James Carr was a rarity in Memphis music history in that although he was born in Mississippi, he was raised in Memphis. Like, Carr, almost everyone else associated with Memphis music had migrated there from somewhere else, but few had been raised in Memphis. It would take a convention of psychologists and sociologists to even hazard a guess as to why the city could produce great instrumentalists but few great vocalists, Alex Chilton of the Box Tops and Larry Raspberry of the Gentrys being the exceptions.

After receiving some recognition as a gospel singer, he approached Stax Records about being signed to sing soul ballads. Stax turned him down. He then went to Goldwax, which signed him to a recording contract two years before Claunch approached Chips and Penn about writing a song for him. Carr's previous songs had been mildly successful. What he most needed at this point in his career was a hit record. Chips was familiar with Carr's previous work for Goldwax because it had occurred during the time

Chips worked at Royal Studios as a sound engineer and session guitarist. Years later, when Claunch reconsidered the recording, he said, "At that point in time you don't think how big it's going to be. Oh, Lord, it just knocked me out . . . It had all the ingredients, a good melody line, it just flowed, and the lyric—um!"[19]

"The Dark End of the Street" was an emotional look at forbidden love that reaches out to the heart almost from the first verse. It is a song one *feels* more so than *listens* to. Peter Guralnick has described it as a "masterpiece and one of the most unforgettable songs of the entire soul era."[20] I would go a step further and say it is one of the best written and recorded soul songs ever. Amazingly, it was the first effort that Chips and Penn undertook as collaborators. Not only did they deliver a hit record— it went to Number 10 on Billboard's R&B chart—it remained the best-selling song of Carr's career and provided Chips and Penn with gravitas as a songwriting team.

To Chips, it was more important than he ever let on. He understood that hit records depended on hit songs. He had had a few in his career up to this point, but he had never had a true writing partner. That is what he saw in Penn, someone who could partner with him at the studio and help him find the kind of success that thus far had eluded him.

In the coming years he would find an even stronger songwriting relationship with Bobby Emmons, but for now Penn was all he had. To hold onto him, he tried to involve him in projects that he knew appealed to Penn, things such as studio sessions and producing. He held those things out as carrots. In fact his new relationship with Penn was the prototype for many of the business decisions he would make over the years. As a businessman, he only *hired* individuals when there was no alternative. He preferred for people to work for him *without pay*, offering incentives through which they could earn money from others by touting their relationship with him. Some people would mistakenly see that as a con, but to Chips it was based on sound economic principles, firmly rooted in the basics of capitalism. Or as he might have put it, getting people to work for him without pay was as American as apple pie.

FOR JERRY WEXLER at Atlantic Records, rhythm and blues artist Wilson Pickett was a great acquisition to the label's talent lineup. For his first album, he put him in a New York studio with producer Bert Berns, who had a history of successful records, including hits such as Solomon Burke's "Everybody Needs Someone to Love," Willie Nelson's "Hello Walls," and the Drifters' "Under the Boardwalk." However, the Alabama-born Pickett was uncooperative and the Bronx-born producer was abrasive. There was zero chemistry between artist and producer. When the album was turned in, Wexler saw that it was unusable.

"Finally, I got an idea—not for a song but for a trip: me and Pickett to Memphis, whose freshness just might give us the edge," Wexler wrote in his memoir. "And instead of providing material, I urged him—with local genius Steve Cropper—to create his own. I put the two of them in a hotel room with a bottle of Jack Daniel's and the simple exhortation—"Write!"—which they did . . . One of the songs was "In the Midnight Hour." I loved the lyric and the gospel fervor. Cropper inspired Pickett's truest passion."

Wexler was so pleased with the May and October recordings he set up a second session for January 1966. One of the songs from that session, "634-5789," also proved to be a hit. It convinced him that he had been right to take Pickett to Stax to record. It was around that time that Jim Stewart informed Wexler that Pickett was no long welcome at Stax. The reason he gave Wexler was that he was tired of other record labels benefiting from their in-house productions.

That was certainly a factor, but there was also Pickett's personality to consider. The singer was temperamental to the extreme, frequently getting into arguments with the staff. He had an athlete's build and when he was upset he tended to get in the face of the person he was disagreeing with, making him very intimidating. Also to consider was the fact that he was

**Wilson Pickett, second from left, Jimmie Johnson, Bobby Womack
Photo courtesy David Hood**

upset that Cropper got writer's credit on "The Midnight Hour."[21] In the end, Stewart, who didn't handle stress well, just wanted him gone. Out of sight, out of mind.

An additional factor, according to Wexler, was his relationship with Chips Moman: "Chips is one of the great Southern musical minds, a manipulator and mesmerizer who, under a full moon in deserted parking lots, has been known to con drug-crazed badasses into handing over their guns. I always got along with Moman, but Jim didn't, and at a certain point he began to resent our relationship."[22]

Because Wexler was so pleased with the Southern vibe he got recording in Memphis, he decided to stay in the South. He booked the next session in Muscle Shoals at Fame Studio. Pickett was none too happy. Returning to his home state of Alabama was not on his bucket list. For one thing, nearby Tuscumbia was the national headquarters for the Ku Klux Klan. Add to that the consideration that Muscle Shoals was around 90 percent white and you can understand Pickett's concern.

When Pickett arrived at the studio and met the band members, he saw that unlike Memphis, where the Stax house band was half white, half black, the Fame house band was all white, except for a couple of black horn players who had been invited to the session. Also invited to that session were Chips Moman and Tommy Cogbill. Over several days ten songs were recorded. At one point, Wexler felt the bass player was not locked into the groove. He asked for suggestions from Chips, who agreed and suggested that he replace the bass player with Cogbill. Wexler felt the switch was "magical," creating the feel he was looking for.

Added to this brew was Pickett's friend, singer/songwriter Bobby Womack, who arrived with several songs: The former lead singer of the gospel group The Valentinos, he shocked the music community by marrying the widow of his friend and mentor Sam Cooke after he was murdered in a cheap motel. He further raised eyebrows when it became known that Janis Joplin had spent her last night drinking with him. Shortly before traveling to Muscle Shoals to be with his friend Wilson Pickett, he was fired from Ray Charles' band. Knowing Womack's troubled history, the Fame house band was not sure what to expect from him. They weren't sure they could handle two explosive personalities.

To everyone's surprise, Womack was friendly, outgoing and eager to do whatever he could to help Pickett have the best recording possible. He contributed songs, backup vocals, and guitar accents. He was fascinating to watch because he played his guitar left handed and reversed the order of his guitar strings. It should surprise no one that Chips was impressed by his songwriting, soulful voice, and skill with a guitar, making a mental note that he would fit in well at American Sound Studio.

Sandy Posey
Photo courtesy Gary Walker

CHAPTER 4
The Making of a Star
(1966-1968)

CHIPS RECORDED about a half dozen acts in 1965 that he released on his Youngstown Records label, but he would not record a follow-up hit to "Keep on Dancing" until 1966—and even then it was almost accidental on his part. It all began innocently enough when MGM Records producer Jim Vienneau, who was based in New York City, made one of his frequent runs to Nashville, where MGM Records had an office and studio that was used to record country artists. As head of the Nashville office, Vienneau was intrigued not only by the success Chips Moman had with the Gentrys, whose hit had been distributed by MGM, but also with the big noise that was being made at other studios in the city, such as Stax, Hi Records, and Memphis Sound Studio. Something magical seemed to be happening in Memphis. He wanted to tap into that for MGM Records.

Vienneau decided to drive over to Memphis from Nashville to meet with the various studio heads. There was no Interstate highway in those days. The road to Memphis was a two-lane highway that was fraught with perils, weather related and otherwise—and finding a safe place to eat along the way was no easy matter. For those reasons and more, he called his good friend Gary Walker, who knew his way around not just Nashville but the South in general.

Gary was an interesting person in his own right. He had begun his music career while still a farm boy in Romance, Missouri, where he grew up with a burning passion to become a country music superstar. Hank Williams was his hero. While enrolled at Southwest Missouri State College, he sent songs he had written to future Hall of Famer Porter Wagoner, who recorded several of them. One of the songs, "Trademark," was covered by Carl Smith who elbowed the song all the way to Number

2 on the country charts. Other songs were recorded by Jim Reeves ("According to My Heart"), Kitty Wells ("Repenting"), and Webb Pierce ("One Week Later"). His success as a songwriter eventually landed him a recording contract with MGM Records, which ended up releasing three singles recorded by Walker. That experience as a recording artist taught him that his lifelong passion to be a superstar was misplaced. He was much too shy to do all the public appearances a recording artist needs to do to become a superstar. He decided to find a less stressful niche for himself.

After several detours, he ended up opening a Nashville office for Atlanta music publisher Bill Lowery whose songwriter roster included Jerry Reed, Ray Stevens, Joe South, and Mac Davis. One day Mercury producer Jerry Kennedy took Leroy Van Dyke by Walker's office to find songs for his upcoming recording session. Walker played them an incomplete song written by Kendall Hayes titled "Walk on By." Both Kennedy and Van Dyke liked what they heard and Kennedy told Walker that if the songwriter would complete the song he would record it at the session. When the songwriter was unable to come up with a suitable second verse, Walker finished the song himself. "Walk on By" went to the top of the charts soon after release. In 1994, when *Billboard* magazine published its 100th anniversary issue it ranked Van Dyke's "Walk on By" its Number 1 hit of all time. In the years after that Walker also worked for Painted Desert Music and Screen Gems-Columbia as a "song-plugger," someone who pitched new songs to producers and record companies.

So when Jim Vienneau, representing MGM Records, set out for Memphis with Gary Walker riding shotgun, he didn't just have a good friend at his side, he had a legendary Nashville music figure who had a nose for hit records. In fact, he counted on Gary being his "rabbit's foot."

When they arrived in Memphis, a drive of about five hours in those days, they parted company and each made his separate rounds. They agreed to meet at American Sound Studio early in the evening so that Jim could talk to Chips and get an understanding of his operations.

Gary called on those people with whom he had been building

relationships so that he could play them tapes of songs represented by his publishing company. When the quality of cassette tapes was good enough to be used to pitch songs (early-to-mid-1970s), song-pluggers used them in their work. However, in the 1960s, they had two choices: they could play songs that were recorded on home tape recorders or they could have acetates (tapes that had been transferred to records). The tapes were used for producers; the higher quality acetates were used for the record labels.

Jim's first stop was at the Sounds of Memphis, a recording studio owned by Gene Lucchesi. In addition to the studio, he and his daughter, Linda, had several record labels (X-L, Crystal, and Pen.) That day, there was one particular act he wanted to discuss with them. The previous year the studio had recorded a song by an unknown band, Sam the Sham and the Pharaohs. Sam's real name was Domingo "Sam" Samudio. He had made his way to Memphis by way of Texas, where he had enrolled at the University of Texas. Lucchesi recorded their song, "Wooly Bully" at Sam Phillips Recording Studio and released it on X-L Records. It tanked in Memphis and the surrounding area. Undeterred, Lucchesi then ran off 1,000 additional copies and distributed them regionally. The record did quite well. It was at this point that Jim entered the picture. Jim told Lucchesi that although "Wooly Bully" was not a country song, MGM would be interested in releasing it. They agreed on terms and MGM presented "Wooly Bully" to a national audience. The first thirty days after its release it sold one million units and went to Number 1 on the pop charts.

As planned, Jim and Gary met at American Sound Studio. If they had wondered why Chips chose the name he did, it was because there already was a Sounds of Memphis. Besides, Chips wanted his studio to represent the whole spectrum of American music, not just Memphis music.

Jim and Chips went into his private office to talk. Gary stayed in the reception area to talk to the twenty-one-year-old secretary, a beautiful woman with dark hair. "I spent an hour or so talking to her," Gary told me. "Long ago as a businessman I learned to get acquainted with the secretaries in the industry because, as you know, they help you get through to the movers and shakers. Sandy was quite interested in talking to me. She said she was an aspiring singer herself and was actually working at the studio, pending a recording session with Chips. He had told her he would do a session with her when he found the right song. She told me this had been a lengthy waiting period for him to find the song. He had also promised to release her from their contract if she had other opportunities."

Sandy had first seen Chips in Nashville while he was living there and working for Tree Publishing. One day she was at Tree recording demos for them, when he passed through the studio for some reason. They didn't speak, but when she later met him in Memphis she remembered the Nashville encounter.

"When I moved to Memphis and started making the rounds of the studios, American was one of them," Sandy told me. "I ran into Tommy Cogbill first and we started talking and then at some point the same day, I met Chips. He didn't have the studio up and running yet. He had nothing going on. I was looking for a job, anything to pay the rent. I was then living with my aunt in Memphis. He told me he was looking for someone to answer the phones and I said I would love to do it. He said, 'What do you need?' Seems like it was thirty dollars a week. I didn't want a lot. I knew he didn't have a lot of money and was trying to get the studio up and running."

Gary didn't talk to Chips that day. When Jim came out of the office, they left Memphis and drove back to Nashville. Chips Moman didn't know it yet, but he was soon to meet his match in the art of negotiation strategy and deal making. Not long before the Memphis trip, Gary had left Lowry Publishing and accepted a job with Painted Desert Publishing. While at Lowry he had a big success with a song titled "Ring of Fire," written by June Carter Cash and Merle Kilgore. It was a huge hit for Johnny Cash. As much as Gary knew about song publishing, he was always learning more facets of the business.

"One day I met June Carter Cash backstage at the Grand Ole Opry," he said. "She was upset because Merle Kilgore was going around claiming he wrote the song, but it was her song. Merle had talked her into writing together and both their names went on the song. Right off the bat she had this very personal song important to her and Merle Kilgore was claiming he wrote it."

Early in 1966, before Gary and Jim went to Memphis, Gary became acquainted with his Music Row landlord's secretary, a young woman by the name of Martha Sharp. She was intrigued that he operated a music publishing office. "How do you write a song?" she asked.

"You have to focus on song ideas. As a new writer, you want to write something unique and that has a different twist or approach to common themes. Of course, you need to learn to play an instrument well enough to get started and as you form songs you need a home recording machine to put your work on tape."

Three weeks later, she flagged Gary down and played and sang him a song on a guitar. "It was not recordable, but I encouraged her," he said. "The second song she brought me was titled 'Born a Woman' and it was something I recognized as a super song. That's what we call songs we know will be hits. As a music publisher I knew I would get this song recorded."

Upon his return to Nashville after his Memphis visit, Gary began putting the pieces together. Rick Hall at Fame Studio in Muscle Shoals had been encouraging him to record some of his demos there, so he called Hall and booked time to record three or four demos, one of them being "Born a Woman." Then he called Sandy Posey and told her he would pay her twenty-five dollars to drive to Muscle Shoals to sing on the demos. She was thrilled.

"I had already sent Sandy the lyrics and the tapes to the songs I wanted to record, so when she arrived we started with one of the other songs, not 'Born a Woman.' Then we started rehearsing 'Born a Woman.' Sandy played Martha's tape to the musicians so they could play the song.

Sandy Posey with Gary Walker
Photo courtesy Gary Walker

Once he heard the song, Rick Hall took over from the engineer. This told me he thought it was a hit song. He started giving advice on the arrangement. In fact, Rick Hall ended up producing the demo. All the magic was there."

Gary suggested to Sandy that she play the tape for Chips when she returned to the Memphis studio. She did. "Chips recognized a hit when he heard one," she said. "He had that genius about him. He knew what he could so with an artist and the right song. I was trying to decide whether I was going to stay in Memphis with Chips or go to Nashville with Gary and Chips said, "Do what you want to do, but I am going to record that song with somebody and it is going to be a hit.' I thought, 'Yep, you will.' I stayed there with Chips."

When Gary returned to Nashville, Gary played it for Jim, whose response was immediate: "I'd like to sign her as a recording artist." Gary played the situation like a maestro. He could have asked Chips to record the demo, but he knew Chips and Rick Hall were competitors. If Sandy told Chips that Rick Hall liked the song so much he took over engineering duties, Gary knew Chips would demand that Sandy honor her contract with him, even if it was only a verbal agreement. Sandy understood that principle, if only because she had sung backup on Joe Tex's "Hold Onto to What You Got." If Chips thought he might be losing her to Rick Hall, he would want to hold onto her even more. Gary counted on that. After Sandy played the Muscle Shoals tape for Chips, she called Gary and told him Chips' reaction. Then Chips got on the line and said he was going to record a master of the song with Sandy.

"Legally, she was still with him, so he could do the recording," Gary explained. "What he couldn't do was record the song without the publisher's permission or license. I told him he could not have the song because I had pitched her to MGM and I reminded him of his promise to release her."

"Well, I'm recording this song with Sandy," he said defiantly. "You can sue me."

"We had to let him record the song," said Gary. "Requiring him to get a license was not very practical at a time like that. Although I can't confirm this, I believe Sandy's feelings about Chips were the same as mine. I think she had terrific faith in him as a producer. A part of her was happy and really wanted Chips to do the session. As it turned out he did the master with a promise to submit it to MGM. That was our deal. MGM would have her as an artist, but he would be the producer."

Chips decided to record the master at Royal Studio, owned by Hi Records, because his equipment was not yet up to speed. Before recording the song, however, he asked the songwriter, Martha Sharp, to change the last verse. According to Sandy, he told Martha, "The last verse can't be negative. I want to record this song, but I want you to fix it. You have to have a positive before the song is over." Martha made changes in the song and Chips loved the final result.

When Gary heard the finished master, he thought it was "spectacular." He conceded it was unique and had a different sound from what they were used to in Nashville. "It was my first experience of being blown away by Chips Moman the producer. In time I came to believe that Chips was my favorite producer of all time. Billy Sherrill was a close second. Allen Reynolds was a close third. Phil Spector had his points, but Chips could do it with different types of songs."

For Sandy Posey, Chips was the "Steve McQueen of the music business." He was good looking in that rugged Southern way, charismatic, drove a sports car, and had his own airplane.

"Chips was quite a character," Sandy Posey told Peter Doggett, "But I wasn't intimidated, because it was so natural for me to be singing in a studio by then. He was very easy to work with, in fact. His talent was that he could recognize a great musician, and he put together a house band at American that was like no other. They didn't get in each other's way; they could just fall into the perfect groove. And they worked all the time." [23]

When the Chips Moman/Sandy Posey collaboration was released in 1966 it was perceived to be a pop record with a country inflection. "Born a Woman" peaked at Number 12 on the pop charts and sold over one million units. It did not chart on the country charts. The song was nominated for two Grammys, Best Vocal Performance, Female, and Best Contemporary (Rock) Solo Vocal Performance. Sandy's second release produced by Chips Moman, "Single Girl," also charted at Number 12 on the pop charts and sold equally well. "Single Girl" was recorded in Nashville.

Recalled Sandy: "Chips didn't want to use strings, not on this session. He put together an arrangement and let Bobby Emmons play organ and Bobby Wood play piano. There were few women on the country charts that year because country music was still dominated by males. The half dozen women on the country charts—artists such as Kitty Wells, Dottie West, and Loretta Lynn—were much older than Sandy Posey, who was twenty-one, and their songs were hard-core country with a double twang: Lynn's "You Ain't Woman Enough to Take my Man," and Wells's "It's All Over But the Crying."

The importance of the Moman/Posey collaboration was two-fold. First, it was pivotal in Chip's development as a producer because it freed him to experiment with a more sophisticated approach to popular music that made use of complicated arrangements and instrumentation. After the success of "Born a Woman," Moman told an interviewer, "People started calling me to produce records."[24] Second, it forever changed the options that women would have in country music in that it opened the door for what became known as Country-politan music that allowed women to venture beyond the fiddle and guitar instrumentation favored by male country artists.

Chips continued to produce Sandy's MGM singles and albums through 1968, at which time they ceased to chart on the pop charts. When she was dropped by MGM, Sandy left music to focus on her family life. There was more to it than that, of course. Her love of studio work and her aversion to performing or talking to the media made it difficult to sustain a career.

In 1971, Sandy decided to return to music. This time she signed with Columbia Records and was produced by the legendary Billy Sherrill, who adopted much the same arrangements used by Moman. This go around Sandy's records targeted country radio and for the first time she began to appear on the country charts. However, she never had a single hit as a designated country artist. The highest she rose on the country charts was Number 18 for "Bring Him Safely Home to Me." After several years of mediocre performance on the charts, she was dropped by Columbia.

One day in 1976, the phone rang.

"Sandy, this is Chips. Do you want to be on Warner?"

It came out of the blue. No greetings or warmup whatsoever. Sandy just about fell out of her chair. All she could think of to say was, "Yeah."

By that time Chips had moved to Nashville and opened an American Sound studio there. He approached Warner about recording Sandy. They said "sure." With their "sure" and her "yeah," they began recording. Her first Warner release with Chips Moman was for the 1976 release, "It's Midnight Do You Know Where Your Baby Is?" It peaked at Number 99 on the country chart. After that session, Chips handled her off to Tommy Cogbill who produced her next Warner releases, including "Born to Be with You," which peaked at Number 21 and "I Believe in Love." Her last hit was in 1979 with "Love is Sometimes Easy."

In 1983, she withdrew from her career in music and has had very little to say in the years since. One exception was an interview she did in 2010 with *Oxford American Magazine*. In the interview, she confided, "I wasn't crazy about any of my hits at all." She described them as "bubblegum." She may have genuinely felt that way or she may have been responding to her interviewer's criticisms of the songs as going "beyond pledges of stand-by-your-man fidelity to become affirmations of acquiescence." If she had a different interviewer, she might have understood her songs better. I don't presume to know what was in the mind of Martha Sharp when she wrote "Born a Woman" and "Single Girl," Sandy's biggest hits, but when I heard the line about a women's place being under a man's thumb, I took it as satire. And when in "Single Girl" the songwriter alludes to finding a "sweet loving" man to "lean on," I hear that as a feminist argument that a woman does not have to accept an emotionally or physically abusive man as a partner. There are plenty of good men out there.

Who knows whether Martha Sharp was a feminist when she wrote those two songs, but after the songs were released she quickly moved up the musical ladder in Nashville, finally landing a position in Warner's talent acquisition department. She was the person responsible for Faith Hill being offered a recording contract. Some reviewers, in the years after the release of Sandy's two big hits, have described them as being poor copies of Tammy Wynette's big hit "Stand By Your Man." In truth, "Stand By Your Man" was released two years after the release of Sandy's "Born a Woman and "Single Girl." What happened was that noted producer Billy Sherrill co-wrote Wynette's song with her precisely because of the success of Sandy's two big hits.

Sandy was a pioneer, but she never understood her importance and because of that she withdrew from music and allowed her musical legacy, whether from shyness and fear of saying the wrong thing, or from true embarrassment about the themes of the two songs, dissipate to the point where today's pop and country music histories ignore her contributions. Chips Moman's decisions about women in music and the instrumentation possibilities for country music, ended up totally transforming the genre, to the point where I am comfortable writing that he is the father of modern country music, whether that is reflected in the music of Sandy Posey or the music of country music's biggest super group ever, the Highwaymen (Willie Nelson, Waylon Jennings, Johnny Cash and Kris Kristofferson).

JERRY WEXLER HAD HIS EYE ON Aretha Franklin for a while. She had recorded six records for Columbia Records, all of them big band efforts that didn't sell. There was just something about her voice that suggested she would be a good candidate to record at Stax Records.

Informed that her Columbia contract had expired, he set up a meeting with her at his office. Present were Wexler, Aretha, and her husband Ted White. No lawyers, no agents. They talked and agreed to proceed, based on a handshake. Wexler wasted no time setting up studio time for his new, Memphis-born acquisition. Columbia's A&R head Mitch Miller had recorded Aretha singing songs such as "Rock-a-Bye Your Baby with a Dixie Melody" and "Sewanee." Wexler pictured her playing piano and singing her heart out on rhythm and blues compositions.

"My first instinct was to offer her to Jim Stewart and have the Stax team produce her," Wexler wrote in his memoir. "Stax was steaming and no one figured to produce Aretha any better than those good folks in Memphis. I told Jim that if he went for the $25,000 advance, Aretha could be a Stax artist with Atlantic promotion and distribution, the same arrangement we had with Sam and Dave. Stewart passed. Thank you, Jesus!"

Rebuffed by Stax, Wexler took Aretha to Fame Studio in Muscle Shoals. Before he left New York, he asked Rick Hall at Fame to please hire black horn players for the session and he asked Chips Moman and Dan Penn to attend. In what would turn out to be an omen, he discovered when he arrived at the studio that Hall had instead hired an all-white horn section. He had learned not to let misunderstandings get in the way of a successful session, so he overlooked the horn section foul-up. They proceeded to record "I Never Loved a Man the Way I Love You" and then discussed the track for the second song, "Do Right Woman, Do Right Man." Chips and Penn had written it for the session, but were having problems finishing the lyrics. As they worked to finish, Wexler noticed that the white trumpet player and Aretha's husband, Ted White, were getting into it while drinking out of the same whiskey bottle. It was yet another ominous sign that it could prove to be a rocky session. After putting down the track for "Do Right Woman"—drums, bass and rhythm guitar—they broke for the day and returned to the motel, where Wexler, Aretha, White, and Rick Hall gathered for drinks. To everyone's horror,

Hall and White got into an argument, with White shouting at the top of his voice what a mistake it had been for him and Aretha to get involved with "Fuckin' Honkies." Of course, in the South those are fighting words. One thing led to another and soon Hall and White exploded from their respective corners like first-round boxers and engaged in an actual fight.

"Rick was kind of a smartass, and back when he used to drink he was a white redneck," trombonist David Hood recalled to me. "He worked with a lot of black people and never had problems, but this uppity black guy from Detroit wasn't having any of it . . . Nobody could tell you exactly what happened because they probably were all drunk. But that was it— Aretha decided she wasn't going to record in Alabama, so they moved the session to New York. I thought it was going to be the end of my career. It was two or three years before I got to work with her again, this time playing bass."

Once he returned to New York, Wexler had an acetate made of "I Never Loved a Man" to give to his favorite disk jockeys. In no time at all, they were on the phone demanding the record. With no side B yet, Wexler tried to get in touch with Aretha to come to the studio to finish "Do Right Woman." For two weeks he searched for her in New York and Detroit, then he got word she had come into the Atlantic studio downtown to finish the song by herself. According to Wexler, she overdubbed two keyboard parts, first piano and then organ, joined with her sisters to do the background harmonies, and finally added her lead vocal. Wexler was astonished when he heard the result. He quickly released "I Never Loved a Man"/"Do Right Woman" as a single and jumped for joy as it rose up the charts, becoming her first ever million seller.

The resulting album, *I Never Loved a Man the Way I Love You*, was completed in New York, with Aretha supplying family members for background vocals. She also worked out her lead vocals and her piano parts before arriving at the studio. Invited to the session were Chips Moman and Jimmy Johnson from Muscle Shoals on guitar, Spooner Oldham on keyboards, Tommy Cogbill on bass, and Gene Chrisman of

American Sound on drums. Neither Rick Hall nor the white trumpet player were invited to the session. The resulting album was hailed as a masterpiece, with the single, "Respect," zooming to the top of the charts in June 1967.

DAN PENN WAS APPROACHED by a Memphis disk jockey in January 1967 about a local group named the DeVilles. Dan talked to Chips about the group. Chips was already familiar with them. His record label, Youngstown, had released three singles the previous year recorded by the group, at that time going by the name Ronnie and The DeVilles. Sales were negligible and no major labels showed interest in the group. The recordings occurred during a period when Chips was tossing musical noodles against the wall to see what would stick. Ronnie and The DeVilles didn't stick. Chips moved on.

When Penn mentioned the group, Chips probably didn't know that Ronnie Angel (his last name was Stoots) was no longer with the group. Previously, Ronnie Angel had been the singer for the Mar-Keys touring band. In those days, disk jockeys and their bosses, the program directors, had a great deal of power in determining which records would be successful and which records would receive no airplay at all. At the very least, record companies, large and small, went through the motions of giving consideration to their personal requests. Chips wanted Penn to say "yes" to the disk jockey, even if nothing came out of the session; he also wanted to say "yes" to Penn because he knew that American Sound needed more producers than himself to thrive as a business. For Chips, it was a win-win situation.

At that stage in their partnership, Chips had not yet told Penn he had decided not to ever again work with an established band in the studio. He found it too aggravating. Anyone who has ever witnessed Chips zoom from a mellow mood to one of great anxiety, complete with purple splotches on his face, understands that aggravation must be avoided at all costs. It's just not worth it, unless of course you are into self-abuse.

Anyone who has ever worked with a bi-polar personality—and let's face it, most of us have at some point in our lives—you learn when to lead and when to dip and bow and follow. You also become proficient at walking on egg shells.

Chips did the only thing he could do under the circumstances: he passed the band along to his new writing partner, Dan Penn, who very much wanted to get involved in record production. "Why don't you invite them into the studio and see if you can get a record out of them," he told Penn. "I've got to go out of town." That was fine with Penn.

After Ronnie Angel left the group, the three remaining members of the group—Danny Smythe on drums, Gary Talley on guitar, and Bill Cunningham on bass—went shopping for a new lead singer and a new keyboard player. Smythe brought John Evans into the group to play keyboards; then they focused on finding a singer.

"Danny said, 'We need somebody who can sing like a nigger,'" says Evans. "In those days that word was not such a derogatory term. Danny admires black music more than any person I know. They asked me if I knew anybody. At that time, it would not have been a viable alternative to have a black member in the band. I called a friend and he said, well, there's this guy who was in a talent show. I said, well, is he any good? He said, yeah, but I don't really know why."[25]

Evans found out that his name was Alex Chilton and he gave him a call. He was surprised to find out that he was only sixteen (they were all nineteen), but he invited him to an audition. Three years difference at that age is a lot, and that concerned some of the guys in the band, but they figured they could overlook the age thing if he could really sing. If they had prepared themselves for the age difference, they had not prepared themselves for what they saw when he arrived for the audition. All the members of the band were dressed in the preppy fashions of the day—Gant shirts, Gold Cup socks and Bass Wegens loafers.

"There was a dress code without having a dress code in those days," says Evans. "Alex came in wearing a faded black T-shirt, jeans with holes in the knees and that was not acceptable in those days—and a blue jean jacket, and no one wore those except farmers, blue collar workers, you know, trailer park people, for heaven's sake. On top of that, he comes in cold weather and he had on a men's dress scarf, like you would wear with an overcoat."

But when Alex sang, he transformed himself into a gritty soul singer, so they forgave his eccentric dress and asked him to be their singer. Later they discovered his mother owned an art gallery and his father was a jazz musician. They lived in the art gallery, and, in the minds of nineteen-old musicians, that pretty much explained Alex's eccentricities.

There was no doubt that Chilton changed the group's focus. "It became a very different kind of a band than it had been—less bubblegum and more soul music," said Evans. "We were basically looking for someone who could sing soul music, but at the time we definitely weren't looking for a black singer. We were looking for somebody that was our contemporary who could sing like a soul singer. Alex was said to be able to do that."[26]

Dan arranged for them to come into the studio for a 10 a.m. session and notified them the day before. He sent word for them to pick up a tape of original songs he had put together for them to learn. That night John Evans and another band member stopped by the studio to pick up the tape.

"Dan wasn't there, but he had left the tape there with our names on it," says Evans. "So we went back and listened to the tape. There were three tunes on it. 'The Letter' was the only one we could stand to listen to. It was short, very simple."

When they returned to the studio the next morning, they got the second jolt of their young careers (Alex's avant garde appearance had been the first of many shocks). "Dan was wearing Bermuda shorts that came down to the middle of his knee caps," recalls Evans. "If that weren't nerdy enough, he was wearing a white T-shirt with the sleeve rolled up around a pack of Lucky Strikes. He was the darnest thing to see. He was wearing high-topped tennis shoes with athletic socks rolled up."

Alex Chilton, lead singer of Box Tops
Photo courtesy Mississippi Valley Collection
University of Memphis Libraries

Dan informed them that Chips wouldn't be coming in that day. He would be their producer. They looked around the studio. Dirty ashtrays and food were piled up everywhere. It looked dark and foreboding. "We didn't know what to think," says Evans. "Dan was primarily a writer, but he worked as an engineer. Dan, thinks, 'Uh, huh, here's my chance to do something.' I think it was the first tune he had ever produced."

Evans showed the other guys in the band the chord progression for "The Letter"—Dan suggested to Alex that he pronounce aeroplane in three syllables—and thirty-three takes later they had a record that re-defined the Memphis sound. When Chips returned to the studio and Penn played him the record they had made in his absence, he was stunned by the shear creativity of what he heard. There had never been anything like it recorded in Memphis.

"There was really kind of an antagonistic thing going on by this time," Penn told Peter Guralnick. "Moman and I are alike in a lot of ways, but really we're opposites. If he asked me about a record—'What you think, Penn?'—and I said, 'Man that's a bunch of shit,' he'd say, 'No, I'm putting it out.' If I said, 'More bass,' he'd put more treble. I mean, I'm overbearing myself, but Moman is overbearing over-bearing. Which I guess is one of the reasons 'The Letter' come out the way it did, because he had antagonized me and fucked around with me, told jokes about me in front of other people, he was really making fun of me."

"The Letter" was released on Mala, a New York-based label that specialized in music for black markets. By then the DeVilles had changed their name to the Box Tops. To the surprise of everyone involved, especially the group's 16-year-old lead singer, "The Letter" peaked at No. 1 in September 1967, thus becoming the first No. 1 pop hit ever recorded in Memphis by Memphis artists.

Four months before the "The Letter" peaked at Number 1, the band performed on the Ted Mack Amateur Hour. During rehearsal, a cameraman noticed that Smythe was playing drums in his socks. He suggested he would get more attention if he played barefoot, which he did when they went on air. The cameraman provided shots of him playing barefoot, delighting the audience, and perhaps as a result of that the Box Tops won the competition.

Fast forward to July 1967, just weeks before "The Letter" topped the chart. Smythe, who was on summer break from Memphis State University, received a telephone call from the William Morris talent agency in New York. Word had gone out that the producers of the hit television show "The Monkees" were looking for a replacement for Micky Dolenz, who played drums with the pretend musical group. Dolenz had received some criticism from fans because it was obvious that he had never played drums in his life. Before each taping, Dolenz had to be given drum lessons on how to hold the sticks. But there was more to it than that.

The Monkees were an obvious reflection of the Beatles and the show's producers wanted a drummer more like Ringo Starr, that is someone a little bit more off the wall. Someone who played drums barefoot and actually knew how to play drums, seemed perfect. Smythe told a reporter for *The Commercial Appeal* about the telephone call from William Morris, and when the reporter asked what he was going to do, Smythe answered that it would all depend on how good the deal was and whether he decided to resume his college studies. As it turned out, producers decided Dolenz was too popular to be replaced and they dropped their search for someone more colorful.[27]

Chips Moman was elated with the success of "The Letter," even if Dan Penn, who had never produced anything in his life, had produced it; but it seemed to confirm his worst fears about what could happen if he didn't stay in the studio 24 hours a day. He would never let *that* happen again.

"There was a ten year period that I might have averaged three hours a night sleep," Chips told me. "I recorded one time for nine days without going home, until I fell unconscious behind the board and people would pick me up and shake me and say, 'Can you do one more mix?' when they should have taken me straight to a hospital."

Of course, with a Number 1 record that sold two million units in the United States and an additional 4 million units internationally, there were calls for an album. *The Letter/Neon Rainbow* followed later in the year. Dan Penn remained as producer, but Chips did the engineering. The second big hit from the group, "Cry Like a Baby," was released in 1968, reaching Number 2 on the Hot 100 list and selling more than one million units.

It is difficult to overstate the importance of "The Letter." Musically, it was the biggest musical event in Memphis since Sam Phillips recorded Elvis, Scotty and Bill, an event that recalled Elvis' energetic and endearing naivety when he first emerged on the scene. Alex Chilton perpetuated that template with statements such as, "Man, I'd never been in a recording studio before," and his admission that he hadn't read the song lyrics of "The Letter" until just before they recorded it.[28]

Not so happy about the success of "The Letter," was Jerry Wexler of Atlantic Records, who wrote in his memoir: "I'd loaned Chips five thousand dollars on a handshake to start up his operation. When he discovered the Box Tops—who hit big with "The Letter" and "Cry Like a Baby"—and gave them to my competitor, Larry Uttal at Bell Records, I was miffed. No Matter; Chips and I remained tight."

Even though Penn remained as the group's producer, turning out three albums over a nine-month period, Chips refused to allow the band members, with one or two exceptions, to play on any of the recordings. He insisted that the 827 Thomas Street Band play on all the records.

Of course, Alex Chilton continued to be the lead singer, but it was a frustrating experience for him because Chips was so quick to dismiss his ideas. For whatever reason, Chips simply was not interested in developing a singer/songwriter career for Chilton. Toward the end of the band's run, they had recorded several albums and had toured with the Beach Boys for a while. When the band folded in 1970, Chilton moved to New York and tried to develop his skills as a singer/songwriter before returning to Memphis to launch a career as a solo artist. When that didn't materialize he joined a local Memphis group called Big Star and recorded two critically acclaimed albums at Ardent Studio on their Ardent Records label. The albums were not well received by the public and Chilton drifted into a sort of self-imposed obscurity.

There were Alex Chilton sightings, of course, just as there had been with Big Foot. There were rumors he was living with his mother and father in New Orleans, where he worked as a restaurant dishwasher. Others said he was holed up in Hohenwald, Tennessee, a small town on the Natchez Trace near where Meriwether Lewis of Lewis and Clark fame was either murdered or committed suicide.

Hohenwald was also the home of the Elephant Sanctuary, the largest natural-habit sanctuary for elephants in America and the home of the Buffalo Valley, a long-term facility for persons recovering from addiction, a combination that somehow makes sense in that the screeching of the elephants at night might have made recovery a more surreal event. Chilton died in 2010 in New Orleans at the age of fifty-nine, but not before going one more round with Chips Moman.

AS THE BOX TOPS' "The Letter" zoomed up the charts, a *Memphis Press-Scimitar* reporter chided the city for ignoring its musical heritage: "Music around the world has been dramatically affected by what happened in Memphis. Nashville and New Orleans capitalize on what their cities have done and it means millions to them, but we just sit on our hands and a lot of people don't even know what has happened and is happening. The Memphis sound is rocking hard being heard louder in more distant places. For a few years the record business here had slowed after the dominant part it played in the mid-50s, when the "rockabilly sound" from Sun's Memphis studios 'influenced the entire course of American music,' according to *Billboard,* the record trade paper. Now Memphis studios are again turning out a phenomenal number of hits. Noted here recently was the fact Chips Moman and Donald Crews put $30,000 worth of new equipment in the American Recording Studios at Thomas and Chelsea."[29]

Around the time the *Memphis Press-Scimitar* reporter was bemoaning the city's lack of support for its music industry, Nashville producer and powerbroker Buddy Killen—and Chips' former boss at Tree Publishing—brought Joe Tex to American Sound to be recorded with the 827 Thomas Street Band. Chips' inability to connect with Tex in Nashville remains one of the mysteries in his career, but Killen was unconcerned about that. This time, he didn't want Chips. He wanted the house band.

Chips was all too happy to let him have the studio. There was nothing he liked better than making money without working for it (one reason he was so attracted to pool and poker). Despite his failure to develop a working rapport with Tex in Nashville, he was always eager to praise his talent' "Joe Tex was an unbelievable talent," he told Allen Smith. "He was a great songwriter but he couldn't play an instrument. He'd have all these songs that he knew the words to but no one knew the chords! . . . But he was brilliant. He was one of the most brilliant recording artists I've ever known."[30]

Joe Tex wrote five of the eleven songs on the resulting album, *Live and Lively*—and, of course, Chips talked Killen into including "Do Right Woman, Do Right Man," the hit he and Dan Penn had written for Aretha Franklin (so that Chips could receive royalties from the album). One of the last songs Tex recorded at the session was one he wrote on the spot, "Skinny Legs and All," a song about a man who berated his skinny wife in public.[31] Ever since the success of "Hold Onto What You've Got," on the pop charts, Tex had incorporated the concept that women should be unconcerned if a man rejects them because there will always be another man down the road who will embrace them, skinny legs and all.

"Skinny Legs and All" proved to be the hit single from the album, but the most publicly discussed aspect of the album was that it was marketed as a "live" album. After Killen completed work on the album in Memphis he took it to Nashville, where he added crowd applause and cheers to the track, allowing it to be sold as a live album. Because the record label never commented on the matter, critics engaged in spirited debates. Critic David Marsh wrote, "Fantastic reproduction of a 1968 show—who knows how much overdubbing was done, and when the feel is this spontaneous and funky, who cares?"

WHEN WILSON PICKETT went to Memphis in July 1967 to record at American Sound Studio, Jerry Wexler did not attend the session. Instead, he sent Atlantic engineer/producer Tom Dowd to co-produce the session with Spooner Oldham. It is not clear whether Chips Moman was even in town during the session. That should not come as a surprise. William Bell was the only black male artist he had successfully produced. Chips' efforts with Joe Tex in Nashville had not worked out for whatever reasons and he may have felt that Pickett was too important from a financial perspective to risk any kind of misunderstanding.

In Chips' defense it should be said that Pickett was an extremely difficult person with whom to maintain a working relationship. In Pickett's defense, it should be said that he did not discriminate: he got along just as poorly with black musicians as he did white musicians. The one person Chips and Pickett mutually considered a likeable person was Bobby Womack, who was invited to play guitar this session and encouraged to bring along as many songs as he wished.

Womack asked Pickett what he thought about that. "[He] had shipped me to the place," Womack wrote in his memoir. "'Bobby,' he said, 'there are some white boys down there; if you closed your eyes, you could not tell they weren't black. Those fuckers can play.'"

Womack found that out himself once he arrived. American Sound guitarist Reggie Young sat opposite Womack during most of the session, with Womack, as usual, playing his guitar, upside down. On Womack's song "I'm in Love," they played around each other's riffs, giving the ballad incredible energy, not something usually associated with a ballad. Womack took three additional songs to the session, all of them recorded: "I've Come a Long Way," "Jealous Love," and "We've Got to Have

Love." They recorded two additional songs at American Sound, but then mysteriously packed up and returned to New York, where they recorded the hit single from the album, "Stagger Lee."

There was definitely a pattern to Pickett's studio work. They would begin at one studio and then finish at another studio. To no one's surprise, about eight months later Wexler booked another session at American Sound, this one scheduled for March 1968. Chips invited Womack to this session and told him to bring plenty of songs so that he could record an album with him once they finished the Pickett session. That was all Womack needed to hear to encourage him to move to Memphis so that he could report to American Sound for session work when needed. "So I flew down to Memphis and found myself the cheapest fleapit in town," he wrote. "The Trumpet Motel, one rackety old room, one bed, single and well used with a tiny kitchenette, Junior Walker, B.B. King, they all stayed there and there were no distractions. Just the music . . . I figured I could really get my schooling from American. It felt right. It was the place to be, I loved the atmosphere and there was a little soul-food place around the corner. Perfect."

What Womack didn't count on was Pickett's arrival in Memphis with no songs.

"What you got in that bag?" Pickett asked, eyeing his satchel.

"Songs, I'm full of them, I'm fresh."

"Why don't you pull out some songs and let me sing?"[32]

"I'm a Midnight Mover" was the major song to come out of Womack's bag. Others included on the album were "It's a Groove," "Remember, I Been Good to You," "I found a True Love," "Trust Me," and "Let's Get an Understanding." Tom Dowd produced the session, using the 827 Thomas Street Band. As they had done the previous year, they returned to New York, where four additional cuts were recorded, with Nesuhi Ertegun and Pickett himself listed as producers for the new cuts. Nesuhi, an executive at Atlantic, was the brother of Atlantic co-founder Ahmet Ertegun. When everyone left American Sound Studio, Womack remained, waiting for Chips to arrive to produce his album. The experience left him someone dazed.

"I gave Wilson Pickett all my songs," says Womack. "Every time he asked for another one, I gave it to him. I was so happy. He got his whole album down and then they said, 'Bobby, what do you want to cut first?' I didn't have a damn song left. I tried my best to write something. Chips came in and said, "Hi, Bobby, how's it going?' I didn't tell him I had given Pickett every song I had. I started playing 'Fly Me to the Moon,' and Chips said, 'Speed it up. That's a smash. Let's cut it.' It was about two o'clock in the morning. He never knew that 'Midnight Mover' and the others were on the Pickett album. They'd have really shit in their pants if they had known that."

Chips was surprised that Womack had no songs for his debut album. The idea had been to record him singing his own songs. Chips was disappointed but didn't let that ruin the session.

Womack played him, "I'm a Midnight Mover," the song Pickett had recorded and Chips liked it, so they re-recorded it, asking the 827 Thomas Street Band to play it one more time.

Other songs included a stunning version of the Mamas and Papas' hit, "California Dreamin'" and the 1944 standard, "Moonlight in Vermont." To the surprise of almost everyone, except perhaps Chips Moman, Womack's version of "Fly Me to the Moon" was a hit, reaching Number 52 on the Billboard Top 100 and Number 16 on the rhythm and blues chart.

AT 6 P.M. MARTIN LUTHER KING stepped out of his room onto the balcony of the Lorraine Motel in Memphis It was April 4, 1968, and the sun was setting across the Mississippi River, casting long, gray shadows that fell across the motel courtyard. The temperature was a chilly fifty-five degrees. King's driver, Solomon Jones, shouted to King that he should wear his overcoat.

"OK, I will," King answered.

Then the shot rang out.

King was struck by a .30-06 slug that ripped into his neck and jaw. When his aides rushed from their rooms, they found him motionless on his back, bleeding profusely. An unidentified white man walked up and covered King's face with a white towel. Then the man disappeared. The civil rights leader was rushed to St. Joseph's Hospital in a fire department ambulance, most likely from the fire station that later would house Chips Moman's "return to Memphis" recording studio. Thirty minutes later King was pronounced dead.

When news of Martin Luther King's murder went out over the radio, Memphis mayor Henry Loeb was in Mississippi, on his way to a speaking engagement at Ole Miss. He immediately turned his car around and headed back to Memphis. Loeb knew he was in for a long night. Ever since the riot that had occurred on March 22, he had kept a loaded shotgun beneath his desk in the mayor's office. He just hoped there would be no more killing.

Hearing the same radio broadcast was James Earl Ray. Like Loeb, he was on the road in Mississippi, speeding toward Alabama. The radio announcer said police were looking for a white man in a white Mustang. Unlike Loeb, Ray did not return to Memphis.[33]

In the wake of King's assassination, outraged blacks rioted in eighty cities, including Memphis. Nationwide, twenty-nine people died and 2,000 were injured. It was the most widespread racial unrest in American history. Mobs of protesting blacks roamed city streets, some looting and setting fires. Memphis officials set a 7 p.m. curfew and called in National Guard troops. If there was ever a turning point in Memphis music, a point beyond which there was no return, it was the King assassination.

Don Nix and Duck Dunn were standing in front of the studio when the rioting began. "There was a lot of activity," recalls Nix. "People were moving around in the streets." But they weren't overly concerned. Stax was located in a black neighborhood, but they knew every shopkeeper on the street. It was inconceivable to them that anyone would hurt them.

"We went back inside and Isaac (Hayes) said, 'Man, ya'll better go home. Let me carry you and Duck home.'"

They said no.

Then they began to see smoke on the horizon.

"As I drove out of south Memphis, I noticed smoke-billowing from dozens of fires. I don't think I realized the danger until I arrived home and turned on the TV. Walter Cronkite was on telling the world that Martin Luther King had died from the bullet through his throat and as he spoke the words I realized he was the same man who told me JFK had been murdered in Dallas."[34]

Meanwhile, American Sound Studio also was in a black neighborhood. As sirens blared and smoke filled the air and radio announcers bordered on hysteria, Chips Moman told everyone in the studio to go home. Then he locked the doors and went home himself. The studio would remain locked for a little over a week.

After Jim and Estelle decided to close the doors at Stax, they stayed closed for a week. "Jim took all the masters home," said Estelle. "We didn't know what might happen. The building might go up in flames. Out of respect we closed until the riots were over and things settled down. We were protecting ourselves. We stayed shut down for about a week."

Estelle smiled, sharing a secret. "I don't think they ever knew we took all the master tapes out of there."

After the riots ended, Jim put a chain link fence around the back entrance to the studio. The gates had locks. "I thought that was when the music started dying," said Nix. "After that, you couldn't go back out on the street. That was my neighborhood. We spent more time there than we did at home."[35]

The news of King's death rocked Memphis and other cities across America. "Although I still spent most of my days in Memphis at the studio, the fun was gone. The days when all the neighbors were invited into the studio and the musicians were invited into the neighborhood were over. So was Mrs. Axton's record shop."[36]

The assassination prompted Booker T. Jones to take a closer look at himself and those around him. "I began to feel a responsibility for voicing the needs of my people and the struggle we were involved in," he wrote in his memoir. "It came to where the social issued demanded us to identify our allegiances. I wanted my bandmates to champion civil rights, not just be willing to play with blacks. It wasn't easy. Dr. King's murder exposed the fact that our group dynamics were more complicated than I realized. After Dr. King was shot and killed at the Lorraine Motel, Steve made these remarks to an interviewer: 'I don't think anywhere in the universe was as racially cool as Memphis was until Martin Luther King showed up. That just set it off for the world, basically. What a shame. There must be something political about that. Let's go to the one place in the South where everybody is getting along and blow that fuse. That's the only way I can see it.'"[37]

At the University of Mississippi, a number of black students enrolled there reacted with anger, some saying it was time to reassess the effectiveness of Dr. King's nonviolent philosophy. By 1968 several dozen black students had enrolled at the university and most were not shy about speaking their mind. "If Dr. King's tactics will not work, we must find new methods with which to express ourselves in order to gain our equality," a student from Jackson told the *Mississippian*. "The system is against the Negro," said another student. "We have been oppressed in every way possible and now it is time for us to do something about it."

The summer of 1968 was especially bleak for Elvis. He had a brand new baby girl, and he was still in demand as a movie actor, but his music career was non-existent. He had not had a Top 10 hit since June 1965, when "Crying in the Chapel" peaked at No. 3, two slots below "Wooly Bully." If he turned on the radio, he heard songs by the Byrds, the Beatles, the Rolling Stones and, perhaps worst of all, a whole gang of Memphis people turning out records at Stax, Hi and American. Elvis was a relic— and he knew it. If he watched television or read newspapers, all he heard or saw was talk of race riots and anti-war demonstrations. He became a virtual prisoner in Graceland.[38]

"There was a period of time for a few months when it was really tough," T.G. Sheppard, who spent a great deal of time at Graceland at that time, told me. "There was a big fear of people breaking into Graceland to kidnap him or Lisa Marie. I remember being in the den, then all of a sudden everyone was scrambling because someone had called the house and said someone had climbed over the wall and had something in their hand and they were pointing it toward the house. Everybody was outside and Elvis was freakin'. He grabbed his gun. There was a fear in him that I had never seen before. He started talking about wanting gun turrets on top of the house and it rubbed off on everyone else. Everybody was scared."

B. J. THOMAS WAS LIVING IN HOUSTON, TEXAS, in late 1967, not doing much of anything. The previous year, he and his band The Triumphs had released a cover of Hank Williams's "I'm So Lonesome I Could Cry." The single sold over one million copies and was certified Gold. They followed up with another single, "Mama," that rose to Number 22 on the charts. Sceptor Records wasted no time signing Thomas and releasing a solo album titled *I'm So Lonesome I Could Cry.* He was invited to go on the road with Dick Clark's traveling show, but his band members, guys he had played in bands with in high school, weren't interested in traveling. He went without them.

Once the Dick Clark show ended, Thomas was literally sitting around the house trying to figure out what to do next when his friend, songwriter Mark James, called and told him that he had moved to Memphis and was now writing songs for Chips Moman at American Sound Studio. He asked Thomas what he was doing and Thomas told him he wasn't doing much of anything. He suggested Thomas drive up to Memphis and check out the music scene.

"My brother and I drove up and hung out at the studio for a while and talked to Chips," Thomas said. "That first night we went to the studio, he was very cordial and said, 'B.J., why don't you go in and sing a song with the band and see how it goes.' He was a great guy and I was in awe of him. We decided on 'Smoke Gets in Your Eyes,' and I sang that song. With that band it was like I had always been their singer and they had always been my band. We just fit together. It was perfect. When we finished, Chips said, 'I love that. Why don't you move up to Memphis and as soon as I get a song I can record on you, you will be close by."

B.J. had no way of knowing, of course, that Chips had a weakness for covering songs that previously had proved to be hits. In fact, Thomas had caught his eye by boldly recording Hank Williams' song, "I'm So Lonesome I Could Cry." It took a lot of nerve to cover a legend and that was something Chips appreciated. Then, when tested in the studio, he chose to sing the Platters' hit, "Smoke Gets in Your Eyes," that cinched it for Chips. He knew then that Thomas was someone he could work with. A novice singer would probably have auditioned with a mediocre original song, but Thomas had the sense to put his own spin on a proven hit.

"I liked Chips from the first," said Thomas. "There was a way about him and you couldn't help but love the guy, especially when he was in the studio doing his thing with music. He was a wonderful guy. Oh, you might have a problem here and there with him. Everyone is like that. I was as much like that as he was. We butted heads every now and then, but I hardly remember what those situations were now. He knew what a hit record sounded like. You could depend on him to know exactly the right thing to do."

As a result of that first meeting, Thomas moved to Memphis with high expectations. He hung out at the studio, getting to know the guys. He also spent time getting to know the city. He visited the various music venues. At that time, Beale Street was shut down and boarded up. There was no central location to go hear music. Nightclubs were scattered all over town. Some in out of the way downtown locations. Others in mid-town. More still were located in more affluent East Memphis. No matter where the clubs were, he could feel the music seemingly radiating up from the ground. All kinds of music. Blues, jazz, pop, country, rock 'n' roll.

B.J. Thomas
Photo courtesy Mississippi Valley Collection
University of Memphis Libraries

Thomas was there for the upheaval caused by Martin Luther King's assassination, and he waited out the studio closing in the aftermath. A couple of months after the rioting, Thomas was hanging out at the studio with his friend Mark James, a soon to be Grammy Award winner for songs such as "Always on My Mind," "Suspicious Minds," and "Sunday Sunrise."

"He played me some things he had written, including 'Eyes of a New York Woman,'" Thomas explained. "It was very different from what I had recorded up till then, but I had only had two hit records and I didn't really have anything to go by. It was more of a rock 'n' roll thing. We went up to New York and visited Sceptor Records, me and the guys and Chips. When we returned to Memphis we recorded the song using an electric sitar on the track."

"Eyes of a New York Woman" went to Number 28 on the pop charts and put Thomas on the fast track for success. The fascinating thing about this song is the way in which it predestinates Chips' working and personal relationship with a dark-eyed New York woman who would come to fill a void in his studio group by becoming the vocal expert he longed for. But more about that later. On a more mundane level, the song went from what most producers would have recorded as a rock 'n' roll ballad to a pop song by the addition of Bobby Emmons' B 3 organ and background strings, and by using a sitar to replace the more pedestrian sound of an electric guitar. Chips was no fan of stripped-down rock 'n' roll. Time and time again he would transform a rock or country song into a pop song with soaring instrumentation, It became his trademark.

Encouraged by that initial success, Chips chose another song written by Mark James, "Hooked on a Feeling," for the follow-up to "The Eyes of a New York Woman." Explained Thomas: "We decided to use the sitar again. Chips brought it in one night while we were recording and gave it to Reggie Young one of the greatest guitar players of all time. It took a while. The first time we recorded 'Hooked on a Feeling' it had like an eighteen-bar ride in it, and Chips spliced what Reggie played on the end as the instrumental he was looking for. It took a while for Reggie to get the handle of the sitar, but once he did he really played it wonderfully. It was mainly Chips' idea. The sitar hung on the wall from then on. I think it is one of the classic guitar rides of all time. Reggie played a lot of different things and Chips was coaching him the whole time, looking for what he was hearing in his mind and finally he got it. We cut the song back in the day when you did things a little more soulfully. We didn't take thirty takes on it. I think we got it in three takes and I immediately straightened a couple of things on my vocal. We overdubbed the percussion and we were done. It really was fun to record that way."

"Hooked on a Feeling" was Thomas's second million-selling record and it was included in his 1968 album, *On My Way*. Included in the album was the song that first attracted Chips' attention, "Smoke Gets in Your Eyes." The album didn't do as well as the singles, primarily because the songs sandwiched between his two major hits written by Mark James seemed weak and lackluster in comparison.

Chips planned another session early in 1970, but before it could take place Thomas was approached about recording a song written by Burt Bacharach and Hal David for an upcoming Paul Newman and Robert Redford movie titled *Butch Cassidy and the Sundance Kid.* The song, "Raindrops Keep Falling on My Head," had been offered to Ray Stevens, but he had turned it down. Thomas was intrigued by the idea of having a song in a movie, so he asked Chips what he should do. Chips told him that he was holding some songs for the next session, including another song by Mark James called "Suspicious Minds," but advised him that he should do the movie song because it would be good for his career. Then he told him that he had been given an opportunity to record with Elvis Presley and he needed to follow through with that. They both would have great projects to look forward to.

Thomas recorded "Raindrops Keep Falling on My Head" with Burt Bacharach producing it, and both the song and the movie were enormous successes. "Raindrops . . ." quickly became a Gold single, a Gold album, a Grammy nominee, and won an Oscar for best original song. Subsequently the song was inducted into the 2014 Grammy Hall of Fame, Recording the song made him two months late for his session scheduled with Chips Moman.

"Finally I contacted Chips," said Thomas. "He told me, 'I have all these songs for your session, but I can't hold back any songs because if I don't cut a hit with Elvis everyone will say it is my fault. I can't hold any songs for you.' Mark James had written 'Suspicious Minds.' It was a given I would do that song next, but I guess that song was destined for Elvis. We were all thrilled he got things together again. We knew he was going to come back big time."

By the time Chips got around to B.J. again, he had only one Mark James song, "The Mask," for him to record. The resulting album, *Everybody's Out of Town,* produced two hits, "Everybody's Out of Town" and "I Just Can't Help Believing," with most of the other songs being standards such as "Sandman" and "Bridge over Troubled Water." Two of the songs on the album were produced by Bacharach and David, with Chips producing the others.

During the next six years, Thomas would gross over $13 million as an artist, "but I never once got my head up out of the mud. I was bogged down in drugs and everything was a failure . . . I was as famous as any singer could ever hope to be, but there was nowhere to rest my head."[39]

By the time Thomas recorded "I Just Can't Help Believing," everything in Memphis was coming unraveled. Explained Thomas: "Chips had a run-in with Scepter over 'I Just Can't Help Believing.' When the song came to the point where you expect him to put in an instrumental, he didn't put anything in that space. Scepter overdubbed on the master some horns and things and it really pissed Chips off and they butted heads. It was getting a little touchy in Memphis. We all had our problems. I had a drug and alcohol problem at that time, so did Chips. Chips and I could really get outlandish and crazy. During that time he and Scepter butted heads over that song."

At Scepter's request, B.J. went to Atlanta to record with the Atlanta Rhythm Section and he didn't see Chips again for another five years. "Chips had a thought process that was unique to him," Thomas told me. "If he got upset he would put your music away. That was a quirk in his personality. He demanded a certain amount of respect and commitment from the people he worked with. If he didn't get it, he could be very displeased and that could be the end."

Years after Thomas and Chips parted company in 1970, I asked Chips what Thomas was like to work with. He said he was one of his favorite artists. Said Chips: "Artists are so different. Some of them are singers, others are artists. Take B.J. Thomas. He was never a problem. He was a singer. He didn't have any idea what song was good and what was bad. You would give him a song and he would sing his heart out. Everything he sang, he went as hard as he could do. But you had to make sure you got him to do what you wanted him to do."

More so than anyone else, Chips understood his inability to sustain long-term relationships, both personal and business. It was not a mystery to him. A lot of time had passed from when he and Thomas had parted company in 1970, but he had forgotten the negative aspects of the parting. He had warm feelings toward Thomas, just as Thomas had warm feeling toward him. Chips was hardly ever surprised by the train wrecks in his life because he could usually see them coming. He felt helpless that he was unable to stop the inevitable from happening. The only exception to this pattern of behavior was with the 827 Thomas Street Band. Defying all odds, they would remain close for more than half a century.

Of course, it wasn't over with B.J. Thomas, either. In 1970, when things soured, Chips still had two more rounds to go with Thomas. It wasn't anywhere close to being over.

BEFORE DUSTY SPRINGFIELD arrived in Memphis in September 1968 to record at Chips Moman's American Sound Studio, she had spent many hours at the home of Atlantic Records producer Jerry Wexler going over song possibilities—and she had experienced a last minute detour from Fame Studio in Muscle Shoals. Dusty turned down more than one hundred songs Wexler had selected for her to record. Finally, after months of nerve-wrenching evaluations, Dusty was able to agree with Wexler on eleven songs. Wexler jumped with joy. It would be his first album with her since she had recently signed with Atlantic Records.

"I was criticized for taking Dusty down South—everyone said the South was for R&B not pop—but I had a hunch," Wexler wrote in his memoir. "You won't hear much of a black influence in her voice, yet she's deeply soulful, her intonation pure. As with Aretha, I never heard her sing a bad note."

Clearly, Wexler decided on his own that Dusty should sing a soul album. She never asked to sing a soul album. Obviously, anyone can have a soulful voice, but there is a vast difference between having a soulful voice and recording a soulful album. Its oranges and apples.

Questioned about his decision by Warren Zanes—"Did you at any point feel uncertain about bringing a pop star like Dusty Springfield into a situation that was associated with R&B?—Wexler responded: "I had my qualms, yes, but I finally decided, 'Let me take the chance.'" [40]

"All Jerry did was talk about Aretha," complained Dusty, "and I was frankly intimidated. If there's one thing that inhibits good singing, it's fear. I covered the fear by being in pain. I drove Jerry crazy."[41]

Dusty Springfield was a British pop singer who had a remarkable voice. If Wexler wanted her to record a soulful album, he should never have mentioned that to her. The soulful sound would have come from the band and the arrangements. It is easy to sympathize with Dusty. Soul singers, white and black, tend to have relatively quiet, laidback speaking voices. Wexler was a New York Jew who had a loud, abrasive speaking voice. Although he was a huge fan of soul, he never possessed an ounce of soul himself. In her mind, Dusty could not match Wexler's voice with his goals for her album.

So, with the songs agreed upon, it was time to head south. But there was a problem. They had taken so long in the song selection process that Fame Studio in Muscle Shoals no longer had an opening. Frantic, Wexler called Chips Moman to book his American Sound Studio. Chips agreed to rent him studio space and he agreed to allow Wexler the use of the 827 Thomas Street Band, for an added fee, of course. Chips would leave town and leave the production work to Wexler, Tom Dowd, and Arid Mardin. That was how Dusty ended up in Memphis to record her first "soul" album. And that was when the nightmare began for Wexler.

To the band's surprise, Dusty refused to sing a "scratch" vocal to each song so that the band would have guidance on what they should play around and behind her voice. Wexler was stunned. He had a singer in a studio who absolutely refused to sing until the track was completed, strings and all. She was nicely apologetic and explained it by saying that is how she always had recorded back home in England. As politely as he could, Wexler tried to explain that the band preferred to work with the singer during the production.

"Oh, well," Dusty sighed.

Keyboard player Bobby Wood, probably the band member most likely to get his feelings hurt by a perceived slight, later told an interviewer: "I thought Dusty was a little strange at that time, but didn't dare to voice my opinion. Dusty was just withdrawn and appeared to not want to be there, unlike most artists we worked with. She just didn't have anything to say. She seemed to not be familiar with the songs."[42]

Guitarist Reggie Young, who did not have an insecure bone in his body, told the same interviewer: "She was quite a professional. I don't think she was very happy when we started . . . she seemed to be in awe. She seemed to have a great time; I found out later that she was scared to death." [43]

Travelling with Dusty was her Australian hairdresser, John Adams. Her behavior in the studio and later at the Holiday Inn Rivermont Hotel, where they were staying, plus her substance abuse at the hotel, concerned him, so he called for reinforcements. Shortly before they left Beverly

Hills, California, to fly to Memphis, Adams had introduced Dusty to a friend of his named Sandy.

"Dusty was sort of taken by Sandy," Adams told Karen Bartlett. "She said, 'You know your friend Sandy, do you think she'd like to come to Memphis?' And I said, 'I'm sure she'd love to.' She said, 'Well, will you organize it?'" Adams agreed to arrange for her passage to Memphis. The two women were reunited in the top-floor suite of the hotel.[44]

Sandy did have a calming effect on Dusty, except when they drank too much and Dusty did not show up at the studio when scheduled. It was around this time that Don Nix was working with Leon Russell and Karl Engemann, an A&R executive at Capitol Records, called him and asked for a favor. "Karl wanted me to be a producer, wanted me to cut something in Memphis," Nix told me." I did one record for him—I can't remember the name of it—then he called me one day and said he wanted to come to Memphis to talk to Chips. It was when Dusty Springfield was there. They flew down and I picked them up at the airport and drove them to American Sound, where they met with him in his office. While they were talking, I went into the studio and Dusty was there and she was sitting on the floor with a girl's head on her lap. I didn't know then that Sandy was a lesbian. But I went, 'Oh, well, think I better go.'"

Obviously, it was Sandy that Nix encountered in the studio, although they never were introduced. Adams's instincts were correct, thus proving the widely held, but not scientifically proven, belief that hairdressers are America's true match-makers. Sandy did have a calming effect on Dusty, there was no denying that.

Chips' meeting with the Capitol Records executive was one of the few times that Chips ventured into the studio while Dusty was booked for her session. For the most part, he was enjoying his time at his farm, located well beyond the Memphis city limits. Incredibly, he had built a full-fledged racetrack on his farm where he trained his own horses to race at tracks around the country, especially Kentucky's Churchill Downs. Gambling was permitted at his racetrack, thanks to county officials who looked the other way to the illegal activities at the farm. Not only did he have a racetrack, he also had an airport where he housed his newly purchased airplane. He had an interest in flying since childhood, but his success in recent years as a producer had now allowed him to purchase his first airplane. He learned to fly and in no time he was airborne, flying anyplace he wished. No doubt he strafed American Sound Studio from time to time, just for the fun of it. Odds are he strafed the studio extra close while he was shut out of Dusty's session.

To the surprise of no one, Wexler, Mardin, Dowd, Adams and Dusty, along with Sandy, packed up and left Memphis with a master tape that had no vocals, just a beautifully constructed instrumental track. Once in New York, they went to the Atlantic Records studio and completed the process of making a record by adding Dusty's vocals and the backing vocals of the Sweet Inspirations. That is not to say that recording with Dusty in New York was any easier than recording with Dusty in Memphis. It was not.

To Dusty's surprise, Wexler deliberately tried to antagonize her by turning up the volume in her headphones "so high she couldn't even hear herself singing." Frustrated, she once tossed an ashtray at Wexler and called Tom Dowd a "prima donna."

"The only prima donna here, Mademoiselle Springfield," retorted Wexler, "is *you*!"[45]

Dusty in Memphis was not a hit when it was first released. However, in the United Kingdom, the single, "Son of a Preacher Man," was a Top 10 hit. But as time went by, the album attracted acclaim for being a masterpiece. When the album was released, music writer Greil Marcus strolled into the *Rolling Stone* office and asked if they would be interested in a review of Dusty Springfield's album. Blank stares and a few snickers later he wrote in a review: "Dusty had a way with words, a soft, sensual box (voice) that allowed her to combine syllables until they turned into pure cream." Then he continues: "There are three hits on his LP, and they are representative of the rest of it. 'Son of a Preacher Man' is as down-home as Dusty gets . . . a vocal that's almost dirty . . . 'Don't Forget About

Me' is to my ears the best cut here . . . her voice almost like another instrument. The song picks up Gene Chrisman's woodblock and the Sweet Inspirations and it's a fast race home."

When the session concluded, she refused to attend a private dinner with Wexler to honor the album, sending her hairdresser instead. In an unpublished interview with *Rolling Stone* in 1973, she said, "I didn't like 'Son of a Preacher Man.' I knew it was a hit song, but I didn't like the record."[46]

Over the years, the album has only grown in popularity, many people saying "Son of a Preacher Man" is one of the best songs ever recorded. In 2001, the album was inducted into the Grammy Hall of fame. In 2020, the Library of Congress selected the album for preservation in the national Recording Registry for being "culturally, historically, or aesthetically significant . . . over time *Dusty in Memphis* grew in stature to become widely recognized as an important album by a woman in the rock era."

The year after the album was released, Dusty gave an interview in which she admitted, for the first time, that she was a lesbian. She lived another twenty-nine years, but sadly died in 1999, two years before *Dusty in Memphis* was put in the Grammy Hall of Fame. She never knew how beloved the album was, nor did she ever truly accept it as one of her best album efforts.

DIONNE WARWICK WAS IN A RAGING STORM on a flight from New York to Kansas City on April 4, 1968, after attending a George McGovern campaign rally in support of his presidential effort, when Martin Luther King was assassinated by a right-wing white nationalist in Memphis. She did not learn of the murder until she landed.

"They told me in Kansas City," she told me. "That was devastating to the world. Still is."

Warwick had been in Memphis eight months earlier to attend a recording session at Chips Moman's American Sound Studio. The August 1967 session was for the Sweet Inspirations, a group she likes to call her

Dionne Warwick in Memphis
Photo courtesy Mississippi Valley Collection
University of Memphis Libraries

126

"church group." As members of the New Hope Baptist Church, Warwick and other family members sang in a gospel group, the Gospelaires, while still in high school. Other older family members such as her aunt Cissy Houston, mother of Whitney Houston, belonged to a group called The Drinkard Sisters.

As the fame of the Gospelaires spread they decided to compete in a gospel contest at the world-renowned Apollo Theater in Harlem, New York. What emerged from those performances were offers from record labels and production companies for backup and demo singers. Both Dionne Warwick and her sister Dee Dee were members of the original backup group.

While singing backup, Dionne Warwick branched out into singing demos for song publishers. One day they were called to sing backup on a Drifters song at the Atlantic Records studio. Also in the studio with them was songwriter Burt Bacharach, the conductor of the session, After the session, Bacharach approached Dionne and asked if she would be interested in singing a few demos for him and his writing partner Hal David.

Dionne, who was twenty-two at the time, had a one word response, "Cool!"[47]

Dionne ended up signing with the Bacharach/David production company. One of the songs they asked her to demo was "It's Love That Really Counts," meant for the Shirelles, who were on Sceptor Records. When Florence Greenberg, founder of the record company, listened to the demo, she reportedly told Bacharach, "Forget the song, get the girl!"

Dionne signed with Sceptor and by 1963 she had her first hit, "Anyone Who Had a Heart," followed in 1964 by her first million seller, "Walk on By." In the *Cash Box Magazine* poll of 1964 she was named "Bestselling Female Vocalist."

As Dionne pursued her solo career, her friends and family members became entrenched as backup singers for artists such as Solomon Burke and Wilson Pickett. When Jerry Wexler of Atlantic Records heard them he hired them as background singers for the album he recorded with Aretha Franklin earlier in 1967. If you recall, Chips Moman and some of his house band members also were at those sessions in New York. Wexler was so impressed with their work on Aretha's album, he pushed them as a star group. He renamed them the Sweet Inspirations and released two singles on the group, neither of which charted. Then he booked them for an August 1967 session to record their debut album at American Sound Studio in Memphis. The resulting self-titled album, *The Sweet Inspirations*, was produced by Tom Dowd and Tommy Cogbill whom Chips Moman had been promoting as a producer. The 827 Thomas Street band provided the tracks.

Led by Cissy Houston, The Sweet Inspirations showed up at the studio accompanied by Dionne Warwick, who apparently was not recognized by the producers or band members because they never mentioned it in subsequent interviews. Dionne went to show moral support to the group, but also because Florence Greenberg at Sceptor suggested she go to see if she wanted to record an album there with Chips Moman. It turned out she did!

When she returned to Memphis the following year to record with Chips Moman, she was pregnant with her first child. When I asked with whom she traveled, she laughed and said, "No one—I was a big girl."

Astonished, I followed up with another question: "What, no big entourage like Elvis?"

"I never did and never will."

She had performed several times in Memphis and been there the previous year with the Sweet Inspirations, so she was not intimidated by the King assassination earlier in the year, nor the city's national reputation as a murder capital. She checked into the Holiday Inn Rivermont Hotel, which was located on the Mississippi River. Only in recent years had blacks been allowed to stay in so-called white hotels in Memphis. She found the view "lovely."

Chips picked her up the next morning to take her to the studio, but first he made a detour to Poplar Tunes, the city's largest record store. To her surprise—the only producers she had ever known, Bacharach and David, had never once taken her to a record store—they entered the store and Chips requested a listening room so that they could listen to records. The store employees thought nothing about it. Elvis used to hang out there all the time to listen to records.

Both Chips and Dionne looked through the album displays and undertook a scavenger hunt, returning to the listening room each time to listen to and discuss their finds. "We were looking for songs that I not only felt I could do, but songs I fell in love with, That's how we chose what would be on the album."

. They ended up with three Beatles songs—"Hey Jude," "A Hard Day's Night," and "We Can Work it Out"—Curtis Mayfield's "People get Ready," the Righteous Brothers' "You've Lost That Loving Feeling," Otis Redding's "I've Been Loving You Too Long," the Penn/Moman song, "Do Right Woman," the Penn/Oldham song "I'm Your Puppet," and others. Chips had learned early on that if he had a song on a hit record he would earn more money as a songwriter than he would as a producer. It was rare for him to work with an artist who did not want to record a song in which Chips had a financial interest.

Trying to picture Chips, with his customary tattered jeans and boots or tennis shoes, and Dionne, certainly one of America's most elegant and stylish singers, even at the young age of twenty-eight, rummaging through the record stalls and then kicked back in the listening room, I held off asking the obvious question for as long as I could: "So what was your first impression of Chips?"

Dionne laughed. "He's a madman . . . but it was wonderful. We laughed a lot. And he knew what he was doing."

She found working with the band a memorable experience. "The musicians had put together such great music. Everything fell into place. I had already learned 'You've Lost That Loving Feeling' because I had worked with the Righteous Brothers several times. And I had toured with the Beatles in the early Sixties. I knew them very well."

The appreciation of her talents by the band was noted in comments made by drummer Gene Chrisman in *Modern Drummer*: "I think one of the first sessions I can remember doing that I really enjoyed was with Dionne Warwick. That was back somewhere in 1968, and we cut 'You've Lost That Loving feeling'" and 'Hey Jude'. . . What I remember about her is that she'd put her vocal down, we'd go into the control room to listen to the playback, she'd go back and put a second harmony vocal on, nail it, the first time, put a third harmony vocal on, and nail it. She's amazing. Working with her was one of the highlights."

When I passed Chrisman's comments along to Dionne, she responded, "Really!—If you happen to speak to him tell him I thank him very much for that."

About Chips, she said: "I had a wonderful time and I was pleased that he and I were successful in thinking of the songs and the arrangements. People loved the album."

Dionne Warwick's album *Soulful* reached Number 11 on the Billboard's Hot 100 album chart and the only single released from the album, "You've Lost that Loving Feeling," reached Number 16 on Billboard's Hot 100 Singles chart. *Soulful* turned out to be one of Warwick's most successful albums of the Sixties.

Dionne Warwick returned to Memphis on two occasions to participate in the annual Memphis Music Awards. The first time, she performed. The second time she served as host for the ceremony. In 1972, the *Memphis Press-Scimitar* reported that Warwick was going to move the headquarters of her record label, Sonday Records, to Memphis, where a company owned by former Elvis Presley associate and current Chips Moman associate Marty Lacker would handle all administrative, distribution, sales and promotion for the record label.

The relocation never happened. Two years later Sonday Records, which was distributed by Sceptor Records, shut down operations after releasing records by Leslie Uggams, the Constellations, and Calvin

Arnold. Asked about the proposed move to Memphis in 2020, Warwick said, "I don't think that would have been a move they [Sceptor Records which distributed Sonday] would ever make. It got overruled."

Elvis Presley during his 1968 NBC "Comeback Special"
Photofest

CHAPTER 5
The Steve McQueen of American Music
(1969-1972)

IF IN THE YEAR PRECEDING 1969, Chips Moman had bragged to his drinking buddies that he would someday produce a Number 1 record on Elvis Presley, he would have been laughed out of the pool hall. The laughter would not be so much because they would have felt Chips was bragging, but because Elvis had not had a Top 10 hit since June 1965 when "Crying in the Chapel" slid onto the charts at Number 3, right behind Sam the Sham's "Wooly Bully." At the time, Sam the Sham and Sandy Posey eclipsed Elvis as hometown stars.

Nineteen-sixty-eight was a terrible year for Memphis. The riots that followed the assassination of Martin Luther King destroyed the perception of many residents that Memphis was a livable city. After a string of inane movies, that threatened to relegate Elvis Presley to has-been status, it was clear his career was in a nosedive. Known for his spontaneous generosity, he no doubt would have been rebuffed by any stranger he handed the keys to a free Cadillac to, something he was known to do in better times, with the words, "No, you better keep it, Elvis. You probably need it more than I do."

About the time everyone expected him to give up music and return to his old job as a truck driver, he surprised everyone in June by recording a NBC television special before a live audience that would be broadcast in December 1968. NBC wanted a full orchestra. The producer/director they hired Steve Binder argued against that, suggesting instead that Elvis perform only with his original core group of guitarist Scotty Moore and drummer D.J. Fontana. Binder won that argument and a second argument with Elvis's manager Colonel Tom Parker, who wanted a big-sounding

133

Christmas album, sometime akin to the movie soundtracks he had recorded in recent years. Blinder won that argument as well. It was the first argument Parker had lost in a long while, but it would not be the last. Once Binder told Elvis that Scotty and D.J. would be joining him, Elvis got on the phone and called Scotty to personally invite him to participate.

The call came late at night while Scotty was at the studio.

"Hello," answered his girlfriend, Emily.

"I'm trying to reach Scotty Moore," said the caller.

"Well, you've reached his home, but he's not here. Can I take a message? Who's calling please?"

"Well, this is, ah . . . Elvis."

"OK, fine," said Emily, thinking it was a prank. "This is Elizabeth Taylor."

There was a pause. Finally, Emily said, "Scotty is at a session. Why don't you call back later?"

When he called back, Scotty was there to talk to him. The last time they spoke was earlier in the year when they recorded "U.S. Male" for RCA. They hadn't done a live concert together since 1961, when they performed at Ellis Auditorium in Memphis. Despite misgivings about performing live again after so many years, Scotty readily agreed. By the time he set out for Los Angeles in the last week in June, Scotty was excited about the reunion. When he arrived at NBC's Burbank studios, he was escorted to Elvis's dressing room. "Elvis looked great," said Scotty. "He was in good physical condition. Once we started talking, it was like old times, really. He was joking and talking about things we had done."[48]

When they walked out onto the small stage their guitars were already in place. Elvis was dressed in black leather. Guitarist Scotty Moore looked almost collegiate. D.J. Fontana looked, as always, like a New Orleans drummer. Also on the state were rhythm guitarist Charlie Hodge and Alan Fortas, from Elvis's inner circle. Unseen and offstage was an electric bass player. Because the stage was in the round, they were surrounded by the audience, mostly attractive young girls. The performance itself was spectacular. They began with some of the early hits, "That's All Right Mama," and "Are You Lonesome Tonight," and it was clear that Elvis was in top form, revisiting levels of talent he had not exhibited in many years. They did two hour-long shows, changing audiences for the second show. When the show aired on December 3, 1968 it was the highest rated program of the week.

Watching with great interest was Chips Moman and his business manager for American Sound Studio Marty Lacker, a longtime friend of Elvis who was a member of his inner circle, sometimes referred to as the Memphis Mafia. Chips was in Memphis during Elvis's rise to stardom, but he had never worked with him or had any direct contact with him, other than seeing him come and go about the city. Chips and Lacker talked about how surprised they were that Elvis had looked and sounded so much like his former self, before his talents were corrupted by the shoddy recordings he had made in recent years to please Colonel Parker.

In 1968 Elvis was a non-entity in American music, replaced by the Beatles, the Rolling Stones, the Beach Boys and a spectrum of other high-energy acts whose music was light years away from rockabilly. Lacker told Chips that Elvis had another recording session coming up in Nashville with his RCA producer Felton Jarvis. Would Chips like for him to talk to Elvis about recording with Chips at American instead? He was working on a session with Dionne Warwick at the time, but, yes, he would be very interested.

Encouraged by Chips' response, Lacker drafted the help of radio personality George Klein, another member of Elvis's inner circle and longtime friend, who also had a history with Chips. They presented the Memphis option over dinner at Graceland just days before he was scheduled to record in Nashville. It was an easy decision for Elvis because he was dreading his return to Nashville. Besides, he was well aware of Chip's success in American Sound Studio. Elvis said yes, as did his Nashville producer Felton Jarvis, who already had collected several songs for the session, including "In the Ghetto" and "Don't Cry Daddy." [49]

THE SESSION ITSELF was put together very quickly and scheduled for January 13, 1969. There was already a session scheduled for that time period with Neil Diamond, but Chips rescheduled the Diamond session and hurried to get ready for Elvis. Luckily, he had the stash of songs he had been holding for B.J. Thomas.

"Elvis wasn't the world's greatest singer, but he had a sound. I worked with people who were more talented, but nobody bigger," he told me, laughing. "He was great."

As was typical for a Chips Moman session, there were some misunderstandings that were not resolved until attention was paid to the fine print. Chips was under the understanding that he would be hired as the producer and receive producer royalties and Felton Jarvis was under the impression that he would be the producer and receive producer royalties. The true terms of the agreement—Lacker was a better talker than negotiator—were that RCA Records would rent American Sound Studio for $25,000. Felton Jarvas would be the producer of record and would receive the producer royalties.

Chips Moman's name would not be listed as producer and he would not receive royalties on record sales. Chips thought about what was obviously a bad deal, but he neither exploded nor imploded. For a man nicknamed the "Front Money Kid," it was a bad deal, the worst of his career. He accepted the terms, but he had a fallback position. He insisted on having songs on which he possessed publishing rights, for which he would receive royalties, and he made up his mind that when Colonel Tom Parker demanded half the publishing, he would say no. He would draw a line in the sand.

As you might imagine, Chips was holding an ace-in-the hole. He controlled a song that he was absolutely certain would be a smash hit, no matter who sang the song—"Suspicious Minds." He had been holding the song for B.J. Thomas, but when the opportunity arose for him to record Elvis singing it, he took the song away from Thomas. When Elvis and his entourage entered the studio to begin the session, Chips was grinning like a Cheshire cat. He was gracious, affable, and without the slightest hint of a bipolar disorder. Neither did he show any indication of alcohol or drug use. The way he showed Elvis and his boys around the studio you would think he was the maître d' of a swanky restaurant.

The recording session began easily enough, with Elvis serenading Chips with his first published song, "This Time." Lacker had tipped Elvis off that many acts began their sessions with Chips by doing that as a show of affection for him. Already in a mellow mood, Chips kicked back and proceeded as if they were there to have fun, a primary factor in whether his sessions would be successful. He appreciated Elvis opening the door to the Fun Room by singing his song to him. That was his cue to take the spurs off his boots.

The first week of the session with Elvis, Chips recorded twenty-one songs. Then after a break, Elvis returned in February and Chips got an additional fourteen songs. That was an incredible feat, something only Chips Moman could bring off. Much of the success was due to his incredible 827 Thomas Street Band. Although composed of individuals, they performed in lockstep as a single unit that simply did not make mistakes. Each musician knew exactly what to do in any given situation. As a result, they did not require constant attention from a producer. Chips put them on auto-pilot and he focused all his efforts on Elvis.

"When he went at it, he was either on or off," Chips explained to me. "If he was off, it was better to do it another day. A lot of people didn't understand how I could get him to do so many takes. I might ask him to sing a song twenty or thirty times, over and over. I'd ask him to back up and fix little lines that he would miss. He went through it without a problem."

One thing that Elvis discovered that no one had explained to him was that when it came to personal charisma, Chips was a close second to Elvis. The King met his match and he appreciated the fact that Chips was a likeable guy whose mistakes could be overlooked. If Elvis and Chips had co-starred in a movie, it likely would have been titled *Butch Cassidy and the Sundance Kid.* So, as it turned out, they made the recording session into a buddy movie that alternated between drama and laughter. Oh, to have been a fly on the wall of *that* session.

"He could take direction—he certainly could," Chips told me. "He obviously hadn't had any direction in a great while. I'm sure he had direction from Sam Phillips. But after he became a star I don't think he had much direction. I know that when I told him he was off pitch, his entourage, said "Oh, no, don't tell him that." They were in a faint. Well, why not? I saw quickly that I didn't want to go on the speaker and give Elvis direction. I walked out into the studio and had a quiet conversation with him, which was not a problem. As a result, when the records were released people said he hadn't sung that well in years. It is just a matter of knowing how to tell a guy without hurting his feelings. I'm sure he wouldn't have taken direction if I had told him he was flat in front of that mob of people. If you do it quietly, one on one, no problem. Producers sometimes have to use tact. It is different with each person."

Chips never records his best songs early in the session because he feels musicians and singers perform best after they have latched onto a groove and sustained it through several songs. He believed that everyone in the studio performed at a higher level while they were tired and needed to overcompensate for that tiredness with a revved up effort. That was the sweet spot where he often found the magic in the recording process.

From the beginning, Chips had understood that "Suspicious Minds" would be the smash hit of the group, so he held onto it until he felt the time was right. It was at that moment the entire session threatened to explode. Freddie Bienstock and Tom Diskin, representing Hill and Range and Colonel Tom Parker, "informed" Chips that they would have to have 50 percent of the publishing on the song. Chips had marveled at how smoothly the session had progressed. He politely listened to Bienstock and Diskin, knowing they spoke for Colonel Parker. He was well aware that none of the songs that Elvis recorded as co-writer were ever his songs.

Using gangster-style coercion, Colonel Parker informed each songwriter that Elvis would not record their song unless they signed over half of the publishing rights to Elvis. No one ever said no.

If they had been watching Chips closely they would have noticed a subtle change in Chips' countenance. If upon greeting Chips, you noticed an impish smile on his lips and sparkling eyes, you knew that he liked you and you were in for a good time. However, if you were presented with tightened lips and hardened eyes, you knew you were in trouble because it was at that point, manic-depressive that he was, Chips would explode, jumping to his feet and shifting his shoulders from side to side. The latter is what Bienstock and Diskin encountered.

Chips told them that he had a message for Colonel Parker. "I'll tell you what," he told them, a distinct edge to his voice. "If you feel that way, we'll just wrap this session up right now and consider these songs very expensive demos." Chips leaned over and pressed the talk button to communicate inside the studio. "Boys, we're wrapping up this session right now. Ya'll can go on home. We' done here."

Band members stopped what they were doing and strained to see inside the crowded control room. It was at this point that a RCA Records executive, who was in the room, stepped forward and informed Chips he would not have to give up his publishing. Bienstock and Diskin left and called Parker to tell him what had happened. Reportedly, Parker informed them that Elvis would never again record with Chips Moman—and he never did.

The American Sound Studio recording session gave Elvis' career new life. Among the songs released were "In the Ghetto," which gave Elvis his first Top 10 song since 1965's "Crying in the Chapel," "Gentle on My Mind," "Kentucky Rain," and "Suspicious Minds," which peaked at Number 1 in November. Chips was named "Producer of the Year" in December 1969 by one thousand radio executives who had gathered in Atlanta for Bill Gavan's Radio Program Conference. Responded Chips: "I was completely stunned. I didn't know what to think or say. It's a wonderful honor for me, but my staff at the studio should receive most of the credit. They make the music. I just turn the knobs and make a few suggestions."

A decade and a half after the session, he told me he did have some lingering regrets about the session. "One of the things I missed with Elvis was his old band," he explained. "I always liked Scotty Moore and Bill and D.J. Fontana. I thought they were really unique. I always thought that it was sad that Scotty and Bill didn't stay their whole career with him. They were unique together."

A short time before the session, Chips had purchased Scotty Moore's Gibson Super 400CESN guitar, the one he had played from 1957 to 1963. He took the guitar to the session and gave it to Reggie Young to play as a tribute to Scotty. "That's what I thought of Scotty," Chips said. "His music changed my life. If I had it all to do over again, he would have been invited to that session."[50]

BORN OF RUSSIAN JEWISH ANCESTRY in Brooklyn, New York, Neil Diamond decided he wanted to be a songwriter while still in his teens. During his final year of college at New York University, a New York song publishing company offered him a contract to write songs for them for $50 a week. He dropped out of college to accept the offer, even though the contract was for only four months. His contract was not renewed.

Undeterred by that setback, he continued writing songs. He was twenty-four before he found success as a songwriter. His first Top 20 hit was "Sunday and Me," recorded by Jay and the Americans. He followed that up with four songs recorded by the TV sensations The Monkees: "I'm a Believer," "A Little Bit Me, A Little Bit You," "Look Out (Here Comes Tomorrow),"and "Love to Love."

Diamond's first success as a solo artist came with "Solitary Man." By 1968 he had signed with Uni Records. His debut album for Uni, *Velvet Gloves and Spit*, did not chart, prompting him to undertake a reexamination of who he was and who he wanted to become. He became

Neil Diamond in Memphis recording "Sweet Caroline"
Photo courtesy Mississippi Valley Collection
University of Memphis Libraries

fascinated with what he read, heard and saw about Christian revival meetings. He wondered if he could do a musical, Elmer Gantry-style album about how people were being taken to the cleaners by fake evangelists. To research his idea, he went to a Harlem church and sat in on a service one Sunday. "It blew my mind," he said. "Because I realized, I think, for the first time that no, this was not a rip-off, these people were getting what they came for. They were finding answers. That there is truth in what these people say. That there is a way to guide your life."[51]

It was at this point that he wrote the song, "Brother Love's Traveling Salvation Show," thinking he would record an entire album based on his "revival" theme. The best place to bring that off, he and his record label figured, was at Chips Moman's American Sound Studios. He wasn't bothered by being bumped by Elvis Presley, and he used the extra time to write more songs. At that time, he wasn't as big a star as the house band was used to. His biggest accomplishment at that point was writing "I'm a Believer," a hit for the Monkees.

When Neil Diamond walked through the doors of American, he looked like trouble to some of the band members. With a black beard and hair longer than the boys in the studio were used to seeing on a man, and a New York Jew personality, defined as acerbic, or as Southerners would call it, snotty, especially if his songs were criticized (and they were on a regular basis by Tommy Cogbill, who possessed none of Chips' homegrown tact), Diamond also carried the baggage of being more of a rock singer than a country or pop singer. Inexplicably, Chips liked him almost immediately. That may have been because he had a collection of Jewish friends that stretched way back. Or it may have been because he knew Diamond's first love was songwriting, something he shared with him and understood about him.

Diamond methodically played the songs he had brought with him to the session, and Chips liked "Brother Love's Traveling Salvation Show" best, so they began with it. Then they moved along to "Memphis Streets," another natural theme for Chips, "Glory Road," and "You're So Sweet,

Horseflies Keep Hangin' 'Round Your Face," written as a satire of country music. After that Chips seems to lose interest, primarily because he didn't hear a hit in the bunch, other than the first song they recorded. Discouraged, Chips stepped away from the session, allowing Tommy Cogbill to do the heavy lifting. By that time, Diamond had dropped his idea for a theme album based on the church revival concept, realizing it was more of an intellectual concept that a musical possibility.

Diamond knew in his heart he could never be part of the "new rock" crowd like the Creedence Clearwater Revival or the Zombies, so he tried to find out more about himself in the hopes that would lead to something musically substantial. "First of all, I was not a teenager anymore," he said. "I was twenty-six or twenty-seven, I had already been married, had two children at that point. I knew I was out of it. It didn't relate to what I was trying to do, which was essentially to try and be Alan Jay Lerner or George Gershwin. 'Hip' was something frivolous people had time to be. I didn't have time to be 'hip' and 'with it' and 'groovy.' I was dealing with something that was much more important—my life and trying to write songs that had substance."[52]

After they had recorded twelve songs, enough for the album, Cogbill asked Diamond, "That all you got?" It was meant as a putdown, a reference to the lack of potential hits produced during the session.[53] Diamond answered that he had two more, a gospel-tinged song, "Holly Holey," and a country tune titled "Sweet Caroline (Good Times Never Seemed So Good)." They recorded both songs. Diamond confessed he had written "Sweet Caroline" the day before in his motel room. They recorded it after only a few takes, but Chips wasn't there because he had left the session in the hands of Cogbill, after giving up on the other songs ever being a hit. There was also his antipathy toward rock music, and although Diamond's music was in a more soft rock vein, it was still rock. A second factor was Diamond's artistic temperament. Given a choice between working with a singer who did not write all of his or her songs, or an artist who wrote all of the songs brought to the session, Chips would always choose the singer.

Despite his sometimes rough edges, Chips was a hypersensitive individual whose feelings were hurt when artists did not follow his suggested changes pertaining to a song's lyrics. The vocals and the instrumental tracks for "Sweet Caroline" were spot on, but Diamond was unhappy with the strings arrangement and decided to take the song to another studio for its finishing touches.

"When you work with a person like Neil Diamond who knows what he wants to do and has a lot of input, a lot of times that is helpful, but a lot of times it is a hindrance," Chips told me. "You make a whole circle to arrive at the right point. You have to go in a lot of strange directions to get what you want. Sometimes I will cut something and try very hard on something I absolutely hate, waiting to get something, but I know if I don't make this come off it is going to blow getting the good song. So I may have to work hard on a piece of trash, maybe, to get a song."

When *Brother Love's Travelling Salvation Show* was released in April 1960, the title cut was issued as a single and went to Number 22 on the charts. "Sweet Caroline" was not on the album because of the delay in replacing the string arrangements. When "Sweet Caroline" was released as a single, it went to Number 4 on *Billboard's* Hot 100 chart and certified gold for sales of over one million singles. Not only was it the biggest hit of Diamond's career, it was one of the biggest hits of the year, qualifying as one of the three biggest hits to come out of American Sound Studio, the other two being "The Letter" by the Box Tops and "Suspicious Minds" by Elvis Presley. It did not go unnoticed by critics that Chips himself produced only one of the three hits.

With the success of "Sweet Caroline," Uni Records called for a second album to be produced at American. This session was scheduled for May 1969. Meanwhile, because of its success, "Sweet Caroline" was added to the *Brother Love's Travelling Salvation Show* album and it was re-released and realized an immediate boost in sales.

The second Neil Diamond album recorded at American was titled *Touching You, Touching Me*, words taken from the lyrics of "Sweet

Caroline." This time Chips Moman produced none of the cuts on the album. Tommy Cogbill produced the album with Tom Catalano, an independent producer who had previously worked with Diamond on numerous projects. The session began with one song, "Holly Holy," in the bank. Unlike the first American album, the second one had four cover songs: Fred Neil's "Everybody's Talkin'", Jerry Jeff Walker's "Mr. Bojangles," Joni Mitchell's "Both Sides Now" and Buffy Sainte-Marie's "Until It's Time for You to Go." Before the album was released in the fall, two singles were released, "Holly Holy," which charted at Number 6 and "Until It's Time for You to Go," which went to Number 53.

In the years following its release, "Sweet Caroline" became Diamond's signature song. Year after year, he was asked the inspiration for the song. He remained noncommittal until 2007, when he did an interview with the *Boston Globe*. This time he said the inspiration for the song was John F. Kennedy's daughter, Caroline, who was seven at the time it was released. Four years later, he was even more specific and said he had seen a magazine cover image of Caroline as a young child on a horse. That image, he explained, had percolated in his mind for five years.

In the beginning, public reaction to his admission was more like . . . aw, how sweet and how noble to honor a presidential family with a song. Diamond perpetuated that perception by singing the song to Caroline Kennedy on the occasion of her 50th birthday celebration. Then, the more people listened to the song, with its references to "touching you, touching me," the more creeped out they became. Finally, in 2014, Diamond admitted the song was about his then-wife Marcia. He needed a three-syllable name to make the melody sound right. His story was believable because people could identify with his not wanting to admit to a former spouse that he had written a lovely song about her. It was also believable that he had lied about the Caroline Kennedy connection to give the song a historical importance or offer a gift to someone he admired.

IN BETWEEN THE NEIL DIAMOND sessions, Tom Dowd, the in-house producer at Atlantic Records, booked a session at American Sound Studio for jazz flutist Herbie Mann. Chips had absolutely no interest in jazz, so he suggested Tommy Cogbill, who did have an interest in jazz, co-produce the album. For Jerry Wexler at Atlantic the project was more or less an experiment. His Atlantic partner Nesuhi Ertegun was the jazz expert of the group, producing avant-garde artists such as John Coltrane and Ornette Coleman, as well as mainstream artists such as Les McCann and Herbie Mann. What would happen, Wexler wondered, if he put a jazz artist with a rhythm and blues band? Neshui apparently approved, but for whatever reason he did not want to venture into the dark and mysterious world of Memphis music.

When they learned they would be working on a jazz album, several members of the 827 Thomas Street Band panicked because they had never listened to jazz records and had no idea what would be expected of them in such a session. The concept was not so much for them to learn to play jazz as it was for Herbie Mann to twist and weave his way into the depths of the rhythm and blues tracks in such a way as to fuse the two types of music into something special.

At that time, Mann was America's resident expert on jazz fusion for a mainstream audience. In 1959 he accepted a State Department tour of Africa, which resulted in an album *Flautista!* an album of Afro-Cuban sensibilities. He did a similar thing after a tour of Brazil, returning to record with Brazilian musicians such as Antonio Carlos to make music with an American-Brazilian flavor. Now, he was going to undertake the greatest challenge of his career. He was going to create a fusion of African American jazz with an all-white rhythm and blues band who played as if they had been trucked in from the Mississippi Delta. These were white boys who just didn't know any better than to play in a style indistinguishable from black musicians.

A look at the song list serves as an indication of how intriguing the challenge was: "Hold on, I'm Coming," a hit for Sam and Dave on

146

Atlantic/Stax; "Chain of Fools," a hit for Aretha Franklin on Atlantic; "Memphis Underground," composed by Herbie Mann; "New Orleans," a rhythm and blues song recorded by Gary U.S. Bond; and the "Battle Hymn of the Republic," arranged by Herbie Mann.

When Mann showed up at American he was accompanied by three top jazz soloists: Vibraphonist Roy Ayers, and guitarists Larry Coryell and Sonny Sharrock. It was at that point that the 827 Thomas Street Band understood the premise of the album. They would play their parts as they would for any other rhythm and blues recording, but the jazz soloists would reshape the texture of each recording with mainstream jazz improvisations while staying within the boundaries set by the band.

Memphis Underground, the album, would go on to become one of the bestselling jazz albums in history. The collaborations of the two styles of music fused into a remarkable body of work. "Battle Hymn of the Republic" was both spellbinding and inspirational. "Hold On, I'm Coming" was hypnotic in the manner in which Mann's flute transformed soul into an even deeper feeling. The reviewer for *Rolling Stone* magazine understood the significance of the album: "Memphis Underground is a piece of musical alchemy, a marvelously intricate combination of the 'Memphis sound' and jazz lyricism . . . The most interesting cut on the album is 'Hold On, I'm Coming.' For those jazz listeners who used to thrive on improvised solos backed up by a driving riff, this will prove a revelation. It turns out that the Sam and Dave riff is a perfect vehicle for all sorts of improvised lines . . . When I talked to Mann about this aspect of his record he explained that his primary task on the date was to make it clear to the 'Memphis rhythm section' that his New York Jazz musicians were not there to flaunt any mistaken 'superiority.' We had come to play with them and it was a privilege to do so.'"

Hunter S. Thompson, the revered godfather of Gonzo journalism, once compiled a Top 10 list of albums from the 1960s. In the Number 1 slot on his list was *Memphis Underground*, followed by albums by Bob Dylan, the Rolling Stones, Miles Davis, and The Grateful Dead. *Memphis*

Underground, Thompson wrote, "may be the best album ever cut by anybody."

AS HE WAS PREPARING for a session with Brenda Lee early in 1970, Chips came across a demo tape from a New York songwriter named Toni Wine that he wanted to use in the session. However, there was a problem. The publisher had not included the lyrics sheet. Because this was before the age of faxes and computer emails, the only way he could get the lyrics would be if the songwriter flew the lyric sheet down herself. Not wanting to lose an opportunity for Brenda Lee to record her song, Toni Wine readily agreed to catch the next plane out of New York. Marty Lacker, who was in New York at the time, was happy to accompany her back to Memphis.

The song was "I Think I Love You Again," something she had co-written with Irwin Levine. It would be in good company on the album with John Denver's "Leaving on a Jet Plane," Barry and Maurice Gibb's "Give a Hand a Hand," John Fogerty's "Proud Mary," Joe South's "Games People Play," not to mention Chips own composition, "Do Right Woman, Do Right Man."

When she arrived at the studio with the lyrics to the song, Chips was stunned by her youth and her attractive appearance, and most noticeably by her high energy level. He was laid back, almost speechless. She was filled with questions about the session, about the studio, about Memphis. Of course, if there was one thing Chips didn't care for it was to spend time answering questions. His favorite mode of communication was understatement and humor. He was most definitely not someone who enjoyed a good debate.

Chips had a few rough edges, smoothed somewhat by the passing years. Toni had razor sharp edges that were sheathed by soft brown eyes and a pretty face not unlike that of a young Natalie Portman. Although in possession of a charismatic personality, Chips had a little bit of Georgia

Toni Wine, left, with songwriting partner Carole Bayer Sager at birthday party for singer-songwriter Tommy Boyce
Photo courtesy Toni Wine

redneck in him. Toni was 100 percent Jewish princess, something she never felt the need to apologize for. Chips was thirty-two and married with a daughter. Toni was twenty-two, ambitious, and single. What could possibly go wrong?

The Brenda Lee session went smoothly enough on her album, which was titled *Memphis Portrait*. There was no reason for it not to. She was a Southern girl born in Chips' home state of Georgia. She had been recording pop hits since 1957, when her song "One Step at a Time," charted, establishing her as a pop star. At the time of her session with Chips she was twenty-six years of age. Her record label wanted a strong pop album to counter lagging sales in the pop market.

Not long after *Memphis Portrait* was released, it floundered. As a young girl pop star she really had no serious competition. As a young woman her competition was Bobbie Gentry, Lulu, Diana Ross, Nancy Sinatra, Carole King, and Petula Clark. Brenda was perfect for the 1950s and early 1960s, but by the late 1960s and early 1970s the yardstick for pop stardom had changed. Pop and rock music reflected the protest and rebellion taking place in American society. The record label wanted a strong pop album and Chips delivered an album that would be a hit for most of the current pop stars mentioned earlier.

The poor performance of *Memphis Portrait* convinced Brenda Lee that she should try a country album next. She did and scored a series of Top 5 hits on the country charts. If Chips had recorded a country album with Brenda it, no doubt, would have been a major hit. The author has interviewed Brenda Lee for previous books, but when he approached her for an interview to talk about *Memphis Portrait,* she declined. In the weeks following the release of *Memphis Portrait* she must have felt her career was over at the moderately tender age of twenty-six.

BRITISH POP SINGER PETULA CLARK was immensely popular in the United Kingdom, Australia, Canada and most of Europe long before she was known in the United States. That changed in January 1965, when her song "Downtown" knocked the Beatles off the top of the charts in America. She quickly followed up with a Number 3 hit, "I Know a Place," that made her the first female singer of the rock era to have her first two chart entries make the Top 3 of *Billboard's* Hot 100. It was a record that stood for almost two decades.

Because of her growing popularity in America, Petula was asked to host her own NBC television special. The director was Steve Binder, who went on to direct Elvis Presley's "Comeback" special later in the year. The format was for her to sing her hits, saving her biggest hit, "Downtown," for last. Her special guest was Harry Belafonte, with whom she was scheduled to sing a duet on "Paths of Glory."

Petula and Belafonte rehearsed together for a week. She was excited about working with him and felt good about the special. However, before taping began a memo arrived from the sponsors insisting there must be "no physical contact between Petula and Belafonte." The reason was because any type of touching would make the show very unpopular in the South. When Petula sang her duet with Belafonte she was advised to sit slightly forward and to one side of the black man. During the actual taping of the show, everything was perfect until they came to the duet. Petula forgot the no touching rule and brushed his arm with her hand as they sang. She barely realized she had done it. Suddenly, the representative from the sponsor, Plymouth-Chrysler jumped to her feet, screaming, "Stop! Cut camera! That's not acceptable. She touched him!" Everyone froze. Then she stridently continued, "Touching is forbidden!"[54]

With that, Petula's husband, Claude, and their lawyer rushed to the basement where they knew the other takes were stored. They asked to see the previous takes and then quickly erased them. When they returned to the studio, the battle was still raging. Belafonte screamed that it was racist. Petula was upset that an innocent hand gesture had caused such an uproar.

Binder told everyone not to worry because he had several takes of the duet. Then Claude spoke up that they had been erased and Petula would not agree to record the scene again. The long and short of it was that the show aired as scheduled and the Plymouth-Chrysler representative was fired. Steve Binder wrapped up his directorial duties and began work on his next special, the Elvis Comeback Special, where instead of doing battle with a racist sponsor rep he did battle with the Lucifer of the music business, Colonel Tom Parker.

In February 1970, Petula Clark flew to Memphis to begin a recording session with Chips Moman at American Sound Studio. After her experience with NBC for the television special in which she touched Belafonte, she did not know what to expect in a Deep-South city such as Memphis, where Martin Luther King had been shot and killed for speaking out in support of black sanitation workers.

Despite the city's violent history against black citizens, Petula was excited about going to Memphis to record. "Memphis is a sort of legendary word all over the world," Petula told me. "It means music and Elvis. I had not met Chips. I fell in love with the place right away. It's a funky little town. It was very hot. I went to the studio and that was very funky, too. I met Chips and I had never talked to anyone who talked like that. He was very cute. I had recorded mostly in London, Paris, Munich and Los Angeles and this was different."

Someone had tipped off the *Memphis Press-Scimitar* that Petula was arriving at the studio, probably business manager Marty Lacker, because the day after she arrived she was greeted by a photographer and newspaper staff writer Brown Alan Flynn, who found her sitting in Chips' office looking "diminutive and pert," sporting frosted blonde hair, and "bubbling over with the magic which brought her success in England, France and the United States."

"Recording was becoming not very exciting for me," she explained to the reporter. "I was searching for a freer, easier sound. I didn't like the idea of knowing what the orchestra would sound like before I started."

Chips and Petula chose the songs she would record the first day. "It was all very casual," she explained to me. "He was playing guitar. I liked the songs. I asked who would be doing the arrangement and he said, 'Well we don't work like that.'

"I was like, 'Oh, really.'"

As Chips played guitar and Petula listened, she noticed that the band members were writing things down on notepads.

"Are they writing down the symbols?" she asked.

"No," responded Chips. "They are writing down the changes."

"It is their own way, their own code," she explained to me. "They

Petula Clark in the Studio with Chips Moman
Photo courtesy Mississippi Valley Collection
University of Memphis Libraries

played it and it just sounded great. There was something about the way they played. I found it totally inspiring and very, very different from anything I had ever felt before in a studio. Of course, Chips was egging us on. It was a totally different experience. I was used to an organized session where you rehearsed and had orchestrations and everything was done live in the studio. All those big hits we did in London were done live. I was absolutely crazy about what was happening in Memphis. I think I sang different on *Memphis* than on the other albums I'd recorded."

As for her impression of Chips, she said: "He reminded me a little bit of Quincy Jones. He never said much. You just felt you knew what he wanted you to do. He never gave me much direction. Quincy Jones never gave me much direction. He felt that the songs were right and I was singing them the way he wanted me to sing them. I liked him a lot. He made me laugh a lot. He would say weird things. To me, the whole experience was on the weird side, but a good weird, something I had never experienced before."

One experience in the weird category that caught her off guard was the time keyboardist Bobby Wood took his glass eye out of his eye socket and popped into his mouth, rolled it around inside his mouth for a while, then removed it from his mouth and popped it back into his eye socket. I explained to her that he was just trying to impress her.

"Well, he impressed me all right," she said dryly.

Two things are notable about the song list that Chips offered to Petula. First, it is a very strong list that offered the possibility of several hits. Second, many, if not most, of the songs were written by songwriters affiliated with Chips, often as publisher, which meant he profited from the publishing royalties in addition to what he earned as a producer. Two of the songs for which he had no publishing "I Wanna See Morning With Him" and "That's What Life is All About," were both written by Toni Wine. However, Mark James (real name Francis Zambon), who was signed to Chips publishing company, had the song, "When the World Was Round." He previously had written hits for B.J. Thomas, Elvis, and Brenda Lee. Johnny Christopher, another one of Chips' songwriters, had two songs, "Nothing's As Good As It Used To Be" and "That Old Time Feeling." Christopher co-wrote one of Chips' biggest hits, "Always on My Mind." Then there was Wayne Carson Thompson, another Chips Moman affiliated songwriter, who had a song "Neon Rainbow," previously recorded by the Box Tops. He also had written "The Letter," the hugely successful hit for the Box Tops. The Memphis album is one of the few albums Chips produced that did not include a song written by him, but in this case he was not known as a songwriter for female pop singers. His strengths as a songwriter were more in the rhythm and blues, and country vein.

Petula's Memphis album does highlight one of Chips' secrets to success—his focus on songwriters. "That is the key to making a Memphis album," Chips explained to me. "That is why so many people in the record business have always failed. It was always just two or three people who had it going. The important part of producing is the song. Writers are who you want to get in there—and song publishers. If you get the songs, artists will do anything to be a part of what you are doing. I got Mark James out of Texas. I got Dan Penn from Alabama. I would have songwriters come visit me. I would put them up when they came to town and encourage them to hang out a week or two. I've always had songs. Everybody in Memphis wants to go into the studio and worry about the singers. I've always had songs. That's why so many people have a hit and then cool off. They don't get more good songs."

Petula told me that her favorite song was Toni Wine's "I Wanna See Morning with Him." "I loved it," she said. "I found a lot of the songs very sexy actually (laughs) in a very different way from anything I had recorded before or since. I wrote a song, 'To Memphis,' fairly recently that I recorded over here and I so much wanted to get that Memphis sound. We did it in London. It was OK, but it was not what I wanted."

In 2016, just weeks before Chips passed away, Petula traveled to Memphis to perform at the Memphis in May celebration, at which time she performed "To Memphis" for the first time in the city. She talked a lot about recording in Memphis, but she had no idea that Chips was lying in a hospice bed only hours away, his life slipping away.

She doesn't recall doing a lot of takes on any of the songs, but there was one song that took more time than the others to get right. "I took more time on 'People Get Ready' I was a little nervous about singing it because it is such a classic. But Chips encouraged me to do it. I wasn't so sure I had the right to do it. When something is so iconic, it is a little difficult going in to do it."

Petula had one song on the album that she wrote herself using the pen name of Al Grant. It was some time after the release of the album that she

155

admitted she was the author of "Right On," a song that was surprisingly serious for a pop singer.

Toni Wine, who was at the session the entire time, later said Petula was one of her favorite singers. "She was so great in the studio. Her voice was bright and clear. She was the consummate professional."

Surprisingly, *Memphis* did not produce any hit singles, but it sold well and went on to be recognized as one of her best albums. Over the years, it has remained one of her favorite albums. She told me the story of a recent encounter with a fan while out shopping in London. Of course, for effect, she used her most theatrical voice.

"This rather eccentric bloke said, 'Oh Petula, you are absolutely marvelous. I tell you what—the best album you ever made was *Memphis*.'

"Really?" she asked. "You think so?"

"I listen all the time. I thought that album was great.'".

Although Petula made it clear she had a delightful time recording at American Sound Studios, her favorite moment was not music related. "We were going to some kind of award thing, so I asked, 'What you going to wear?'

"Chips said, 'I don't know. I had a suit once, but I lost it.'

"I thought that was a funny thing to say. He was full of it. The English have a great sense of humor, but I found his sense of humor absolutely delightful. I loved him dearly."

When I conducted this interview Petula had not yet heard that Chips had passed away. I had the unfortunate task of informing her of his death. I heard a gasp, and she said, "I didn't realize he had left us, so this is all very difficult for me."

AFTER THE COMPLETION OF PETULA CLARK'S album, Bill Medley formerly of the Righteous Brothers, recorded several singles at American Sound Studios for MGM Records early in 1970—"Keep One Eye Open," "Smilin' in My Sleep," and a re-make of Chips' "Dark End of the Street"—but they quickly dropped out of sight without charting.

Creating more excitement at American Sound Studios was the lawsuit filed against Chips by his partner Don Crews. Few people maintained long-term relationships with Chips, personal, business or romantic, without suing him or being sued by him. At the time, Crews was president of the company. As a result of the lawsuit, Chips called for a board meeting. Crew was voted out of office, and replaced by Chips. Other officers were Tommy Cogbill, vice president; Marty Lacker, general manager/treasurer; and attorney Jay Taylor, secretary.

It was during this high drama that Columbia Records called to book a session at American Sound Studios for Bob Dylan. That grabbed everyone's attention until the record company representative said that Chips could not be listed as the producer of the album. He would have to be the engineer. Not surprisingly, that demand rubbed Chips the wrong way. He told Marty Lacker to tell the record representative that he simply was not interested in Bob Dylan recording in his studio. [55]

UPON COMPLETION of the Brenda Lee project, Toni Wine returned to New York City, but only long enough to pack her bags to return to Memphis in time to be there for the session with Petula Clark. Chips encouraged her to relocate to Memphis. "I loved the magic coming out of that studio," Toni told me. "The music being made in that studio was incredible."

As Chips once explained to me, Toni was "the most professional person I have ever worked with." Not until he sat down and talked to her in the studio did he realize how successful she had been as a songwriter and singer. By accident he had stumbled upon the missing link in his vision for a recording studio. Vocally, her voice could be heard on the Archies "Sugar, Sugar" (the Archies were a fictional group; the vocals were done by session musicians of which Toni was the female duet lead and background singer) Tony Orlando's "Candida" and "Knock Three Times" (in the studio Toni was one of the two female voices; Dawn sang the songs in performance; Toni sang in the studio) and Gene Pitney's "It Hurts to be in Love." It was her voice on commercials that became pop-culture sensations: she was the "Meow-Meow-Meow" on Meow Mix's jingles; on "I'd Like to Teach the World to Sing" for Coca-Cola; and "Sometimes You Feel Like a Nut" for Peter Paul's candy; other artists she sang background for were Frank Sinatra, James Brown, and Lena Horne. In Chips' mind she was perfect to work in the studio with both recording artists and background singers. Not having such a person on the team was the weak link in his organization.

As a songwriter, she had written the theme song for Dick Clark's "American Bandstand," a song for the movie *To Sir With Love*, songs such as" Groovy Kind of Love" for Wayne Fontana and the Mindbenders, "Black Pearl" for Sonny Charles and the Checkmates (written with the legendary Phil Spector); "Candida" for Dawn, the male lead of which was Tony Orlando, but they kept that a secret because he was signed with another record company; the group would later become Tony Orlando and Dawn and record her song "What Are You Doing Sunday," on which she sang background); and others.

Thus far the songwriters who had affiliated with Chips had all been male. He needed a female songwriter who could give a female perspective, especially on ballads. To that end, he envisioned possibilities of him co-writing songs with Toni, just as he had done with Dan Penn and Bobby Emmons. To talk Toni into moving to Memphis, Chips turned on the charm, something he had a knack for doing. Steve McQueen could not have done it any better.

"We became fast friends," Toni explained to me. "I admired his talent and he mine."

Not only did Toni and Chips have polar opposite personalities, they also had polar opposite backgrounds. He came from a poor, rural part of Georgia, where his father worked the land to support his family, when he was not working in one of the textile mills. His education ended in the eighth grade. By contract, Toni was the daughter of a Jewish mother and father who divorced when she was a child. Her mother worked as a legal secretary at MGM in New York, a prestigious job, the envy of anyone trying to break into the music business.

Toni's introduction to music came at the age of fourteen when she heard the radio of a babysitter playing rock 'n' roll.

"What is this? I heard rock n' roll and I went nuts."

Prior to that moment of discovery, she had studied as a classical pianist at Juilliard School of Music for nine years. A child prodigy, she gave her first concert at the age of ten at Carnegie Hall. Everything changed after he heard her babysitter's radio. She asked her mother to introduce her to the people in the record division of MGM. Soon she caught the eye of record producer Don Kirshner. As a result, she was signed at the age of fourteen as a songwriter by BMI. She was the youngest songwriter they had ever signed.

"Six months after he signed me, they merged with Columbia Pictures, which was Screen-Gems Music," she told me. "They moved Mother and me to California for a year. I started writing them songs for movies and television."

While in California, she looked up her father and was surprised to learn that he owned a bookstore. She was never heard to speak ill of her father, but neither did she gush over him the way many daughters do of their fathers.

From movies and television, Kirshner redirected her talents to music. At age seventeen she had a hit with the Shirelles and her career just went upward from there, thanks to Don Kirshner—or maybe not. "Donnie put me in the music business," Toni told me. "I love him for that. I hate him dearly for not being honest with me. I would rather have had him tell me, 'Toni, this is a freebee.' OK for Donnie to get paid and for me not to. I sold 13 million records with the Archies and got a dozen roses. I didn't sign anything because he was the Daddy. It was a sad thing in my life that I am still paying for."

Just hearing that story from Toni would have made Chips' blood boil because he had similar experiences, beginning with Stax and continuing with record companies in New York and elsewhere. Once frustrated with a record label's slow payment of money owed him, Chips went to New York City to collect the money himself. He was greeted warmly by the record executive, but when Chips asked for his money the executive had only more excuses. At his wit's end, Chips grabbed the record executive by the lapels and dragged him over to a window of the skyscraper.

"You've finally pushed me to the point where I'm ready to die for this," Chips told the startled executive. He pushed the man up against the glass. "Is this something you're willing to die for?" The record executive did not feel the issue was of such magnitude that he was willing to forfeit his life. Chips left with his money.

The Chips Moman-Toni Wine friendship began because of their mutual love of music, especially songwriting, and it was then amplified by their mutual struggles within the industry to get their just due. It was the stuff of which firm bonds are forged.

THE NEXT MAJOR PROJECT Chips focused on was a new recording session with B. J. Thomas. Unfortunately, Thomas' return was marred by the band's overreaction to Toni Wine's move to Memphis. They had worked with Chips for most of their careers in a Boys Club environment that excluded women as equals, unless they were major stars. All Chips could talk about was how talented Toni was. Was it his intention to alter the chemistry of the 827 Thomas Street Band? Would he now write songs with Toni instead of Bobby Emmons.? Toni was a classically trained pianist from Julliard. Would she be put in charge of supervising Bobby Emmons and Bobby Wood in the studio?

On top of their jealousies and insecurities, band members were mindful that they only got paid when they worked. They counted on Chips keeping the studio booked. They all had families to support. Of all their fears, this was the one that had the most credibility. They saw Toni as someone who was distracting Chips from his work. Chips had never allowed his wife, Lorrie, or any woman, to intrude into their space, but now they found themselves eyeball to eyeball with Toni. She was verbally aggressive in that she was outspoken, but it never occurred to her that others would see her outspokenness as aggressive behavior. She rubbed the band members the wrong way because of her incessant questions.

A typical conversation would go something like this:

"I went to the store today to get a gallon of milk."

"What store?" asked Toni.

"Safeway."

"Which one?" asked Toni.

"The one on Union."

"What kind of milk did you get?" asked Toni.

"I didn't notice."

"Do you drink skim milk?" asked Toni.

Like most songwriters, she was sensitive to human feelings, whether they belonged to her or someone else. It is probably closer to the truth to say that Toni was probably just as threatened by the band as they were of her. When you look at her remarkable career before she arrived in Memphis, she had no history of failure. As a teen, when her elders commented negatively on her musical choices, she looked at it as a learning experience. By contrast, each band member, by then in their thirties, had experienced failure of one kind of another. They were battle scarred. Chips thought he had found the missing link to even more success, but it was not so much a link as it was a pin to a hand grenade that everyone saw but Chips and Toni.

Enquiring minds at the studio were so flustered that when Thomas arrived for his session, some members boycotted the event. The studio was in turmoil. In the days and weeks after the Petula Clark session, there were times when Chips disappeared, usually in his airplane, for days at a time. Band members would show up at the studio and wait around, killing time, until they heard from Chips. He was not the kind of boss to call in and keep others updated on his whereabouts. He valued individual band members, indeed he considered them family, but when they were out of sight they were out of mind. It was the same situation with his wife, Lorrie.

Despite the emotional riptide beneath the surface, Thomas' new album, *Everybody's Out of Town*, slowly but surely took shape. The title song and "Send my Picture to Scranton, PA," were written by Burt Bacharach and Hall David, but songwriters affiliated with Chips, Mark James, Johnny Christopher, and Wayne Carson, had four songs combined. The album had covers of already popular songs, always a trademark of a Chips Moman album, "Bridge Over Troubled Water, "Everybody's Talkin'" and "What Does It Take." As flawless as the album was in execution, it produced no Top 10 hits. The album itself made the album charts, but lingered only a short time in the 70s before disappearing.

NEXT UP IN THE STUDIO was Carla Thomas. A session with Carla, an artist under contract with Stax Records, would have been impossible three years earlier because of the bad feelings between Chips and Jim Stewart, but a lot had changed in recent years at Stax. It began with the 1968 buyout of Estelle Axton's half-interest in the company. Estelle explained it to me this way: "I saw that they were going to beat me out of part of mine. So, in 1968 I dealt with them and got my part before they gave up on Stax. The good Lord has been good to me. I got out before they dumped Stax and I got five-year's salary in that deal."

Internally, Al Bell, the African-American promotions and A&R director, was a rising force in the company, building his importance almost to the point where he had equal status with Jim Stewart. So, it was Al Bell who thought a Carla-Chips pairing would be a good thing. The band was delighted to work with her because, almost to a man, they felt she had one of the best rhythm and blues voices around. She had a tone and a delivery that suited the band's instrumental temperament. They were not far into the album before they realized their worst nightmare was coming true.

Chips accepted five Toni Wine songs for the album one of which "I Loved You Like I Loved My Very Life," was earmarked to be the first single released. On the B-side was "Hi De Ho (That Old Sweet Roll)," written by Gerry Goffin and Carole King, one of Toni's favorite writers. The album is a mixture of country soul and California glitter. It is a very commercial sounding album, but unfortunately the first—and only— single released was not well received. As a result, the album was fast-tracked to the Stax vault where it remained for forty-three years until its release in 2013 by Ace Records.

Burdened by the artistic successes—and commercial failures—of the Petula Clark, B.J. Thomas and Carla Thomas albums, Chips flew off in his airplane and disappeared into a cloud bank for an extended time. His productions were as brilliant as ever, he knew that; but were they brilliant by 1960s standards and not by the sounds being played on the radio in the 1970s? There was also the challenge of determining the role that Toni Wine would play in his professional and personal life. Could the professional relationship he had built with the 827 Thomas Street Band survive turmoil Toni had generated inside a group of men he considered family? Was it going to come down to choosing between the two? His bipolar personality pretty much had him going up and down on the issue.

When he returned to the studio in late summer 1970, he had two projects looming: Another recording session with B.J. Thomas and one with Jackie DeShannon scheduled to begin in January 1971. The new album with B.J. Thomas was titled *Most of All* and it was released in December 1970 by Scepter Records.

Chips always felt he had a good chance of recording a hit with Thomas, but when the album was released there was only one hit single, "Most of All," and it was the only song on the album *not* produced by Chips. "Most of All" was produced by Buddy Buie and Steve Tyrell. It went to Number 2 on the adult contemporary chart and Number 38 on the *Billboard* Hot 100. As 1970 drew to a close, Chips was beginning to feel jinxed.

CHIPS BEGAN 1971 with his first session with Jackie DeShannon, one of the first female singer/songwriters of the 1960s to score an impressive string of hits. She was probably best known for hits such as "What the World Needs Now," "Put a Little Love in Your Heart," and "Needles and Pins." She also was known for dating Elvis Presley and 827 Thomas Street Band guitarist Reggie Young. They recorded several sessions from January 1971 to April 1971.

DeShannon wrote three of the songs on the album titled simply *Songs*, with others written by two of Chips' writers—Johnny Christopher and Mark James. Several covers were on the album, including Bob Dylan's "Lay, Baby, Lay" and the old traditional "Down by the Riverside." When the record label received the album they did not release some of the songs and re-recorded others. Only one of the Moman-produced songs stuck, Christopher's "Show Me." The producer of the album was listed as Eric Malamud, DeShannon's future husband. The rejection of several month's work was devastating to both Chips and the musicians. Everyone associated with the studio was accustomed to Chips' sudden mood swings, but to have such bad luck with their work product over the past year was unreal. There was a sense that their lives were spiraling out of control. Of course, half the men in the band blamed it on Toni. The other half blamed Chips for listening to her. It was around this time that Don Nix stopped by the studio to ask if anyone knew where he could get a good deal on a window air conditioner for his parents.

"Come with me," said Chips.

They went outside to the parking lot and Chips unlocked the trunk of his car. Inside was a big box with the name of a well-known air conditioner brand printed on it.

"How much?" asked Nix.

"$200."

"Sold."

Nix laughed telling the story, adding "You just never knew what Chips might have in the trunk of his car."

After the sessions finished in April 1971, Chips flew to Los Angeles to visit his old friend Dorsey Burnette, who wanted to promote his son Billy as a rising rock star. The three of them met at the Continental Hyatt House, a favorite among rock musicians. Chips liked what he saw and signed Billy to a singer/songwriter deal.

Before he knew what had happened, eighteen-year-old Billy Burnette, who has just graduated from high school, was on a plane with Chips to New York to meet the President and Vice President of Columbia Records. They signed him to one of their imprints, Entrance Records. They advanced him $150 a week, $75 for writing and $75 for being an artist.[56] It was hardly a good deal, but Billy knew that and felt the real payoff would come from working with Chips at his Memphis studio.

When they returned to Memphis, a recording session was just wrapping up for a new artist named John Prine, a country/folk singer/songwriter from Illinois. He was discovered by Kris Kristofferson, who invited Prine to open for him at the Bitter End Club in New York City. Subsequently, he was signed by Atlantic Records and sent to Memphis to record an album. It was produced by Arif Mardin, a Turkish-American producer who had worked with a diverse group of artists such as Queen, Bette Midler, and Aretha Franklin. Many of the songs recorded on the album went onto to become classics—"Sam Stone," "Hello In There," and one of my favorites, "Angel from Montgomery." The album was nominated for a Grammy and was subsequently ranked by *Rolling Stone* as number 452 on its list of the 500 greatest albums of all time.

As Billy Burnette recorded his album at the studio, Reggie Young produced two of the songs, probably because he saw Chip's interest waning. Billy also helped out in the control room by running the tape machines. In the studio with Billy, Chips was confronted by his aversion to rock music. Although a rock song was his first post-Stax hit, he had avoided rock music in the years since because he was never a fan, partly because it was rare for a rock artist to not be attached to a band—and Chips didn't have the patience to work with musicians unschooled in studio work. Sure, he had played on the road with Gene Vincent and the Burnette brothers, but it was mostly rockabilly, a transition genre to full-scaled rock. .

Billy Burnette's self-titled debut album was released in 1972. It received little radio airplay, not even in Memphis, the city of his birth, despite receiving favorable coverage from *The Commercial Appeal*. Typically, Memphis news media did not report on Memphis-born artists until they received publicity from national publications. Chips blamed the failure of Billy's album on local radio stations. It made him furious.

Astonishingly, Chips had no successes in 1971. His band members blamed it on Toni Wine, but they were not without blame themselves. They mutinied among themselves, sniping at one another and complaining nonstop, but rarely did they confront Chips to his face over the lack of work being generated for the studio. To support their families, they needed monthly sessions, or sessions that extended longer than a month. He could do one or two sessions a year and make money, especially if each album contained songs for which he owned publishing or songwriter rights. As musicians, they couldn't live on two albums a year.

Besides feeling a sense of failure about his recent work, there were other things playing with his emotions. His marriage had about run its course. His home life was stressful because his wife, Lorrie, felt left out of things, stuck at the farm while he flew away in his airplane for weeks at a time. He resented the way the band treated Toni, but that was complicated by the fact that he did not yet know what he wanted to do with her. Beneath all of this was an undercurrent of fear and loathing over what was happening across town at Stax Records. He had not had a Number 1 record since 1969's "Suspicious Minds" with Elvis Presley. Since then Isaac Hayes had produced a Number 1 record for Stax with "Theme from *Shaft*." Willie Mitchell had produced a Number 1 record for Hi Records, Al Green's "Let's Stay Together." And Al Bell had produced a Number 1 record for Stax with the Staple Singers' "I'll Take You There." Although he had been on the ground floor of building Stax Records into a rhythm and blues powerhouse, he had lost his edge for his first-love of soul music. It didn't help things that none of his band members were black. His bitterness over that came out years later in a newspaper interview.

"Everyone within the Memphis music organizations were promoting Memphis as Soul City," he told Bill Burk of the *Press-Scimitar*. "It should never have been that way. Memphis should have been called Music Town, or something like that. When you call yourself Soul City, you're typing the music that comes from here. American Studios was getting left out. I said to myself, if this is the way things were going to be, we would go somewhere else."

Dark clouds began to form over Stax Records in May 1967 when Atlantic Records was purchased by Warner. That meant Stax could either sell out to Atlantic/Warner, sever that distribution relationship and operate totally as an independent, or sell to a third party that would allow them to continue with business as usual. They chose the latter and signed with Gulf & Western. It was at this point that Estelle Axton sold out her interest in the company to her brother Jim Stewart, who soon brought Al Bell into the company to appease the Memphis black community. After the assassination of Martin Luther King in 1968 and the subsequent riots, race relations in Memphis rapidly deteriorated. Bell brought into the fold a tough guy New York record executive named Johnny Baylor. He owned a small label that only had one artist, Luther Ingram. Baylor was not hired as a talent scout. He was hired as an enforcer.

With his ear to the ground Chips heard the unmistakable click-click-click of flashing caution lights. In 1971, according to the Associated Press, Stax lost almost half a million dollars in a kickback scheme with Stax distributors. Talk on the street was that Stax had become a "gangsta" organization in which employees carried weapons. There were rumors of FBI and IRS investigations. By early 1972, everything that was going on—the investigations, his personal life, his relationship with the band—all added up to one conclusion: It was time for Chips to leave Memphis and start over somewhere else, where he could again find peace of mind in his work. He scheduled one last session in 1972. According to Chips. it was with rockabilly artist and musician Billy Lee Riley. Riley had begun his career at Sun Records, Jack Clement producing hits such as "Rock with Me Baby" and "Red Hot." His band, Little Green Men, ended up serving as Sun's house band for a while. Several songs were recorded, but only one was released as a single on CBS Records. It was titled "I Got a Thing About you Baby." The single didn't do much, which probably didn't surprise Chips. Most likely, the session was just something he wanted to do with an old Sun Records veteran. The other recordings from the session were put away in Chips' vault, never to be heard.

In June 1972, Chips packed up his studio equipment into trucks and asked friends to help him drive his vehicles to Georgia, where he wanted to build a new studio. He left behind his estate, Shelby Farm, though he arranged for it to be put on the market, but he took his wife, Lorrie, and his twelve-year-old daughter Monique with him. He didn't try to sell the building that housed his Memphis studio; he just closed the door and walked away. By then, Toni Wine had returned to New York to visit her mother.

In the months and years after Chips left Memphis, Stax Records sort of imploded and exploded at the same time. Black activists saw the company as a political arm of the black-power movement. "Things started getting rough around the studio," said Estelle Axton. "Street people were walking in with guns and taking money. Artists were carrying guns. It just got rough."[57]

Jim Stewart sold his interest in Stax to Al Bell but stayed on as president to provide continuity to the company. A federal grand jury was sworn in to look into the company's corporate affairs and Jim Stewart and Al Bell were ordered by a judge to turn their records over to the grand jury. Right in the middle of this activity, Johnny Baylor went to the Memphis airport to catch a flight to Birmingham, only to be stopped by authorities and asked to open his attaché case. Inside the case, according to the *Memphis Press-Scimitar* was $130,000 in cash and a check for $500,000. No charges were filed but the IRS kept the money because it already had a lien against Baylor. Soon banks were filing for payment of $10 million in unpaid loans.

In August 1975 Jim Stewart sent Shelby County Sheriff Roy Nixon a letter requesting that Al Jackson, a member of Booker T. and the MGs and a drummer in the Stax house band, be granted a permit to carry a pistol. About six weeks later, Jackson was shot and killed by a burglar he caught ransacking his home. After being forced to lie face down on the floor, he was shot five times in the back. His killer was never found leading some to conclude it was a professional hit.

Newspaper headlines tell the rest of the story:

Probe by IRS of Stax Reported by Attorney

Inquiry Growing Into Payola Case

Stax is Accused of Covering Up in Payola Case

Bankruptcy Judge Gives Stax Chance to Regroup

Stax Owner Acquitted, Ex-UP Officer is Guilty

Jury Finds Stax Payments Fraudulent

Stax Records to Reopen Here Soon

Stax Label is Revived by Fantasy

Waylon Jennings and Jessi Colter
Photo by James L. Dickerson

CHAPTER 6
Triumph in Nashville
(1973-1984)

"MOM AND I WERE NOT HAPPY about moving," said Monique. "That took her away from her family and it was a culture shock for me. I hated it!"

Not all of the band members were happy about it, either. Bobby Wood resigned and moved to Nashville. Gene Chrisman didn't want to move to Atlanta, or to Nashville either, for that matter, so he stayed behind in Memphis and got out of music entirely. "I just got a daytime job at a collection agency for a while, and then I went back working for a commercial air-conditioning filter company I had worked for years before," explained Chrisman. "I was crazy back then. I'd had about all I could stand for a while."[58]

A wealthy man at this point, Chips had two reasons for moving to Atlanta: to open another recording studio and to create a record label, something he had repeatedly tried doing in Memphis, without success. He flew his plane to the tiny airport at Warm Springs (population 450), about seventy miles from Atlanta, where his parents lived. He left Lorrie and Monique with them while he commuted to Atlanta, constructing a family home next to his parents while finding accommodations for himself in Atlanta, where he began work on a new studio.

"Dad used to fly his plane back and forth to Atlanta," said Monique. "And we would go pick him up at the Warm Springs airport."

With Chips in Atlanta were Bobby Emmons, Reggie Young, Mike Leach, and Billy Burnette. They built the second version of American Sound Studios and sat back and waited for the work to come in as Chips tried to organize a record label. To do that he needed, to raise money, find business partners and develop a business plan for the label. After more than a year of false starts and no major recording contracts, Chips decided in 1973 they needed to all move to Nashville because that was where the money was when it came to music. Billy Burnette remembers helping to lay the carpet in the studio that was christened American Sound Studio Nashville. He also remembers that the studio was "busted for drug use, which landed some of the crew in jail, so they were a bit paranoid around there."[59]

Shortly after that both Bobby Wood and Gene Crisman rejoined the 827 Thomas Street Band, although they could no longer think of a good reason to keep using a name that had no relevance in Nashville. After a while the music professionals in Nashville they dealt with started calling them the "Memphis boys." People outside of Nashville continued to refer to them as the 827 Thomas Street Band.

Chips did not exactly hit the ground running in Nashville. In addition to the aggravation of tearing down a studio in Atlanta and moving it to Nashville and finding a place to live, and building a house next door to his parents for Lorrie and Monique, he spent the latter half of 1972 and the first part of 1973 dealing with personal issues. He obtained a divorce from Lorrie and accelerated his relationship with Toni Wine. Friends called them the Desi and Lucy of the music business, as in the "I Love Lucy" couple of the 1950s. On Thanksgiving Day 1974 they were married. Their son Casey was born March 1978.

Chips did not make a smooth transition to Nashville. It was not as easy to establish himself in Music City as he had thought. No one was knocking his door down with offers. Finally, one day he received a call from B.J. Thomas, who was then living in New York City. He had signed with a new record label, ABC Records, after Spector Records had declared bankruptcy, and he wondered if Chips would be interested in doing another album with him. It had been about three years since they had been in a studio together. They talked about the possibilities and decided to record a country album. They would call it their "reunion" album. The sessions took place in the fall of 1974 at Chips' studio on 17th Street in Nashville.

Chips gathered an assortment of songs, including: Toni Wine's "Beautiful Things for You," Roy Orbison's "Crying," Dan Penn's "Doctor God," and John Phillip Baptiste's "Sea of Love," which was a Number 1 R&B hit in 1952. Interestingly, long after the completion of this album "Sea of Love" returned in 1984, a Top 10 hit for The Honeydrippers, a band fronted by Robert Plant, and again in 1989 with the movie of the same name starring Al Pacino and Ellen Barkin. Chips' production of the song was excellent but it was never released as a single.

After recording the required number of tracks, they sat down and listened from beginning to end. At the end of the listening, there was silence. Finally, Chips said, "I just don't hear a hit on this album."

"I don't think I do either," said Thomas.

Then Bobby Emmons said, "Why don't you play him that song you wrote with Larry Butler."

"Chips' face got really red and he hemmed and hawed," recalled Thomas.

Emmons said, "Play him 'Another Somebody Done Somebody Wrong Song.'"

Chips sang and played it on a guitar.

"It was obviously a great song," said Thomas. "This was one of those things that I was positive would be a hit. I said, 'Let's do it.' I don't know if he planned to do it with someone else or what the embarrassment was about, but we recorded the song immediately and it was obvious it was going to be a smash."

"(Hey Won't You Play) Another Somebody Done Somebody Wrong Song" was a Number 1 hit on both the pop and country charts. It was Thomas's first hit country song. The album itself went to Number 2 on the country album chart.

("Hey Won't You Play) Another Somebody Done Someone Wrong Song" was written by Chips and Larry Butler while Toni Wine was on a two-day trip to New York City to record jingles. Chips was in a pensive mood with his new wife on her first solo trip to New York City since their marriage. When she returned home, Chips saw her coming in the door and jumped to his feet to greet her.

"Come listen to this," he said excitedly.

She put her bag down and approached the piano. With Butler playing and Chips singing, they went through the entire song and looked at Toni seeking approval.

"Are you crazy?" she said.

"What are you talking about?" said Chips, puzzled.

"You are going to get sued. Play it again."

They played it once again.

Smiling, she went to the piano and nudged Butler aside to play "Hey, Look Me Over," from the Broadway play *Wildcat*, starring Lucille Ball. The song was written by Cy Coleman and Carolyn Leigh.

Chips and Butler looked at each other, stunned.

"Don't you hear it?" Toni asked. "It's the same melody."

Chips shook his head. "I don't care."

Ninety days after the song was released they were sued for plagiarism and lost. To this day, both sets of songwriters are collecting royalties on the record.

Despite the lawsuit, it was an auspicious beginning for Chips' new focus on country music as a Nashville resident. Because of his success with Sandy Posey's first singles, his production techniques were copied by Nashville producers and the end result was a more female-friendly recording environment for women in Nashville that opened the door for Shania Twain, Faith Hill, and eventually Taylor Swift. It also raised high expectations for Chips in his new Nashville home, where a tightly knit music industry maintained an ever-present vigil to prevent elements of rhythm and blues, pop or rock from infecting traditional country music.

The sudden success of "Another Somebody Done Somebody Wrong Song" caught everyone off guard, including ABC Records which found itself with its first hit single ever. It did not take them long to decide they needed a second Thomas-Moman album. Chips quickly gathered together another batch of songs, including two co-authored by himself, "We Are Happy Together" and "Lyin' Again," and a song written by Bobby Emmons, "Help Me Make It (To My Rockin' Chair), obviously written to play off of the success of what had come to be called the "Wrong Song."

For whatever reason, *Help Me Make It* never got off the ground. That may have been because ABC Records marketed it as a rock and pop rock album. It may have been because there were no obvious hits on the album, not the sort of hits that immediately grabbed you the way the "Wrong Song" did. The album's release gave B.J. Thomas two albums in 1975, but the feeling offered up by the recordings did not translate to the joyous vibes given off by the "Wrong Song."

If you looked behind the scenes it would have been evident why the album did not have the right "feel" to it. For starters, Thomas was high on drugs the entire time and Chips' emotions were on their perpetual journey to find a safe place in-between the bounces that sometimes made communication with Chips difficult. When his moods were bouncing, dealing with him was like walking on egg shells.

"Chips and I were at each other constantly," Thomas wrote in his memoir. "We are, I believe, of similar talent levels, but I was so out of it that he couldn't respect me. The big blowup came, however, over money."

Thomas asked Chips if he would loan him five thousand dollars so he could take a vacation once the taping was finished. Record Companies advance money for production costs, all of which is charged to the artist's royalty account. It was not an unreasonable request. Chips said he would do that. Later, when the album was completed, Thomas brought it up again. This time Chips told him he could not loan him money until he was paid by the record company. Thomas, feeling he already had been paid, called Chips a liar.

They had words and Thomas stormed out of the studio and went to a party where he snorted several thousand dollars of cocaine. Once he was soaring at his maximum altitude, he returned to the studio and again confronted Chips about the money.

Again, Chips said he didn't have it

Thomas pulled out a hunting knife with a six-inch blade. Chips hurried over to his golf bag and pulled out a club and turned around to face his attacker, but Thomas was already upon him, the knife blade pressed into his chest.

"You even think about hitting me with that club, and I'll kill you."

As that transpired someone came up behind Thomas with a golf club in his hand. Thomas insisted that they both drop their clubs. They did and Thomas backed away.

"I know I would killed him, and it horrifies me to think about it even now."[60]

A couple of years later, Chips called him and suggested they record again. He never mentioned what happened in the studio. For Chips, the music always came first. It's not so much that that he forgave. He just forgot. He had co-written some songs—"Everybody Loves a Rain Song," written with Mark James (it would become the title song for the album when it was released in 1978), "She's Rolling Over & Over," written with Bobby Emmons, and "Blues River," an emotionally infectious song with references to the Peabody Hotel and the Delta Queen. The later was an intricately layered production with a banjo, harmonica, and strings. Listening to the songs today, it is easy to understand why Chips chose to forget the incident with the knife: clearly, there was no better voice to interpret those particular songs than B.J. Thomas.

After the song was recorded, while still in the control room, Chips gleefully said to no one in particular, "You're listening to one of the greatest singers in the world." Then turning on Thomas's earphones, so he could speak directly to him, he said, "Put the chairs on the wagon, son: the meetin's over!"[61]

That scene says more about Chips Moman, the producer, than any testimonial ever could.

CHIPS WAS APPROACHED about recording another album with Petula Clark in 1975. He jumped at the chance, especially when he learned it would be a country album. She once had been to Nashville to appear on a television show, but she had never performed or recorded there and she didn't have strong positive feelings about the city like she did about Memphis. However, she was eager to work with Chips again.

Late that year she flew to Nashville from Los Angeles, where she and her husband, Claude, had rented Hope Lange's magnificent Hollywood mansion. Their nearest neighbor was Helen Reddy. Lange rented the house out on a regular basis. The previous tenant had been Dustin Hoffman. Petula and Claude's two children, Barra and Katy, had attended a school in Geneva for a number of years, but they were relocated to Hollywood and enrolled at the prestigious Lycee Francaise, where students and teachers communicated in French. The children found themselves in classes with Hollywood royalty because at that time the "in thing" for movie stars was to send their children to this particular school. That fact was hammered home by the drop-off lanes where there were long lines of limousines. Barra and Katy, who preferred Switzerland, were not all that impressed.

Petula and Claude were giving serious thought to establishing a residency in California because of the way her career had taken off in the United States, not just in music, but in television and movies as well. She had begun an album in Los Angeles, recording three tracks—Tom Jones's "Loving Arms," Petula's song, "I'm the Woman You Need," and "Never Been a Horse That Couldn't Be Rode"—when she and the record label realized the album was not coming together.

That's when Chips entered the picture.

Chips pulled together ten songs for the session, including: Bobby Emmons's "It's Midnight (Do You Know Where Your Baby Is)," an Emmons-Moman song, "Charlie My Boy," a Toni Wine song, "Gimme a Smile," a Johnny Christopher-Pat Bunch song, "You're the Last Love," and the only known recorded song written by Chips and Toni, "Pickin'

Petula Clark
Photo courtesy Mississippi Valley Collection
University of Memphis Libraries

Berries." By this time the band had ended its rebellion and everyone was back in a familiar grove. Most importantly, Emmons had realized that Toni was no threat to his songwriting partnership with Chips. Bobby Emmons had a laidback personality and was not in the least argumentative. Toni was outspoken and never hesitant to argue her point. Chips and Toni were not a natural songwriting team.

"I was timid about my own songwriting," said Petula. "There is a different feeling when you go out on stage and sing one of your own songs. Chips encouraged me. He loved 'Blue Lady,' the title of the album."

Petula found Nashville to be a relaxed place to work. Interviewed by me in 2020, she remembered staying with Chips and Toni while in Nashville. She told Andrea Kon, "Our studio was a beautiful room intact with all the lovely old American antiques. There was a kitchen, too, where the guy who did the engineering also did the cooking. In the middle of a session, he would say, 'Hang on a minute. I've got to see if the ham's OK,' or 'I've got to do the beans."

Petula's favorite songs on the session were Emmons's "It's Midnight" and the Bacharach-David song, "Don't Make Me Over." She also liked "Pickin' Berries," telling the author, "Someone mentioned that one to me today. They asked, 'what is that song all about?' I said, 'Oh, yeah, picking berries. It was a cute song, but weird. I loved singing it. Do you know what it was all about?" Petula also loved what Chips did with her song, "Blue Lady," explaining, "It was great. What can I say? I don't have an extraordinary song, but I was with Chips and for me Chips could do no wrong."

As they were finishing up the session, Claude called Chips with some astonishing news. The police had called and told him that they had intercepted a telephone call that indicated that the mob had put out a hit on them. He said he thought it best if Chips didn't tell Petula right away so that she could finish up the session. Chips agreed and promised to protect Petula from harm in Nashville. After the call, Chips notified the band and

Petula Clark, left, with Toni Wine Moman in Nashville
Photo courtesy Toni Wine Moman

production staff of the call and asked them not to bring up any news they heard of the matter because he wasn't going to tell Petula just yet. Then he disconnected the television and radio so that she wouldn't hear any news while in the studio.

"Everything was going well, very pleasant, and then one day it all stopped," she told me. """People stopped coming in. There were no newspapers, or television."

Petula proceeded in ignorance, unaware that their rented home in California was under siege. When Claude talked to her, he was careful not to say anything that would make her suspicious that anything was wrong. Everything went as planned until Petula insisted, despite Chips'

180

objections, that they attend the Country Music Association Awards. He gave every excuse in the book, saying he "didn't know about that," but she was adamant that she wanted to attend.

"What do you mean, 'You don't know about that?' I love country music and I want to go. We had a to-do about it and finally he said, "OK, OK. I will get a special box where we all can sit.' So we went and the show is going on and the show is great. Then some people started waving to me, waving me down to the floor. Chips said, 'No, you don't want to go down there.' I said 'Chips, 'I do,' so I ran off and went downstairs and people gathered around me and were saying they were so sorry about what had happened in L.A. Is everybody OK? I had no idea what they were talking about. Chips comes and gets a hold of me and pulls me out of there."

Outside, it was pouring rain.

I said, 'What's going on Chips?'

He said "OK, OK, Claude told me not to tell you.'

"So, he told me there had been as assassination threat. This actress who owned the house was close to the mob and they had received a message that they were going to get rid of everyone in the house. The house was surrounded by the police for three days. I knew nothing about this. It had all been kept from me. I was beside myself."

Chips said, "It's all calmed down now. Claude said you wouldn't finish the album if I told you."

"By the time I got back there was just one police officer in the house. The police told us if we wanted more protection we would have to pay for it. They insisted they had taken care of the problem. After that, Claude and I had a very important conversation. He said, 'I don't want us to stay in this town anymore. I don't want our children to grow up in this town and we are out of here. I agreed with him."

The Nashville stay did not sour Petula on either Nashville or Chips.

"I really would have loved to work with him again. I did speak to him when he was in Atlanta, asking his advice. It was lovely to hear his voice, but for some reason we just couldn't get it together. I think if I could have worked with him some more we could have done some really great things together."

Sadly, when *Blue Lady* was turned in to ABC-Dunhill it was rejected without explanation during a change in leadership and shelved for twenty years. It was not released until 1995. *Blue Lady* contained not only the ten songs Chips had produced, but also the three songs produced by Phil Gernhard and Tony Scotti before Petula went to Nashville. Listening to it today, it is perplexing to understand why the album was not released immediately after it was recorded. Petula is at her best vocally, and the production was letter perfect, although it could be argued that the album was ahead of its time in its production values for a country album. In a 1995 review, a *Billboard* reviewer wrote the album was a "fascinating mix of Los Angeles and Nashville . . . vintage Clark."

David Hadzis, project manager of United Music Foundation and a consultant to Petula Clark, successfully retrieved both the Memphis album and the Nashville album. "I have a DAT transfer somewhere with rough mixes Chips made for Petula in the 1990s," he told me. "That's how I found out about 'Another Major Tragedy,' which was not in the Universal Music vault. I also heard quite a few alternate takes. I wonder where the tapes are now."

"Another American Tragedy" is a song that was recorded during the Nashville session but not submitted to the record label. It was Hadzis who rescued it from a Swiss tape vault that included almost all of Petula's Warner tapes, including the backing vocals to "People Get Ready" that had been erased to "audition some singer on that very same backing track."

FRUSTRATED BY THE REJECTION of *Blue Lady*, Chips approached Warner Records about a deal for Sandy Posey. She had been out of the music business for several years, but he felt he had a hit with Bobby Emmons's "It's Midnight (Do You Know Where Your Baby Is?). Besides, he already had the instrumental track. All he needed was for

Sandy to provide the vocal. She had given him hits at a critical time when he needed them. Now he was in need of some more good luck.

One day the phone rang and Sandy answered.

"Hey, this is Chips. Do you want to be on Warner?"

That was it. No fuzzy-wuzzy greeting. No small talk. Just a question.

"Yeah," she said.

She told me, "I almost fell out of my chair."

Soon they were in the studio.

Sandy sang "It's Midnight" and then did the vocal for the B side, "Long Distance Kissing," a Toni Wine song for which Chips also had an instrumental track. After he moved to Atlanta, Chips decided to pitch Toni as a solo artist. He landed a deal for Toni as a solo artist with Entrance Records for a single using a demo of Toni singing "Long Distance Kissing." The record was released in August 1972 but didn't chart. Undeterred he recorded a demo of Toni singing a song she had written titled "My Point of View." Warner released it in August 1973.

Not until Chips finally gave up helping Toni to become a successful solo artist did they get married, with him focusing on his career as a producer and songwriter, and her focusing on her career as a songwriter and vocal coach. Instead of dreaming of becoming a solo artist, Toni got pregnant and gave birth to a son who then became the focus of her life. From what I saw of her relationship with her son, she never once regretted the tradeoff.

Sandy was pleased to be working again. She especially enjoyed recording with Chips. "Chips never told me how to sing, never," she told me. "Where so many producers make mistakes is when they try to tell a singer how to sing. Chips never did that, not with me."

Chips was stunned that "It's Midnight" did no better than 99 on the country singles chart. Before the next Warner recordings were due he landed a contract to record an album with Waylon Jennings. Discouraged by his effort with Sandy, he allowed Tommy Cogbill to take over as Sandy's producer using his studio and his studio musicians. Chips must have wondered about his ability to cut hit records with female singers because from that point on he chose to work with only two female singers for the remainder of his life.

Cogbill was not in the least intimidated. He bested his boss and produced two singles with Sandy, one in 1978 and another in 1979, both of which made the Top 20. Posey's records were among the last Cogbill produced. In December 1982 he died of a stroke at the age of fifty. At his funeral, which was attended by Chips and members of the 827 Thomas Street Band, Chips' old nemesis from Stax Records, Jim Stewart walked over to where he was standing and attempted to begin a conversation. Chips looked at him a moment, not sure how to respond, then he turned and walked away without saying anything.

BY 1976 WAYLON JENNINGS had released two consecutive Number 1 solo country albums: *Dreaming My Dreams* (1975) and *Are You Ready for the Country* (1976). A third Number 1 album, *The Outlaws,* that included Waylon along with Willie Nelson, Jessi Colter and Tompall Glaser, came out in 1976 and became the first country album in history to go Platinum. Helping it along were nine producers, including Waylon, Willie Nelson and the legendary Chet Atkins.

Feeling that he could produce an album by himself with Waylon that would go Platinum, Chips asked for a meeting with the artist. The request pleased Waylon because Chips was a "name" producer who had worked with heavyweights such as Elvis Presley and Dionne Warwick. Waylon had done all right basically producing himself, but with his recent successes he wanted to step it up a notch.

At the meeting, Chips handed him the lyrics sheet, saying, "I got a song here and you can't do it because your name's on it."

Waylon carefully read over the lyrics.

"I knew it was a hit song, even though I didn't like it, and still don't," Waylon later wrote in his autobiography.[62]

The song was "Luckenbach, Texas (Back to the Basics of Love)."

Chips played it on his guitar for him.

"It had a laidback rhythm I kept wanting to rush. I've never been to Luckenbach. Neither had Chips or his co-writer Bobby Emmons."

What he said was true. Neither Chips nor Bobby had ever been to Luckenbach, a tiny town outside of Austin, Texas. The seeds of the song were planted by friends of Chips, Guy and Susanna Clark. One day they stopped by the studio at 1111 17th Avenue South, right next door to Waylon's office, for a visit that extended all night. They told Chips the story of Hondo Crouch, who owned Luckenbach, Texas. He lived there and owned the only store, half of which was leased to the U.S. Postal Service. It was a terribly funny story and Chips was still laughing when Bobby Emmons reported for work at 9 A.M. that morning.

"Hey Bobby, let's go to Luckenbach, Texas."[63]

Knowing a hook when they heard one, Bobby sat at the piano and Chips picked up his guitar, and they wrote "Luckenbach, Texas." Nothing about the song made much sense, which is part of why it is so irresistible. Willie Nelson agreed to sing the song with Waylon. He was at a point in his life when he had made up his mind that the rest of his life would run smoothly. When they went to record "Luckenbach, Texas," he told Waylon about his plan.

"Your life ain't ever gonna run smoothly, hoss," Waylon told him.

Willie asked why.

Waylon told him to take a close look at the lyrics of the song they were about to record.

Willie did—and chuckled.

"Don't you see, Willie?" Waylon continued. "Until you get back to Luckenbach—or Abbott—or wherever the hell you came from, things ain't ever gonna run smooth because the outside world is too fucked up and filled with confusion."

Willie confided that he had wanted to return to his home of Abbott, Texas, but it just didn't work out.

**Left to right, Toni Wine Moman, Chips Moman, BMI CEO Frances
Preston, Connie Nelson, Willie Nelson
Photo courtesy Toni Wine Moman**

"Of course, it didn't. That's 'cause life ain't letting you. The best you
can do is sing this song and pretend that you're going back."[64]

Willie and Waylon both loved the song, as did most of America.

In addition to "Luckenbach, Texas" Chips added a song he had
written with Reggie Young, "Brand New Goodbye Song," Jimmy Webb's
"If You See Me Getting Smaller," Neil Diamond's "Sweet Caroline," and
Waylon Jennings's "Belle of the Ball," among others.

For this album, which would be titled *Ol' Waylon*, Chips did not work
with his house band, with the exception of Reggie Young and Johnny
Christopher, who were part of the session. Instead, he used members of
Waylon's band. Toni Wine and Waylon's wife, Jessi Colter, were included
as the background singers.

186

After "Luckenbach, Texas" was released as a single, it went to Number1 on *Billboard's* Hot Country singles chart and Number 25 on *Billboard's* Hot 100 singles chart. *Ol' Waylon* went to Number 1 on *Billboard's* Country Album Chart and remained for thirteen weeks, going Platinum, thus becoming country music's first solo album to ever sell one million units. It was quite an accomplishment for Chips and put him on top again. Just as he had changed Memphis music, so was he now changing Nashville music. He would never be a country music insider, but he would for the remainder of his life set the pace for the insiders.

One outgrowth of the recording session was that Toni and Jessi became friends. Chips and Waylon also became friends. In effect, they became friends as couples, something you rarely see in the music business. Once Waylon and Jessi went out on the road to promote the album, Chips and Toni went with them. One of the venues they played was in Las Vegas. During the show Waylon asked Toni, who was singing background with Jessi, to sing her meow commercial for the audience, "Meow, meow, meow, meow . . ." They loved it. Why not? The commercial was as well-known as many hit records.

Later, Toni was standing in front of the hotel, when a woman recognized her from the show and walked up to her.

"Oh, dear, my cats just love you," the woman said.

"I gave her a hug and said, 'Thank you.' What could I do? Then she asked me if I would make a long distance call and do it over the phone to her cats," said Toni, laughing. "I did not do it."[65]

Soon it became evident Waylon's tour was costing more than he was taking in. Despite a Number 1 hit with "Luckenbach, Texas" and the first country album to ever sell one million copies, Waylon was in deep financial trouble. Added to the expense of touring were his expenditures for cocaine which easily exceeded $50,000 a month. Bill Robinson, his business advisor, asked him if he wanted to declare bankruptcy.

"The figures didn't lie," Waylon wrote in his autobiography. "I was swimming in red ink and about to go down for the third time.

**Chips and Toni in costume for a 'Fifties" party at Waylon and Jessi's home.
The 1955 Caddy formerly belonged to Roy Orbison
Photo courtesy Toni Wine Moman**

"You're broke," Robinson said. "Everything you've got is in hock: your buildings, your home. The bank has closed your accounts. You've spent your advances."

"The worst thing was that I had been giving it away. So much money was flowing through my office that I never bothered to count it. And after a while, nobody else did either, except to take out their share. There were a lot of shares."[66]

Ordinarily, the first response a recording artist would make upon hearing such news would be to go out on tour. That was no good in this instance because his tours cost more than he earned from them because of his expenses. He cut his touring entourage down to bare bones. Then he started shutting down his business locations and staff. The quickest way to bring in revenue, of course, was to record another album. The advance would bring in money immediately, followed by record royalties.

In late 1981, Waylon and Chips began work on the album that would be titled *Black on Black* and released in 1982. It included another duet with Willie Nelson, "Just to Satisfy You," written by Waylon and Don Bowman; two songs written by Emmons and Chips, "We Made It as Lovers (We Just Couldn't Make It as Friends)" and "May I Borrow Some Sugar from You"; another Emmons song "Get Naked With Me"; Waylon's song, "Shine", with others by Hank Williams, Rodney Crowell, Johnny Cash, and Paul Kennerley.

To no one's surprise, *Black on Black* was a commercial success, with "Just to Satisfy You" going to Number 1 on the singles chart and the album going to Number 3 on Billboard's country album chart. Two additional singles, "Shine" and "Women Do Know How to Carry On" made the Top 5 singles chart. The album itself did not rescue Waylon financially, but it certainly bought him some breathing room.

Despite the album's commercial success, reviews were mixed. "'Get Naked with Me' is a stupid song in the old, tired outlaw frame," wrote Thom Jurek in a caustic AllMusic review that had Trumpian overtones. "Given its presentation as a singalong country song . . . it only serves to showcase Jennings' tired voice and the strange textures Moman added to the rather simple songs on this set . . .Jennings is as inspired as could be, but Moman ruined this set with his trademark over-production."

When people accused Chips of over-production they were referring to the pop sensibilities that had made him one of the most successful record producers in history. It was all part of the cultural wars that were developing in country and rock music production. Chips' critics preferred a most acoustic sound they considered raw and thus more artistic. Chips understood that only a minority of record buyers wanted a raw, acoustic sound. He was in the business of recording hit records. He was not interested in appealing to music purists, most of whom had secure day jobs not directly related to music. Such reviewers were an irritant to him that sometimes drove his blood pressure up, but he was usually able to bring that spike down by looking at his bank statement and basking in the praise offered by the artists he worked with.

IN 1977 PHILLIP RAULS, who worked for Stax Records' publishing company, West/Memphis Music, which just recently had been taken over by Union Planters National Bank during the record label's bankruptcy, stopped by Chips' recording studio in Nashville to promote the Stax song catalog. He hoped to interest Chips in using a Stax cover song in an upcoming production. It took about thirty minutes for him to play the tapes he had brought with him.

Chips responded by playing him a song from his most recent Petula Clark recording session. Midway through the song, his secretary called with some bad news. Elvis Presley had been pronounced dead.

"Man, you should have seen the look on Chips' face as he still had the phone stuck to his ear," Rauls told me. "His face turned reddish-blue. He laid the phone down and froze for a second. One of Chips' engineers was in the control room at the same time and Chips told him to 'Shut the studio down. That's right, we're closing up right now. I'm going home.' He walked out the back door to the parking lot with me still standing there in the control room. It was an unbelievable circumstance for all, including myself."

All the music-related businesses on Music Row did the same thing. The following day, according to Rauls, Music Row looked like a ghost town. *If Elvis could die, anyone could die.*

On a follow-up visit, Rauls was invited to stay at Chips' home while in Nashville. Chips had decided to start up a record label. It had been his passion since he began playing music. Undeterred by his failures to establish a record label in Memphis, he had come to consider Nashville a better platform. His renewed interest in a label might explain why he played a song from his Nashville session for Rauls. He may have been considering the possibility of launching the country album he did with Petula Clark on his new label, Gibraltar Records.

Chips encouraged Rauls to contact Alex Chilton and Carla Thomas about recording for Gibraltar Records. Rauls followed up with Chilton who drove to Nashville to investigate the offer.

"While there Alex demanded that Chips pay him some of his past due royalties before he would consider any future endeavors," Rauls told me. "Alex later told me that Chips advanced him seven hundred and fifty dollars from his credit card and he had returned to Memphis and they never spoke again."

Rauls did not have a personal rapport with Carla, so he talked to her brother Marvell Thomas, who told him flat-out, "She would never do that."

GARY STEWART BEGAN HIS MUSIC CAREER as a rock musician, singing and performing in Florida in a gritty, roots style that was midway between traditional rock and traditional country. One night country recording artist Mell Tillis heard him perform in a nightclub in Florida and encouraged him to move to Nashville and focus on songwriting. Stewart did exactly that, writing hits such as "When a Man Loves a Woman" and "There's a Whole Lot About a Woman a Man Don't know." Soon Roy Rogers, Jimmy Dean, Cal Smith and others were recording his songs.

Those successes landed him a spot in Charlie Pride's band, where he was allowed to perform his own songs on occasion. Eventually, he was signed to a recording contract by RCA Records. Throughout the 1970s, his singles and albums showed up on the charts, but a big hit always eluded him. His drinking and legal problems, and his self-destructive lifestyle, kept him from becoming a major star. However, among musicians he was legendary because of his skills with a guitar and the raw emotion of his songwriting. If he were a race horse in the Kentucky Derby with one hundred to one odds of winning, Nashville musicians would have bet on him for sentimental reasons, hoping he would finally get his due.

It was at this point in his career that Chips Moman landed a deal with RCA Records to record sort of a honky-tonk, Southern rock album with Stewart that would be promoted as a country album. Chips and Bobby Emmons contributed four songs for the album: "Okeechobee Purple," "Staring Each Other Down," "We Made it as Lovers (We Just Couldn't

Make it as Friends)," and "Cactus and a Rose," which became the title of the album. Stewart wrote songs for the album with Gregg Allman and Dickey Betts. Billy Burnette and Johnny Christopher also wrote a song together that was used on the album. Sitting in on the session were Allman, Betts, and Bonnie Bramlett.

Cactus and a Rose had everything going for it—great songs, assists from the likes of Allman, Betts, and Bramlett, and a hit-making producer—but the finished product never rose higher than 49 on *Billboard's* Top Country Album chart, meaning almost every album put on sale in recent weeks scored higher on the chart. Critics said it was overproduced, too layered to suit Stewart's rough voice and stage persona.

Chips should have known better than to even try. Anything close to rock just did not interest him as a producer. He liked the idea of it better than he ever did the reality of it. That's because he would hear something raw and ragged on the tape and try to smooth it out. Chips was disappointed to have another failed album, but he certainly enjoyed making it.

"One time I was in the studio, and I was gonna put a vocal down, and I kept turning the mic up, but I couldn't get him," Chips told EDD Hurt in the Cream Interview. "I couldn't pick him up—it was muffled. I couldn't figure out what it was. I went back there, and he was laying down on the floor. And that's the way he was. That explains everything. He was just a funny guy."[67]

In 2003 Stewart lost his wife of many years, a loss so devastating that he took his own life with a gunshot to the neck.

Chips was never one to wallow in self-pity, at least not for long, especially if there was a challenge on the horizon. For his next project, he landed a deal with Epic Records (CBS) to record an album in January 1981 with country music legend Tammy Wynette. Still the reigning queen of country music, she had just come off a traumatic tour with her ex-husband George Jones. At a show in New York, he was asked to open for Tammy. It was unheard of in country music for a man to open for a women, so he protested to no avail. He was asked to limit his performance to forty-five minutes because Tammy had a rented plane waiting for her. He showed Tammy who was "boss" by singing for two and a half hours. It would be their last performance together until well into the 1990s.

Soon after that she went into the studio with Chips to record an album that would be titled *You Brought Me Back*. It was the first album she had recorded since completing her final solo album with Billy Sherrill. Chips and Bobby Emmons contributed four songs to the session: "Cowboys Don't Shoot Straight (Like They Used To)," "Easy Street," "I Don't Think I See Me in Your Eyes Anymore," and "He's Rolling Over and Over (In Someone Else's Clover)".There was also a Carole King song, "Crying in the Rain," a Billy Burnette song, "You Brought Me Back," a Mama Cass Elliot cover, "Easy Come, Easy Go," and others. Toni Wine sang backup.

Two singles were released after the album went on sale in June 1981, "Cowboys Don't Shoot Straight" and "Crying in the Rain," neither of which cracked the Top 10. The album itself failed to even make *Billboard's* Country Albums chart. Judging by the songs chosen for the session and the production values used for the album, Chips had hopes of having a hit that would crossover to the pop charts, where he excelled at finding the mark. Tammy's "Stand By Your Man" had been a Number 1 hit on the country singles charts, Number 11 on the Hot Adult Contemporary charts (Pop), and Number 19 on the Hot 100 chart (Pop). Tammy still had the voice to bring it off, but unfortunately the songs missed the mark for female record buyers.

About the album, Tammy said, "I think Chips saw me as being more pop than I am. I'm not pop. And I think I held back a little bit."[68]

There was one more female singer on Chips' list to produce. After that he would be done with women singers, success or not. More and more his thoughts were on the creation of a record label at which he could call all the shots. He was no longer satisfied being one of the best record producers in the world. He wanted to be one of the best business executives in the world.

PEDERNALES IS A GHOST TOWN in Texas near Spicewood, which is about thirty miles southwest of Austin. Willie Nelson's 700-acre ranch, called Luck Ranch, is located near Spicewood. One day Nelson heard that the only grocery store in Pedernales had filed for bankruptcy. He purchased it with the intention of converting it into a recording studio so that he would not have to travel so far to make records. He asked Chips Moman to put the studio together for him and Chips agreed on the condition they do some recording once it was up and going. That was fine with Willie. Chips arrived at the former grocery store in his yellow Blue Bird RV, along with Toni and their son Casey, his engineer David Cherry and the 827 Thomas Street Band.

Some of the first recordings done at the Pedernales Recording Studio (Willie's first name for it was "Cutt and Putt") were: "A Whiter Shade of Pale" and Chips Moman's "Do Right Woman, Do Right Man." They kept recording until Chips felt they had a smash hit, something that didn't happen right away. Chips was a patient man when the occasion demanded it, so they took a break to record a duet album with Merle Haggard.

Willie camped out in his tour bus parked near the studio. Merle pulled his tour bus up nearby. And Chips made do in his traveling mobile home. They surrounded the studio the way the wagon trains going west circled when it was time to bed down for the night. They were in the middle of nowhere, but that was good because there were absolutely no outside distractions.

Among the songs recorded for the duet album were three songs written by Willie—"My Own Peculiar Way," "Half a Man," and "Opportunity to Cry"—and one written by Merle Haggard, "No Reason to Quit." They did two versions of "Half a Man." In one version they sang a duet; in the second version, Willie sang the lead vocal.

Merle sang the lead vocals on "No Reason to Quit" and "My Mary," written by Stuart Hamblen and Jimmie Davis. They also recorded "Still Water Runs the Deepest," on which Willie sang lead. It was written by

Jesse Ashlock, who wrote another song they recorded, "My Life's Been a Pleasure."

Still, they had not recorded a song Chips thought would be a smash hit. If Chips wasn't happy, then no one was happy. He found himself at the same street corner onto which he'd stepped from Willie's solo album. The duet album did not have a solid hit you'd want to bet money on. He had recorded Johnny Christopher's "Always on My Mind" with Elvis Presley and B.J. Thomas, so he thought why not with Merle? They were well into the song, when Christopher, who was playing guitar at the session, shouted out, "This ain't shit," meaning Merle's vocal. Merle got mad, stormed out of the studio, and boarded his tour bus and locked the door and refused to come out.

Chips instructed the band to keep playing. He would use the song for Willie's solo album. The band kept playing, but when they reached the point where Reggie Young played his guitar solo, Christopher stood up and put his finger to his lips, indicating he wanted the band to stop. Chips ignored him, which infuriated Christopher even more. This time Christopher blew a whistle, which he figured would put a stop to the session for certain. Wrong again. Chips kept the band playing and the tape rolling. Later, he listened to the tape and decided he didn't mind the whistle. He had just the song he needed to finish off Willie's solo album.

That still left them without a hit for the duet album.

That night Willie's daughter Lana called him and said she had a song she thought he'd like. It was Emmylou Harris singing something written by Townes Van Zandt. It was a narrative song titled "Pancho and Lefty."

Willie hadn't heard it, so she told him she would drive over and play it for him even though it was late at night.

"One listen told me that she was right," said Willie. "I loved Emmylou's version—I love anything Emmylou does—but I could hear how the song lent itself to a duet sung by two men. It had two male characters. Pancho was a Mexican bandito, Lefty, his pal. When Pancho is killed by the Federales, he may or may not have been betrayed by

195

Willie Nelson   **CBS Records publicity photo**

Lefty. I loved the line that said, 'The dust that Pancho bit down south, ended up in Lefty's mouth.' I loved the song's essential mystery."[69]

Willie took the tape to Chips and played it for him. Chips was ecstatic. Now, he had the hit song he wanted for the duet album. They went to the studio to record the track. Once the arrangement was in place, Willie went to Merle's bus and banged on the door. Merle asked what the hell was going on and Willie told him he had a song he wanted him to listen to.

Willie played him the song. Merle nodded that, yes, it was a good song, but he wanted to go back to sleep. Willie told him there was no time for sleep. The band had worked up the arrangement and Chips was waiting for them in the studio. Willie practically dragged him into the studio, where they proceeded to record the song in one take. Said Willie, "It was like we'd been singing the song for years."

Unfortunately, "Pancho & Lefty" got off to a rocky start. As they began, Merle called for a halt. He told Chips he heard a B 3 organ and he didn't want the organ on his record.

"I don't like organs. I don't have them on my records."

"Yeah, I'm the same way," said Chips, adding, "Except just the opposite. There is not a record I am going to make that doesn't have a B 3 on it. If you don't want a B 3, then don't let me produce it."

Merle backed off and delivered his vocal, B 3 and all.

Later, Chips said, "If Merle was going to get pissed he should have just stayed on the bus like he did with 'Always on My Mind.'"

The next morning, Willie got up early and played golf to work off the excitement of the evening before. Around the fourth hole, Merle showed up. He, too, was excited about "Pancho and Lefty." He asked Willie if he could go back to the studio and re-record his part because he felt he could do a better job if given an opportunity.

Willie told him it was too late. Chips had overnighted the tape to New York, where the suits had listened and declared it a smash hit. Chips had sarcastically told Willie that he had done that. He had done no such thing. The album still needed work and it needed to be mixed. It is unclear whether Willie knew Chips was being sarcastic and passed the message along to Merle as the straight man to the joke, or whether he believed it to be the gospel truth. The bottom line was that Chips had no intention of giving Merle another shot at the song, not after he had bad-mouthed his B 3 organ.

After Merle left, Willie and Chips went into the studio to put Willie's vocal on the "Always on My Mind" track. Chips could not believe his good fortune. He had rolled the dice and won the entire casino. Within the space of a few hours he had recorded the smash hits he needed for both the solo and the duet albums. How lucky could one guy be?

Always on My Mind was released in February 1982. It was Willie's twenty-seventh solo album. Not only did it go to Number 1 on the country album charts, it stayed on *Billboard's* Top Country Albums chart for almost five years. *Billboard* saluted it as the Number 1 country album of 1982. In addition, the album placed on Billboard's 200 album chart that included all albums for almost two years, peaking at Number 2. Merle went to his grave never knowing that Willie's vocal on the "Always on My Mind" track was the same one he had walked away from in a huff, blowing whistle and all.

Most of the reviews were positive, a reflection of the public's love of an album that won a Grammy for "Record of the Year." Unduly caustic was a *Rolling Stone* review by Paul Nelson that read, ". . .almost nothing works here. Nelson's hammy performances and Chips Moman's hothouse production somehow manage to inflate understatement to the point of pomposity while letting all of the air out of what might have been genuinely moving and dramatic. The band plays competently but carelessly."

Pancho & Lefty was released in January 1983. No surprise to anyone, both the album and the single went to Number 1 and dominated country music for the entire year. The second single, "Reasons to Quit," peaked at Number 6 on the country charts. At that point, it was clear that Willie and Merle, two of country music's biggest stars, were at their peak. Music writer Robert Christgau wrote, "Haggard hasn't sung with so much care in years, which is obviously Nelson's doing." In 1983 the album won a Grammy for "Best Country Performance by a Duo."

With these two albums, Chips Moman proved that he could dominate Nashville music just as he had dominated Memphis music. By any measure, Chips had become country music's most successful producer, a distinction the Music City establishment was reluctant to acknowledge.

These two albums with Willie provided Chips with his new "go-to" artist for country music, just as B.J. Thomas had been his "go-to" artist for pop music. For Chips, Willie Nelson had extraordinary abilities as an artist. "When Willie Nelson walks into the studio, I know what the song is all about, but he doesn't," said Chips. "But I know he will learn it quickly. I have cut an entire album with him never singing a song over twice. He has an incredible memory. He can hear a song over the speakers and without a lyric sheet, sing it back to you—and play it on his guitar without making any mistakes. That is extreme talent. That is probably the reason he didn't make it in his early career. There were no producers ready for that back then. I guarantee you that."

Willie told me that he works fast to fight off boredom. "I don't think it should take long to do a song. It's all individual taste, but for me I have to do it pretty quickly or I'll get tired of it. Probably got used to working fast in the studio because when I started in Nashville they all expected you to do four songs in three hours. It might be your first and last time to go into a studio and you got three hours. I learned songs before I went to the studio and I've always recorded that way, especially now that I use my band to record more."

Willie went on to explain that he only records songs that he loves. That was the criteria he used for "Always on My Mind" and "Pancho & Lefty." That way, he doesn't mind playing them every night. "It would be hard if you recorded songs all of the time just because of the commercial value you think they might have. If you don't really like them very much and they become a hit you have to sing them every night and that really could be a drag if you didn't enjoy singing the song."

By the end of 1983, Chips and Willie returned to the studio to record another album titled *City of New Orleans*. In addition to the title song, the album included one song written by Willie Nelson, "Why Are You Pickin' On Me;" Dave Loggins' "Please Come to Boston"; Larry Henley and Jeff Silbar's "Wind Beneath My Wings"; Buffy Sainte-Marie's "Until It's Time for You to Go"; Danny O'Keefe's "Good Time Charlie's Got the Blues" and others.

"City of New Orleans" was written by Steve Goodman, who recorded it in 1971. It told the story of a train ride from New Orleans to Chicago aboard the famed City of New Orleans. Willie's version of the song really resonated with the public, which was why both the single and the album went to Number 1 on *Billboard's* country charts. The song quickly became a favorite with Willie's fans, who would not let him play a concert without singing it. The City of New Orleans ran overnight north and south through Memphis, which made the song a sentimental favorite with Chips, the late-night call of a lonesome train whistle appealing to his musical wanderlust.

To people who have never lived in the Mid-South, it must be difficult to imagine the importance of the City of New Orleans to the residents who live along its route. One of its stops is in the city of Greenwood, Mississippi. It passes near the department store managed by my father and to this day I associate the train whistle with the good times father and son shared, complete with the scent of honeysuckle and the authoritative deep voice of the conductor shouting, "All aboard for New Or—leans!" With apologies to the late Steve Goodman, no one has ever sung the song as well as Willie Nelson.

At this point in his career, Chips Moman could seemingly produce a Number 1 record with a blink of an eye. It was his genius that he could hear the artist singing the song and the band playing the song in his head before the recording tape even rolled.

NOW THAT HE WAS the top country music producer in Nashville, Chips again succumbed to his obsession with starting up his own record label. This time he chose two high-profile partners—Buddy Killen, a Nashville music mogul with whom he had signed at Tree Publishing, and Phil Walden, co-founder of the Georgia-based Capricorn Records. Killen began his career in the 1950s playing bass on the Grand Ole Opry. Later, as a producer he worked with artists such as Dolly Parton, Roger Miller, Joe Tex, and Exile. In 1980 he took over ownership of Tree International Publishing and subsequently worked with artists such as Faith Hill, Reba McEntire and Kenny Chesney. Walden began his music career as a manager, representing Otis Redding from 1959 to his death in 1967, Al Green, Sam & Dave, and Percy Sledge. His record label was affiliated with Atlantic Records. The roster included Allman Brothers Band, Bonnie Bramlett, the Marshall Tucker Band, Kitty Wells and Dobie Gray.

Moman, Killen and Walden formed a company in March 1984 named Triad Entertainment Corporation to oversee the formation of a record label they named Triad Records. At this point, all three individuals were wealthy men, but instead of investing in the corporation themselves they applied for a loan for $300,000 from Commerce Union Bank, of which Killen was a board member. The loan would be made available to Triad by means of a $300,000 line of credit. Each of the three signees to the loan agreed to a suretyship agreement that guaranteed repayment of the loan.

By the time, the company went into business Chips already had several completed high-profile projects in his tape vault. Because of his experience with Stax Records when it affiliated with Atlantic Records, Chips insisted that Triad should not affiliate with a major label.

"It took some talking to convince Phil and Buddy not to go through one of the major labels," Chips told the *New York Times* for a story published May 9, 1984. "I said that if we were going to depend on the majors for distribution and promotion, then we'd really be nothing more

Robert Duvall in the film, *Tender Mercies*   **Photo: Photofest**

than a production company, and we'd have to direct our main promotional efforts inside the major label, rather than directly to radio stations. I wanted to do something meaningful."

Chips announced to the newspaper that Triad already had on their roster Tony Orlando, the Atlanta Rhythm Section, Jessi Colter, along with actor Robert Duvall, who had won an Academy Award for his role as a country singer in 1983's *Tender Mercies*. For his role in that movie, Duvall had contacted Chips to ask if he minded if he based the character he played on Chips and his mannerisms. Chips told him he didn't mind at all. By then Chips had recorded an entire album of country songs with Duvall doing the lead vocals. Most likely the album was recorded in 1982. I know of no one who has actually heard the album, not even Duvall himself, who has publicly said he never received a cassette and has no idea what happened to the album. Whatever its strengths and weaknesses, Chips was unable to place it with a major.

In late1982, Chips produced two songs with Tony Orlando that were included in the soundtrack for the film *All the Right Moves,* starring Jennifer Warnes and Chris Thompson: "Easy Street," written by Chips and Bobby Emmons, and "Have I done Anything At All (To Make You Love Me Today)," written by Emmons. Chips never recorded just two songs with anyone, so it is likely he recorded an album's worth so he could make a deal with a major for an album to accompany the movie's release. That never happened, so apparently this was the Tony Orlando album he had to offer to Triad.

In 1982, The Atlanta Rhythm Section went to Nashville to work with Chips on a new album. Earlier that year, they had recorded an album titled *Longing For a Feeling* for CBS Records, but the record label wanted them to drop some tracks and record replacements and the band refused. As a result CBS dropped its contract with them.

The new album was titled *Hardball*. It was completed, but two of the band members, bassist Paul Goddard and drummer Danny Biget, left the group because they were dissatisfied with the direction of the music. That probably should not come as a surprise since Chips had not produced a successful rock album since his first big hit at American Sound Studio, The Gentry's "Keep on Dancing."

The only artist on the roster Chips announced who appears to have been recorded specifically for Triad was country artist Jessi Colter, whose 1975 country-pop song, "I'm Not Lisa," was a crossover hit. In 1981 she released a duet album with husband Waylon Jennings, *Leather and Lace*, that was a major hit. Her last studio solo album was 1981's *Ridin' Shotgun*. At the time Chips approached her to do an album for Triad, her contract with Capitol Records was up and if she signed a renewal that would have blocked her from doing the album with Chips.

Actually, Chips approached Waylon first, told him that he thought it best if Waylon was not around if he worked with her.

"Why is that?" Waylon asked.

"Because Jessi will look to you for direction."

"And is that a problem, hoss?"

"It is," said Chips, "If I'm the one in charge."

"When it comes to Jessi," said Waylon, "She's the one who's really in charge. She'll just fool you into thinking you are."[70]

Waylon delivered the message and she asked what he thought.

"Your guess is as good as mine. Musically, no one's better than Chips. But in terms of worldwide distribution, no one's bigger than Columbia."[71]

Jessi signed with Chips, putting the music first.

The resulting album, titled *Rock and Roll Lullaby*, was recorded at Chips Nashville studio. Chips and Bobby Emmons had two songs, "Partners After All" and "Easy Street," previously recorded for the movie soundtrack with Tony Orlando; covers of Lena Horne's "Stormy Weather," not recorded by Chips since his single with Tommy Burk and the Counts, Don Gibson's "I Can't Stop Loving You," and The Davis Sisters' "I Forgot More Than You'll Ever Know," Barry Mann and Cynthia Weil's "Rock and Roll Lullaby," which Chips had produced for

B.J. Thomas in 1972; and Basil McDavid's "I Want to Be With You." Oddly, Jessi, an excellent songwriter, had no songs of her own on the album. All the songs were chosen by Chips.

Shortly, before the album was scheduled to be released, Chips drove his Harley out to meet with her at their Tennessee home, named Southern Comfort. She wrote about the encounter in her memoir, *An Outlaw and a Lady*. She offered him coffee and he said sure, but added that perhaps he should give her the bad news first.

"What's wrong?" she asked.

"Phil Walden and I had a falling out."

"Which means?"

"Your record's not coming out."

"Why in the world not?"

"We're folding the label."

"Even before you get started?"

"Afraid so."

However, *Rock and Roll Lullaby* was released in 1984, with "I Want To Be With You" earmarked as the first and only single. Jessi Colter's vocals were exceptional, but the songs were not country radio friendly and neither the single nor the album charted. It foundered, generating no reviews. It is unclear whether the album actually was released prior to Chips' meeting with Jessi—and the argument with his partners was over its failure—or was released subsequent to the meeting, only to die because there was no promotion with radio stations or with print media. Jessi was never asked to do a single interview to promote the album. It would be a decade before she would go into a studio again. Figuring into that decision may have been Waylon's addictions and his declining health.

The Triad Entertainment Corporation was dissolved shortly after the album was released. When Commerce Union Bank requested payment of $150,000 from Chips and Toni under the terms of the surety agreement they had signed, they refused and claimed that the bank had exhibited

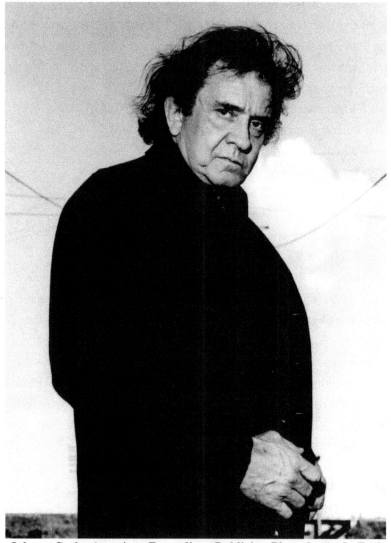

Johnny Cash, American Recordings Publicity, Photo by Andy Earl

duress in getting them to sign the agreement in the first place. Chips ended up filing a lawsuit against both the bank and his former partner Phil Walden. When he lost the lawsuit, he filed an appeal to the Tennessee Court of Appeals. The application for permission to appeal was denied in October 1986. He didn't know it yet, but he had one more swing at scoring by launching a record label, but it was strike two with two outs at the bottom of the ninth.

SHORTLY BEFORE CHRISTMAS 1983, Johnny Cash was flown from Jamaica in a private jet to Palm Springs for treatment for drug rehabilitation at the Betty Ford Center. Forty-three days later he left the center to return home for rest and relaxation before heading out on the road for an eight-city tour. When he returned to Nashville, CBS Records head Rick Blackburn had an album recording session lined up for him with Billy Sherrill. The last pairing with Sherill had not worked out very well, but Blackburn, who had risen up the ranks at CBS as a marketing executive, had a novelty song titled "The Chicken in Black" that he felt could be a hit for Cash. The chicken in the song told the story that Cash needed a brain transplant because he had worn his out. Cash agreed to record the song, perhaps recalling the success he had with a previous novelty song, "A Boy Named Sue." After the session, he told friends he felt good about it.

Blackburn also felt good about it and ordered a video about "The Chicken in Black" to be released when the song was released. As the star of the video Cash dressed like a chicken. Most of his family told Cash they didn't like the video or the song, as did Waylon Jennings, who told his old friend he looked like a buffoon in the costume.[72]

At that point Cash refused to promote the record, even though it was moving up the charts, a decision that did not endear him to CBS marketing executives. Cash had been with CBS for years, but his sales were no longer competitive with the younger artists they signed. In desperation, Blackburn turned to a record producer whose work with Willie Nelson and

Merle Haggard had given the record label some of its biggest hits ever.

Chips Moman said he would be happy to work with Cash, someone he had admired for many years. Aside from Elvis Presley, it was Cash who had the biggest impact on the music coming out of Memphis. Right away, Chips began gathering songs for the album that would be given the optimistic title *Rainbow*, including two songs from himself and Bobby Emmons, "Easy Street" and "Borderline," two songs written by Cash, "I'm Leaving Now" and "You Beat All I Ever Saw"; two songs from Kris Kristofferson, "Casey's Last Ride" and the title song, "Here Comes That Rainbow Again"; a John Fogerty cover, "Have You Ever Seen the Rain?"; a Willie Nelson song, "They're All the Same"; and a Bobby Braddock-John Prine song, "Unwed Fathers."

Chips pulled together a solid song list and they began recording late in the fall of 1984, at a time when Chips was still dealing with the crash on takeoff of his dream project, Triad Records. They didn't get far into the project before Cash informed Chips he needed to take a break to go to Montreaux, Switzerland, to tape his annual Christmas television special. His special guests that year were Waylon, Kris, and Willie. Cash suggested Chips accompany him and supervise the sound. Chips readily agreed. He needed a break and it would be fun hanging out with them, Kristofferson being the only one with whom he had not recorded.

Chips was impressed with the chemistry the four men displayed working together. All of them were stars, all of them where top songwriters, all of them had big egos. One evening they were just hanging out, exchanging musical war stories, when someone suggested they should all record an album together. No sooner had they returned to Nashville, than Chips had them all together in his studio with his house band. They tried out different material, trying to find a song that could match the magic of their combined voices.

Finally, they got to a Jimmy Webb song, "The Highwayman." It had four distinct verses about four distinct characters. They taped "The Highwayman" and Chips took the tape to Rick Blackburn at CBS Records, and he agreed with Chips and the four artists—they had a smash hit. He authorized an entire album.

Chips returned to the studio to listen to more songs, leaving it up to Blackburn to gather the necessary permission for Waylon and Kris to participate (Willie and Johnny already were signed to CBS). The interesting thing about the song collection was that of the five participants, only Cash contributed songs to the project—"Big River" and "Committed to Parkview." For the first time in a long while, there were no songs written by Chips and Bobby Emmons.

Of course, everyone suggested songs: Ed Bruce's "The Last Cowboy Song," Woody Guthrie's "Deportee (Plane Wreck at Los Gatos), Bob Seger's "Against the Wind," Steve Goodman-John Prine's "The Twentieth Century Is Almost Over", Paul Kennerley's "Welfare Line," Cindy Walker's "Jim I Wore A Tie Today," and perhaps the best song in the album, Guy Clark's "Desperados Waiting for a Train."

With his recent hits, Chips had become a hit-making phenomenon at CBS Records with his recent successes with Willie Nelson. Blackburn was delighted when he heard the entire album. Willie Nelson was the hottest thing in country music. Waylon was second. And Johnny was one of the most beloved country artists of all time, despite—or perhaps because of—his struggles with addiction. Blackburn knew he had a hit with *Highwayman*; he hoped that the still unfinished album Chips was recording with Johnny would be catapulted into hit status as well because of Johnny's association with *Highwayman*.

Shortly after its release, as expected, *Highwayman* went to Number 1 on both *Billboard's* Country Albums chart and its Country Hot Singles chart and would stay on the country charts for sixty-six weeks. The second single released, "Desperados Waiting for a Train," peaked at Number 15 on the country single charts. No sooner did the four of them take to the stage together than they started calling themselves the Highwaymen. The name stuck and soon became the official name of the super group, although on the first album they were billed as Jennings, Nelson, Cash and Kristofferson.

"When we first took the Highwaymen out live, it looked like four shy rednecks trying to be nice to each other," Waylon wrote in his autobiography. "It almost ruined it . . . We had just come back from Australia, and were set to play a week at the Mirage in Las Vegas. After the opening night, I was fixin' to quit. I talked to John about it and he was feeling the same way. 'I get a little nervous,' he said. 'I don't want to look like I'm trying to steal your thunder.'"

As a result of that conversation, the four artists got together and talked it out and realized that they were all of one mind: each artist should feel free to do whatever occurs to them on stage. If they want to comment on another artist, they don't have to ask permission. If it suits them, they can run up and down the stage doing cartwheels and lean in and sing into another artist's microphone. It was the NFL equivalent of if the ball lands in your lap, run with it. The audiences responded just as Waylon had predicted and the unpredictable stage personas of the artists became a part of the group's appeal. For example, once while Willie was singing his hit, "I'm Crazy," Waylon leaned over into his microphone and sang what he knew to be the original title of the song, "I'm Stupid." It was an inside joke, but the audience loved it and Willie broke out into a broad smile.

ABOUT A YEAR AFTER I WAS HIRED by *The Commercial Appeal*, the Mid-South's dominant newspaper, to write editorials and columns, editor Mike Grehl brought up the deplorable state of Beale Street during an editorial board meeting. For more than ten years, the Beale Street Development Corporation, a racially diverse organization, had struggled to make progress on redevelopment. Efforts to development the historic street into an entertainment district were stalled by city and county government, mostly along racial lines.

At the time there were only two nightclubs that specialized in blues and rhythm and blues—Blues Alley, which was located downtown, and Club

Handy, which was one of only two or three businesses open on Beale Street. The street itself looked like a war zone, with boarded up windows and doors. White city and county officials were afraid redevelopment would bring a "bad" element downtown, meaning it would become a congregating place for blacks.

However, the blacks involved in city and county government considered Beale Street a historically important expression of black culture worthy of being saved. Plus, they argued, new restaurants, bars and entertainment venues on the street would help make Memphis a tourist destination. Grehl pointed out that the influence of the newspaper was such that it could tip the balance, either in favor of or against redevelopment. Because Grehl knew that I had helped pay my way through the University of Mississippi by playing in rhythm and blues, and rock bands, he suggested I take my girlfriend and spend a couple of weeks hanging out on the street, especially Club Handy, and report back to the editorial board with recommendations. The newspaper would pick up the tab.

My girlfriend, Laura, and I spent evenings hanging out on Beale Street. We discovered that Club Handy had a thriving music scene. At that time, the cub's feature act was the Duncan Sisters, Phyllis and Helen. Natives of Mississippi they had toured with Little Richard, and as the New Supremes. The band, which featured an outstanding horn section, was easily the best in the city.

When I reported back to the editorial board, I made the case for supporting redevelopment. Grehl asked me to write a series of unsigned editorials in support of breathing new life into Beale Street. The editorials had the desired effect and soon the opposition to redevelopment faded away. The City of Memphis agreed to allow the Beale Street Redevelopment Corporation to begin applying for grants. Under the terms of the agreement, all leases offered to new businesses would have to be approved by the redevelopment corporation, the City of Memphis, and a management company named Performa. Soon, the redevelopment corporation had secured over $5 million in grants—and Beale Street was

211

well on its way to recapturing its glorious past.

As new nightclubs and restaurants opened on Beale Street, people became nostalgic about Memphis's history as a music center. Whatever happened to the music? By 1984, the city was a music ghost town. There were several recording studios in operation—Ardent Recording, owned by John Fry; the Daily Planet, owned by former Stax Records founder Jim Stewart and Stax alumnus Bobby Manuel; and a handful of others—but there had not been a hit record that had come out of Memphis since Estelle' Axton's 1976 hit, "Disco Duck." Mostly, the existing studios were vanity operations, renting out time for demos or to record singles and albums for artists who lived elsewhere. Where there were once a half dozen producers in the city churning out hit records, now there were none.

This situation was discussed by *The Commercial Appeal* editorial board and it was decided that the newspaper would promote a public discussion of the situation by running a series of Q & A interviews on the editorial page, placed next to the editorials to demonstrate their importance to the newspaper. I was tapped to conduct the interviews. In all, there were twenty-one interviews with twenty-seven individuals, all of which focused on what could be done to bring music back to Memphis.

Subsequently, *The Commercial Appeal* published the interviews in a book titled *Coming Home: 21 Conversations About Memphis Music*. Some of the individuals interviewed were: B.B. King, RCA Records executive Gregg Geller, Bonnie Raitt, Jerry Lee Lewis, Willie Mitchell, Booker T. Jones, Steve Cropper and Duck Dunn in a joint interview, Rita Coolidge, Miles Davis, Johnny Cash and June Carter Cash, and Chips Moman.

IN DECEMBER 1984, Chips resumed work on Johnny Cash's solo album, *Rainbow*, and on his duet album with Waylon Jennings to be titled *Heroes,* both commissioned by Rick Blackburn at CBS Records. Blackburn wanted the solo album to go on sale in October 1985 and the duet to go on sale in June 1986. *Rainbow* was released with high expectations, but interest in it was so slight that both the single, "I'm

Leaving Now," and the album failed to chart. How was it possible for the *Highwayman* album to soar while *Rainbow* sank? Perhaps the duet with Waylon would help keep Cash afloat—or so Blackburn hoped.

Blackburn clearly did not want to give up on Cash, but a 1986 interview with me revealed insight into his thinking process. Asked if CBS Records planned to put an emphasis on new talent, he responded that the company had received a clear signal from the market place.

"The fan base is now responding to a sound first and the artist second. It used to be they were extremely loyal. Whatever Conway Twitty or George Jones put out was fine because it was George and Conway. They still love George and Conway, don't get me wrong, but they will hear [a new artist] on the radio and like that and purchase the music and know little about the artist . . . The new artists who are coming in, the ones we are having success with, it's an exciting time right now to be in country music. But you're happy on one hand and you're saddened on the other because there is a displacement process. The newer ones are displacing the seasoned veterans . . . You wrestle with that issue. Do we as an industry owe them more than that?"

In January 1985, I travelled to producer Chips Moman's Nashville studio on a bitterly cold day to interview him for the newspaper series. Actually, I had set up a joint interview with Chips and two additional producers who had experience with Memphis music. The other two producers never showed up, perhaps intimidated by Chips' daunting reputation.

There was no name attached to the studio. Just an address: 656 Iris Drive. The structure looked as if a windowless warehouse had been attached to a cottage. The closed door had three locks on it. There were windows along the cottage side of the structure, but no windows on the larger attached structure. I knocked on the door and waited. Minutes later, the door opened and revealed a man dressed in jeans, a pullover shirt, and a Greek sailor's cap perched jauntily atop his head. The author had never seen photos of Chips Moman, so he had no idea what he looked like.

Rick Blackburn   Photo by James L. Dickerson

"Is Mr. Moman in? He's expecting me."

"I'm Mr. Moman," answered the man, speaking through a cautious crack in the door. He turned loose of the door and pushed it open in an inviting way. "You thought I was the janitor, didn't you?"

He laughed. He thought it was funny.

I admitted I had thought exactly that. I was wearing a sports coat and tie, the uniform of the 1980s journalist.

During the interview, which took place inside the dimly-lit studio control room, Chips explained that the secret to his success has always been songs. "While everyone else was wining and dining other people, I wined and dined songwriters . . . I do a lot of things that work. I don't know why they work. I'm not smart enough to know why. All I know is that somehow or another when I love something other people usually love it. It's just a gift. It took me years to realize that there's nothing clever about it. It's just what I do best. I don't give any thought about how to creatively do an album. I just get the best musicians I know, the best songwriters, the best artists, and I just go to a studio and have a good time."[73]

Chips went on to say that what Memphis needed most was a leader to pull all the loose ends together. I asked if he would consider returning to Memphis. "Yes, under the right circumstances, I would."

During a pause in the interview, there was a knock at the door.

"Come on in," called out Chips.

Toni Wine entered the room, followed by June Carter Cash. They had come to the studio to sing background on the album that Johnny Cash was doing with Waylon Jennings.

Chips introduced me and June's eyes brightened when he told her I was writing about Memphis music. I liked June right away. "I think my strongest Memphis connection is with Johnny Cash, with him coming out of that rockabilly group that came out of Memphis in the 1950s . . . my first connection with the Memphis sound at that time was with Elvis Presley. I had a manager called Colonel Tom Parker . . . [he] also had Elvis

. . . so as a result of him having Elvis and me both at the same time I worked a lot of dates with Scotty Moore and Bill Black and D.J. Fontana. I used to do a little comedy act in the beginning and do my little set and then Elvis and Scotty and Bill went on."[74]

As we were talking, Waylon Jennings, wearing a long coat and a black hat, appeared in the doorway, pausing until June waved him into the room. Minutes later there was the sound of heavy footsteps in the hallway outside the door. Dressed in black, Johnny Cash stuck his head inside the control room and paused, spotting me sitting next to Chips. June introduced him to me and he came in and sat down. The control room quickly filled up.

Everyone fell into an easy banter, often with everyone talking at once. The conversation got more focused when they started talking about health food diets and vitamins. Suddenly, Johnny Cash, his eyes dancing, looked directly at me and said, "See, those are the kinds of drugs you talk about when you get our age." Everyone laughed. Each of the men had experienced some rough years before they got interested in health food.

It was at that point that Johnny asked, addressing no none in particular, who had seen the movie *Scarface*, starring Al Pacino. Everyone said they had. Then Johnny said, "At the end, he is sitting at this desk with a pile of cocaine this high (indicating with his hands), and then he buries his face in it and raises up and it's just all over his face."

Everyone was laughing at that point.

"Yeah, I taped it," said Chips, "And re-ran that part about eight times. I never thought of doing that."

Everyone paused, thinking, you could tell by the darting eyes, that perhaps someone had said too much.

"Let's go into the studio," said Toni Wine, adept at crowd control.

Later, everyone was sitting in the control room, listening to what they had put on tape. Abruptly, Chips paused the tape and addressed Waylon.

"Tell Jim the lyrics to that Jack Clement song we were talking about."

Waylon cleared his throat and recited the words: "There's something about Memphis that comes on strong, like something that's lost between right and wrong. Like the words to a familiar old love song. There's something about Memphis that turns me on."

At the end of his recitation, Waylon said to me, "Be sure and put it down that those words were written by Jack Clement."

Johnny worked on overdubbing vocals for a while, and then he and June left. Still there were Waylon, Jessi, their five-year-old son, Shooter, Chips, and myself. When Waylon went into the studio to sing a love song, not an easy thing to do in the morning, Jessi left with their son to fetch a bucket of fried chicken for lunch. Meanwhile, Waylon's 21-year-old daughter Jennifer arrived with her son, B.J. It quickly became a down-home family gathering.

Asked to join them for lunch, I declined because I didn't want to intrude on a family moment. Waylon and Jessi sat at the table, but the children, including adult daughter Jennifer, sat on the floor to enjoy the meal picnic-style. As we talked, I noticed Waylon was eyeing the camera dangling around my neck. I quickly found out why.

"You know, there was this photographer from a news magazine who once shot a picture of Jessi eating barbecue," he explained. "I thought that was unfair—and I never could figure out why the magazine would want to publish a picture of people eating."

Getting the message, I excused myself and told them I would be outside when they were ready for me to shoot a picture or two. Waylon looked relieved to see the camera go.

Outside, while I was shooting the photographs, Jessi played to the camera to Waylon's amusement. Finally, he reached out and good-naturedly grabbed her hand and said, "Time to go ... I think he's got enough shots of you."

I flew back to Memphis the following morning. Halfway there the jetliner jerked, lurching back and forth several times. Minutes went by, then the pilot notified the passengers that those ticket holders who were going beyond Memphis would be put on another plane for their "convenience." What the pilot didn't say was that we had lost an engine and were going to limp into the Memphis airport with one engine.

The Chips Moman interview ran in *The Commercial Appeal* on January 31. The next day, when I opened my office door at the newspaper the telephone was ringing. Moman's comments that he would return to Memphis under the right conditions had energized the music community. Everyone in the city, it seemed, wanted to talk about it.

"Vanity record production is out of control in Memphis right now," said record producer Jim Dickinson, a former member of the Dixie Flyers. "There are people who call themselves producers who aren't qualified to turn the equipment off and on . . . Chips Moman not only is a fantastic producer, he can do business, which is why he was successful in Memphis while others were not."[75]

Later that morning, at the editorial board meeting, Grehl suggested that the author interview Ron Terry, the chairman of First Tennessee Bank, so that the business community could have input into the music series. In his interview, Terry recalled the first time he met Johnny Cash. Just out of the Navy he was working at the bank as a trainee when Johnny and June came in one day to tell everyone goodbye because they were moving to California. He said, "If you could talk Chips Moman into coming back to Memphis that would be a major first step . . . It is something the banks would love to see."

Terry suggested I interview Memphis Mayor Dick Hackett for the series. Hackett had been mayor for little more than one year. Prior to that he had served as county clerk. He knew next to nothing about the music business, but he saw it as an opportunity to bolster the music industry in the city. The interview took place in his office and centered on how government could assist the business community in a meaningful way. He felt the music industry should be treated no differently than any other business.

Suddenly, out of the blue, he made an amazing statement: "For the right producer or studio, listen, I can make them a bargain on some land—

and I'm talking about like one dollar—if they will contribute toward creating that atmosphere or climate in the city. The city has a lot of land scattered around. There is some land on and around Beale Street."[76]

Hackett went on to explain that the property would be sold outright for one dollar with the understanding that the purchaser not turn around and sell it the next day for "$100,000."

In view of what Chips had said in his interview, I asked Hackett if he would be willing to go to Nashville to talk to the producer. He said he would make arrangements as soon as possible.

"Should I take someone with me?" he asked. "Someone in the business community?"

I said, "Sure."

"Who should I take?"

"Take Ron Terry," I answered, recalling Terry's commitment.

"But I don't know Terry that well," he said, slightly embarrassed. "He wasn't really one of my supporters. Do you think he would go?"

"Yes," I said.

Less than two weeks later, on February 12, Memphis Mayor Dick Hackett and Ron Terry flew to Nashville after making arrangements with Toni Wine for her to pick them up at the airport. She had jokingly asked Hackett to carry a red carnation in his mouth so she could identify him.

After the two men wearing dark business suits arrived and entered the lobby, they looked around to see if they saw anyone who looked like Chips Moman (they had only seen one photo) or his wife, Toni Wine, of whom they had never seen a photo. Hackett carried the red carnation in his hand, trying to brandish it so it could be seen by others. In the distance they saw a man wearing a cap similar to the one they saw Chips wearing in a photo. With him was a woman. Certain they had the right couple, they approached them with the red carnation extended as a greeting.

"I wasn't about to put this carnation in my mouth," explained Hackett. He handed the flower to the astonished woman and said, flashing a broad smile, "My name is Dick Hackett."

"Who *are* you?" demanded the woman.

The woman's companion glared at the two men in dark suits.

Shocked, Hackett looked at the man. "Aren't you Chips Moman?"

The man shook his head and the woman handed the flower back to Hackett. As the couple walked away they exchanged bewildered looks that caused Hackett to wilt like the flower he now held rather limply in his hand. The banker and the mayor sat down and waited for something good to happen. Soon they heard a page over the public address system that instructed them to meet Toni at the rental car booth.

"It was a white-knuckle ride all the way," said Toni about the 25-minute drive to their 330-acre farm along a highway covered with ice. Once, with expletives erupting in unplanned harmony from the dark-suited men, the SUV skidded through a red light. "By the time we got into the house, talk about loose neckties."[77]

Hackett reiterated his offer to sell a city-owned property for one dollar to the right producer or studio. The only conditions were that the producer or studio have a proven track record of success and agree not to re-sell the property for a profit.

For his part, Terry agreed to put together a financial package that would guarantee Chips the loans he would need to remodel the building.

Within two months, the mayor and the banker had put together a package of financial incentives that lured the Momans back to Memphis. Seldom in the city's history had government and business joined hands to work for a common goal—and succeeded so quickly.

CHIPS AND TONI drove to Memphis in April 1985 to meet with Mayor Dick Hackett to sign a letter of intent to move Chips' studio from Nashville to Memphis. At a press conference, Hackett said he got involved in trying to bring Chips back to Memphis after reading a series of articles in *The Commercial Appeal*. The tentative agreement provided for the sale of an old fire station at Third and Lindon about a block from Beale Street.

The two-story, brick and concrete structure was built in the 1920s. There was a stone façade at the entrance.

Chips said the building would have to be inspected to determine if it was structurally suited for a recording studio. He left open the possibility that he might want to build an adjacent structure for the studio itself, much as he had done for his Nashville studio. Chips explained that he wanted to get this studio "right" because he planned on living in Memphis for the rest of his life.

After the press conference, Chips returned to Nashville, where he resumed work on the duet album with Johnny Cash and Waylon Jennings. His song list included Bob Dylan's "One Too Many Mornings," Rodney Crowell's "I'm' Never Gonna Roam Again" (Crowell was Johnny's son-in-law), Kris Kristofferson's "Love is the Way," Tom T. Hall's "Ballad of Forty Dollars," Johnny Cash and Jack Wesley Routh's "Fields of Diamonds," and Jennifer and Thomas Kimmel's "Heroes."

Interestingly, Cash had only one song on the album and Waylon had none. It is also noticeable that Chips did not have songs from the writers who had given him hits in the past, including himself and Bobby Emmons. Essentially, it is an album of cover songs. Why would Chips not try to find an original song he felt could be a Number 1 hit when both Johnny Cash and Rick Blackburn were counting on him to do just that? Perhaps it was because he was almost totally absorbed with working out the details of his relocation to Memphis.

When the album was released in June 1986, the reviews were generally good. Bill Stuart wrote in *Nine-O-One Magazine*: "Of the album's ten songs, eight are duets. But Jennings' plaintive ballad, "I'll Always Love You," and Cash's reflective ode to the stars, "Field of Diamonds," are two of the album's stronger cuts. *Heroes*, unlike many collaborative albums, seems genuinely inspired. As long as we have musical heroes such as Johnny Cash and Waylon Jennings, the integrity of country music is safe indeed." Writing for AllMusic Bruce Eder said: "It is one of the more obscure records in either artist's output, a fact that's astonishing, given the quality of the music, the singing, and the overall production . . . there's not a weak point anywhere here."

In spite of everything going for the album, it peaked on Number 13 on the country album chart, and of the two singles released—"Even Cowgirls Get the Blues" and "The Ballad of Forty Dollars"—only the former charted and it didn't rise about Number 35 on the singles chart.

The lack of sales was an ominous sign for Johnny Cash.

BY THE END OF MAY 1985, Chips, Toni and their son Casey came to Memphis for an extended stay to look for a house. The owners of the Peabody Hotel, the city's only luxury accommodation at that time, generously allowed Chips and his family to stay free of charge in the hotel's penthouse where they could dine on room service anytime they wished. On June 5, Chips threw a birthday party for Toni at the upscale Four Flames Restaurant. Attending were radio personality and Elvis friend George Klein, noted restaurateur John Grisanti, county mayor Bill Morris but not city mayor Dick Hackett, Dan Turley, and Gary Belz, whose family owned The Peabody. With Belz was his 21-year-old date, Ellen, a student at the University of Memphis. At one point Toni and Grisanti made comments about Toni being a Jew.

"Oh," said Ellen, "Some of my best friends are Jewish."

"I'm Jewish," said Belz, perplexed.

"Oh, I didn't know that," said Ellen, who then dropped that line of conversation.

The following day Chips signed his first and only recording act in Memphis, Reba & the Portables. Reba (Becky Russell) was a rhythm and blues singer who had the best voice in the city. "This is the best group I've heard in years," said Chips. "They were playing 'Do Right Woman.' She sings the song every night. She had no idea I wrote it. You know how good Linda Ronstadt is? This singer is better than Linda Ronstadt ever thought about being."

Chips said he planned to invite them to Nashville and rehearse in the studio so they could get used to it. The day after signing Reba & the Portables, Chips was asked to judge a band contest at a Beale Street restaurant. "There were two bands," he said. "One consisted of a man reading the lyrics of a song and the other was a singing secretary. The radio ads for the event made it sound like I was an act. I felt used."

Chips was getting a crash course in what it is like to be a celebrity. Throughout his career as a record producer, he had gone to great lengths to avoid publicity. He had only given a handful of interviews in his life. He was not a recluse, he just didn't like being the center of attention. He found it tiring and unsatisfying.

Chips was also learning that there were limits to what people would do for him. He and Toni had researched the elementary schools in Memphis and determined that the highest rated one was the Campus School at Memphis State University, as it was then called. They contacted the school and talked to university president Thomas Carpenter about enrolling Casey in the school since Toni had agreed to teach a songwriting class at the university, but he said that would not be possible since Toni would not be a full-time teacher. The children of part-time teachers did not qualify. Chips' response to the rejection was the first time I witnessed him in the manic phase of his personality. He was outraged. This was his son, the university was rejecting. He called Mayor Hackett and told him that if Casey could not enroll in the school they would just stay in Nashville. In a huff, Chips and Toni left Memphis and drove back to Nashville. The next day the school called and told Chips that Casey could enroll.

With that, they loaded up the car and returned to Memphis.

Not long after that, Chips called me and asked if I wanted to sample a Hueyburger at Huey's Restaurant. The co-owner of the restaurant was Thomas Boggs, who had been the drummer for the Box Tops. During the meal, Chips disclosed that Johnny Cash and Waylon Jennings were at his lakeside retreat in Arkansas. Would I like to drive over there with him and do more interviews?

Early the next morning Chips called to say that the trip to Arkansas

Chips Moman, left, Jerry Lee Lewis, Gary Belz
Photo courtesy Gary Belz

would have to be cancelled. He told me that Gary Belz had told him that a young singer named Jason D. Williams from Arkansas was going to claim that Jerry Lee Lewis was his illegitimate son.

"I need to stay in town to talk to Gary to make sure it is on the level," said Chips. "I told Gary that Lewis and Williams needed to have blood tests."

I subsequently interviewed Jason D. Williams to flesh out the story. He said he believed Jerry Lee Lewis was his father because of the similarities with their hair and nose, and because of the way he plays piano. "I have known I was adopted all my life, but my mother and father never told me. I never asked my parents who my natural parents are. If Jerry is not my natural father, I could care less who actually is. My parents are the icing on the cake. Jerry is just a little extra icing."

I called Jason's mother to ask about his claims.

"I'd rather not talk about it," she said politely, and then hung up the phone.

One night, several weeks later, Chips called and asked if I wanted to go with him to visit Jerry Lee Lewis at his penthouse apartment in downtown Memphis. The building was still under construction. The elevator was not enclosed and many of the apartments were unfinished. The only lighting was a flickering lightbulb tied to the frame of the elevator. When the elevator stopped at the penthouse floor, it was apparent that Lewis was the only person living in the entire high-rise building. It was as spooky as a Stephen King novel.

Inside the apartment everything was bright and well-decorated.

Lewis was seated in a white wicker chair and seated in other chairs were Gary Belz and Jason Williams, who looked considerably more nervous than he did when the author previously interviewed him. Chips and I sat on the couch and Chips picked up an acoustic guitar that he began to quietly strum. The discussion was all about whether Jerry Lee felt he could be Jason's father. "I don't know, man," he said. "Jason here was born in 1959. I was pretty active then, but that was a long time ago and I don't know anything about getting anyone pregnant in Arkansas."

"Would you have any interest in recording with him?"

"That's something I'd have to think about."

Jerry Lee was surprisingly cordial and polite, but he understandably was not much interested in claiming Jason as his son. The legal ramifications were daunting. At the same time, he didn't want to dismiss the possibility that he might have a son.

"He's a good person," said Jerry Lee. "He's no dummy. He's a very determined young man. It all depends on the man upstairs, Killer."

SOON AFTER CHIPS ARRIVED in Memphis, Michael Grehl, editor of *The Commercial Appeal*, asked me to invite Chips to the newspaper to meet the editorial board. At the appointed time, Chips arrived with a man the author had not met, Herbie O'Mell. He later explained to me that his name was actually Herbie O. Mell, but he preferred to be called O'Mell. As a Jew he felt it opened more doors to be associated with an Irish name. His paternal grandfather, a Russian Jew, had immigrated to Memphis and opened a downtown liquor store.

Not long after graduating from high school, O'Mell landed a recurring role in the hit television show "Route 66," which shot several episodes in Memphis. He had a long history in Memphis as a music promotor and nightclub owner. Chips knew him from the days when his cash-hungry bands performed in O'Mell's nightclubs and earned enough to pay their grocery and light bills. When Chips started giving serious attention to relocating to Memphis, he called O'Mell and asked him if he would be his business manager.

Chips wore a long-sleeve shirt to the meeting to cover his tattoos. He did a good job of answering questions about his plans in Memphis, but each time he seemed uncertain of an answer, O'Mell stepped in and answered the question for him. Grehl, who seldom smiled and could be quite intimidating, sat behind a massive desk, which was elevated, so that if he looked straight ahead his gaze went over the heads of the people he was talking to. For direct eye contract Grehl had to look down at the people he was addressing.

Chips thanked Grehl for the support *The Commercial Appeal* afforded his return to Memphis, and the overall support it gave the Memphis music industry. By the time the discussion was over, both Chips and Grehl felt good about the meeting. Chips left the building at a full run and didn't slow down for weeks. Working out of the hotel penthouse, his list of things to do included finding a house to live in, making plans for the renovation of his new Memphis studio, putting together a recording project big enough to excite the imaginations of the music community and the local news media, and getting set up in an office. The latter was accomplished when The Peabody gave him free office space on the third floor of the hotel.

Shortly after the office opened, the author stopped by to check out their progress. He got off the elevator on the third floor, where hotel business operations are based. To find Chips' office you had to go through double doors that were closed and marked "employees only." Once you pass that checkpoint you find yourself in a long, unpainted corridor upon which is scribbled graffiti. The entrance to the office does not have a sign outside to identify the occupants, but Herbie always left the door open so passersby could see into the office.

The first thing the author saw was Chips Moman playing Scotty Moore's guitar, the one he used when out on the road with Elvis Presley. Listening was a pretty young woman just out of high school who was the reigning Miss Memphis. She was there to talk about a possible career in music. Also there were Stephony Smith and Mike Porter, two songwriters Chips had just signed to his publishing company. At that point, Stephony was an unrecorded songwriter, but she would go on to write hit songs for Tim McGraw and Faith Hill ("It's Your Love" for which she was nominated for a Grammy), "Perfect Love" for Trisha Yearwood, and "How Was I To Know" by Reba McEntire.

Also in the office was a black songwriter who had written numerous hits, including Bob Segar's "Old Time Rock and Roll." The songwriter told me that Chips had just signed him to a recording contract. He couldn't sign a song-publishing contract because he was already under contract to someone else. "Chips is going to record an album with me," he said. Then without explanation, the songwriter opened his mouth wide to show his missing teeth. "But I got to get my teeth fixed first."

I asked Chips what he thought about the funky entrance to his office. He grinned and said, "That suits me fine. It's my style."

Most of August was spent looking for a house. Every time they visited a house they thought they would be comfortable in, the owner raised the price once they learned who was interested. That became a major annoyance and slowed the process. Finally, they found a suitable house at 191 Waring. Actually, it was more of a compound with two houses and a metal fence that encircled the property. There was an electronic gate and a speakerphone that had to be used to gain access to the property. They took out a loan from First Tennessee Bank to purchase the house. They planned to keep their Nashville farm, which was appraised at one million dollars and already paid for.

The biggest challenge facing Chips now was to make certain his first recording session in Memphis would be a success. After all the fanfare associated with his return, he needed a surefire session that would deliver a hit record. He pondered his choices. B.J. Thomas? B.B. King. Dionne Warwick? Neil Diamond? His most recent smash hit was the *Highwayman* album. Was some kind of group album the best way to go? He pondered all the possibilities and then decided that the biggest splash he could make would be with a group album that somehow highlighted Memphis music history. There were three possibilities. One would be to have a Stax Records reunion with four of that label's biggest talents. Of course, that wouldn't work because there still were hard feelings between him and Stax founders Jim Stewart and Estelle Axton. Another possibility would be to have an American Sound Studio reunion. However, the problem with that was choosing four individuals whose work was similar enough for them to be able to work together as a unit. The third choice would be to have a Sun Records reunion that focused on the legends of the rockabilly and early rock music nurtured by Sam Phillips.

It was the final choice that won out. He decided to check into the availability of Johnny Cash, Charlie Rich, Jerry Lee Lewis, Carl Perkins and Roy Orbison. They were all his heroes, the artists he looked up to while he was struggling to establish himself in Memphis. His last two albums had been with Cash so he figured that would not be a problem. Neither Charlie Rich, Jerry Lee Lewis nor Roy Orbison were currently under contract to a record company, or so he thought.

When he called Carl Perkins, who had just signed with MCA Records, Perkins told him about his upcoming record.

"If Jimmy Bowen will let you do it, do you want to?" asked Chips.

"Sure."

"I didn't think I would be able to do it," Perkins confided to me.

Chips told him he would get back to him.

Two weeks went by and Chips called with word that Bowen, who was head of MCA Records, had agreed he could do the Memphis project.

Chips' final lineup was Cash, Lewis, Perkins and Orbison.

The challenge facing Chips was to convince the public this new project would not be *Highwayman*, part two. He did not want to be viewed as copying himself. However, despite the clear similarity, he fully intended to follow the same blueprint—solos, duets, and at least one group song. Another challenge facing him was that Cash, Lewis, and Perkins had converted to country music over the years. The last thing he needed was to produce a country album that would have to be marketed as a reunion of early rock recording artists. To be successful, he would have to find a way to record these early rockers performing music that would be viewed as current by today's radio listeners.

ON SEPTEMBER 16, 1985, Chips held a press conference in the lobby of the Peabody Hotel to announce his upcoming album with Johnny Cash, Carl Perkins, Jerry Lee Lewis, and Roy Orbison. The lobby was packed with people as well as the mezzanine. Several tables were pulled together and covered with a white tablecloth. In the center was a lectern, and on both sides sat the recording artists—Roy Orbison, Jerry Lee Lewis, Johnny Cash and Carl Perkins—with Chips Moman and Sam Phillips seated at each end of the table.

Chips announced that the recording session was scheduled to begin the following morning at the Sun Records studio where they all had begun their careers. "We're talking to the labels," said Chips. "They're all interested. We've got to get it cut first."

"We're here to recapture the spirit," said Cash. "We felt that spirit when we hit the city limits."

After spending almost a week recording at Sun Studio, Chips explained, the session would be moved to his old studio, American Sound Studio, where the final session would take place. At the end of the press conference the artists rose and shook hands with those individuals who had fought their way through the crowd to be within handshake range.

Later, Chips confessed to me that the large crowd on hand at the Peabody was no accident. "I went to the Memphis Federation of Musicians and said I needed all the members. I need a crowd. These are the kinds of things you do to make it happen. There is a certain amount of smokescreen you have to use. This was a calculated deal. We did a number of things to get people there. You think I would allow my heroes to sit up on that podium with a handful of people there? I am fighting the biggest battle I have ever fought. I have to use all my artillery. Six months ago none of those legends could get a deal. Now people are fighting over them. That was the way P.T. Barnum and Colonel Tom Parker would have done it. People can believe in lucky horseshoes all they want."

It was after the press conference, while everyone was still in the lobby doing interviews with recording artists, that Chips lost control of his perfectly staged event. "Panic was running throughout my body," he said. "I was trying not to show it. There were some things that went down that I don't handle very well. Jerry Lee kept hogging everything during the interviews."

As television reporters, surrounded Johnny and Jerry Lee, Roy and Carl were pushed to the side and ended up over in a corner, alone. "That slipped by me that he would try to hog it," he said. "I had a meeting in the corner with Roy and Carl and said, 'Look, I'm aware of the situation and I will take care of it. I want everyone to have the same shot.' They both said they knew I would."

That afternoon Chips was pulled in a hundred different directions at once. Chips had asked each recording artist to bring some original songs they wanted to record. He had to listen to their demo tapes or listen to them play their songs. Throughout their careers, all of the artists except Jerry Lee had written hit songs. His only self-penned song was "High School Confidential," written for the movie of the same name. It was a Top 20 song in the United Kingdom but did not chart in the United States. Chips was so confident of his ability to get good songs from them that he and

Bobby Emmons wrote only one song for the session, "Class of 55."

After he listened to the songs, he realized they were not hit material. Faced with that reality, he put out feelers in Nashville with music publishers for new material. But inexplicably he did not approach any of the songwriters who had written hits for him over the years. He was going into the most important recording session of his life with the weakest song selection with which he had ever begun a session.

Additional time had to be spent at the Sun Records studio. He had brought in an 18-wheel truck filled with a soundboard and high tech digital equipment to do the actual recording on the session. Microphones had to be set up inside the Sun Records studio and cords run outside to the truck. Chips planned to communicate with the artists from the truck through a speaker-and-microphone system. Parked near the recording truck was a video truck with a control room for the video crew that would film the session for a television special that would be produced by Dick Clark Productions. Gene Weed, vice president of Dick Clark Productions, was there to supervise. He said it was the first time he knew of that a recording session would be filmed from start to finish.

"We think the marriage of the two—recording and television—could not only be a revival for the music situation in Memphis, but a revival for the music on television, which has been lacking greatly," Weed said. "We knew that some of the old pickers would be here and that's really all we knew."

The night before the session was scheduled to begin things started falling apart shortly after midnight. Johnny Cash and Carl Perkins were in solid, but Jerry Lee Lewis and Roy Orbison were wavering. At that time, the IRS had seized much of Jerry Lee's property and every time he performed they were there to get their share. So that he could get paid for the session, Jerry Lee set up a production company to receive his payment, but at 2 A.M. in the morning he wanted to know if there was any way part could be paid in cash directly to him.

"They are drowning the man," explained Chips to me. "I feel for him.

He can't pay his band or fuel an airplane."

When Chips was told Jerry Lee wouldn't be able to participate unless there was cash involved, Chips refused. "There is no way we are going to do that," said Chips. "We have made a deal and as far as I am concerned this can be a trio or Charlie Rich can replace him."

The drama with Lewis raged on through the night and was not resolved until the morning the session was scheduled to begin at Sun Studios. The problems with Roy Orbison's participation were less clear. "Roy's manager was so insanely jealous," said Chips. "He'd had Roy for ten years and without a snapshot of him taken in this country. He was telling me what he was going to do and what Roy's wife was going to do.

"I said, 'I tell you, hoss, you had to take him overseas to get anyone to take his picture. Just manage him when I'm not involved' These kinds of things cause a tenseness inside me.'"

The problem with Roy's management was not solved before sessions began the next day, but by mid-week everyone had reached an understanding. Roy Orbison participated in four group songs, but the only solo recording he made was "Coming Home." In essence, Roy did the least he could do on the session and still remain on equal financial standing with the other three artists.

Class of '55: Jerry Lee Lewis, seated, Johnny Cash, Roy Orbison, Carl Perkins Photo: Dave Darnell, The Commercial Appeal

CHAPTER 7
Goin' Back to Memphis
(1985)

ON THE FIRST DAY, when the four artists walked into the 18-by-29 foot studio, they were surrounded by a horde of television and newspaper photographers. The air was electric. The four men seemed to bounce off one another like energized cartoon figures in a video game. When Cash strolled in with his wife, June Carter, he walked up to Lewis, leaned over, and kissed him on the forehead.

Lewis, seated at a microphone, looked stunned. For an instant he froze. He wasn't used to being kissed by men. Then he smiled, looking pleased but slightly embarrassed.

After a minimum amount of polite conversation, the four men gathered at the piano and clowned around for the cameras as Lewis pounded the ivories with his customary flare. That evening CNN and the three major networks all carried footage of the reunion. But the television lights had raised the temperature of the room considerably and, by the time the media left, the four men were exhausted. Chips asked the quartet to rehearse one of the songs. After a few bars, Lewis screwed up and pleaded with the others to stop playing.

"What are you trying to do to me?" he said to Cash.

"What do you mean?" Cash asked, puzzled.

"I idolize you and you make me nervous," Lewis said, laughing.

Cash shook his head, speechless and embarrassed by the compliment.

Once the rehearsal was completed, Chips called it a day and sent everyone home. He and I retreated to a pancake house for dinner. He ordered an omelet and an order of strawberry blintzes. I ordered a waffle. His eyes sparkled with excitement. What had impressed him most that day was the respect the four men had shown for Sun Records founder Sam Phillips. "All four of them still call him Mr. Phillips," he noted with

Chips Moman, Jerry Lee Lewis, Sam Phillips, Carl Perkins
Photo courtesy of Gary Earhart

amazement. "That says a lot for these guys."

TUESDAY GOT OFF TO A WOBBLY START. Cash abruptly left town because of a family illness and Orbison stayed shut up in his hotel room all day with an upset stomach. Perkins and Lewis returned to the studio, bursting with energy. Lewis began the session with "Keep My Motor Running." At age forty-nine, Lewis was trim and wiry. With Lewis and the band inside the studio, and Chips outside in the truck, the session began. Several times Lewis made mistakes on the piano and the music had to be stopped. Lewis was concerned his playing would not be up to par for the house band.

"The guitar is playing lead, but I'll be playing piano—and you know me, if I put a lick in, just call me down on it," Lewis says.

Chips told him not to worry about it, to just keep playing.

Toward the end of the day, Chips suggested Lewis sing a ballad,

"Sixteen Candles." Lewis tried the song while wearing earphones, then complained they got in the way. "I can't cut with earphones," he said, laughing. "That's faking it."

Without the earphones Lewis gave a flawless performance.

Later one of the musicians commented he had never heard Lewis sound better. A string of personal tragedies, including the deaths of two wives and a son—and a serious tear in the lining of his stomach in 1982—may have scared his body and his spirit, but it had left no mark on his art. Lewis was still, well . . . the Killer.

After knocking down "Sixteen Candles," Chips called a break and everyone fled to the back parking lot for a breath of fresh air. Lewis detoured into the tiny bathroom in the studio. I was standing nearby when he emerged. He looked at me and grinned. "In 1958 Elvis put my picture on the toilet," said Lewis. "I wish he hadn't done that."

I walked with Lewis outside. After pacing around the parking lot for a few minutes, and throwing pulled punches at friends, the hyperactive Lewis said he thought "Sixteen Candles" had the best feel of any song he had recorded since "Whole Lotta Shakin'."

"I usually do my records in one cut, but Chips wanted three," Lewis said. "It was a blessing for this man to record me. Anything he says to me, Jerry Lee Lewis ain't going to argue with. Playing in here again gave me a great feeling. Nothing could ever hold me back in that studio."

I brought out a small tape recorder I had used many times to interview Lewis. Suddenly, Lewis snapped. His eyes glazed and fixed in place, resembling cat's eye marbles. He grabbed the tape recorder and tried to pull it out of my hand. Unfortunately, the tape recorder had a strap that had looped around my finger and I could not have turned it loose if I had wanted to. What might have been going through his mind at that moment I cannot even guess.

Jerry Lee Lewis was a music legend and here I was seemingly fighting with him in a parking lot on a hot September night. The irony would have floored me had the pain shooting through my finger not distracted me from a proper overview of my situation.

For what seemed like an eternity, Lewis and I scuffled elbow to elbow, our feet grating against the loose gravel of the parking lot as we went round and round in what from a distance must have looked like a weird new dance. The spectacle attracted attention from the other side of the parking lot. Within seconds, Lewis' manager ran over, calling out Lewis' name. Lewis never demanded the tape recorder. He just grappled for it, his eyes fierce with determination. Inexplicably, he leaned over and began biting the tape recorder. Sparks seemed to fly from his demonic eyes. Abruptly, the strap broke and the battery cover on the tape recorder pulled off, ending the altercation.

Lewis retreated to the other side of the parking lot with his manager, J.W. Whitten. They spoke for a few moments, and then Whitten came back over to where I stood trying to put the tape recorder back together.

"Jerry wants to apologize," he says. "He'd like to buy you a new tape recorder."

"That's not necessary. It's not broken."

Whitten reported back to Lewis. After a few minutes of conversation, the manager returned. "Jerry really feels bad," he says. "He'd like to buy you a couple of new recorders. That way you'll have a spare."

I shook my head.

Whitten went back to Lewis. After a few minutes, he returned with a new offer. "Jerry wants to buy you a hundred new recorders," he says. His eyes pleaded, as if screaming out, "Please, for God's sake!" Again, I shook my head.

Whitten relayed that message to Lewis, who threw up his arms and shook his head. By then it was time to return to the studio. Lewis came over and shook hands with me, a smile on his face.

"I'm sorry, man," he says.

It was enough to right the situation.

I told him not to worry about it. Then I changed the subject. I asked how it felt to be back in Sun studios. "I beats playing in the rain," Lewis says, laughing. The lame joke was his way of getting back on track. "No, it gave me a great feeling. I knew I should have been back in that studio all the time. Chips Moman knew it. These fellows knew it. And you knew it."

Years later, I spoke to a psychologist about Lewis' symptoms. He said it sounded like Lewis might have had an epileptic seizure. That sounded reasonable. Lewis had a history of drug abuse, but I saw no indication of that on that day (although Elizabeth Kaye a writer on assignment from *Rolling Stone* subsequently reported she had seen pills spill from his shirt pocket). Interestingly, a few weeks later, I saw him do that "eye thing" again. I was seated at a table in a hotel bar in The Peabody Hotel with a small group of people. Lewis entered the room and joined the party. He sat next to me. He was in a good mood and his conversation was animated. We talked a while, then after about 30 minutes he suddenly turned to me and looked me squarely in the face. His eyes fixated, giving off sparks.

"Who are you?" he asked, looking puzzled.

Earlier I had noticed the handle of a snub-nosed .38-caliber pistol protruding from his back pocket. That information, along with the sudden return of his sparkly dancing eyes, convinced me it was time to go home. It wasn't the pistol that bothered me. It was those eyes. Everyone in the music business carried a gun in those days. People felt a little more comfortable if they were packing a piece. Chips carried a palm-sized .25 Beretta automatic in his back pocket. I carried a .380 palm-sized Bulldog.

Elizabeth Kaye wrote in her *Rolling Stone* article that Lewis was summoned into Chips' trailer after the singer "arrived one evening, dressed in jeans, his comb in one back pocket, his gun in the other . . . only to emerge in a fury half an hour later, gun-less and carrying a drink that he hurled against a tree as he stormed into the studio."[78]

Once Chips and I were sitting outside his downtown recording studio, enjoying the celestial fireworks of a summer sky and listening to the music wafting overhead from a nearby music festival on the river. Chips was on his big Harley, reclining against the handle bars. I sat in a chair a few feet behind him. As we talked, a black youth crossed the street and walked in our direction. He pulled a straight razor from his pocket and began tossing it into the air, eyeing us with a menacing look. I saw Chips' hand slip into his back pocket at the exact time my hand slipped into my back pocket. Luckily, the youth stopped tossing the razor and walked on past, grinning broadly. I asked Chips about the pistol.

"I'll take a whipping," he says. "I'm man enough to take a whipping. But I'm not gonna let anybody kill me. That's the only time I would use it—if somebody was gonna kill me."

BACK IN SUN STUDIO AGAIN, Carl Perkins showed none of the scars of thirty years of hard living and fan neglect. As comfortable as a country preacher at a church picnic, he mixed well with the musicians and the others in the studio, glad-handing his way around the room. He had been born again, and he knew it and he was damned grateful. Before the session began, he walked about the room, almost in a daze, looking at the pictures on the walls. He told me about the first time he had walked into the studio.

"I left my two brothers and a drummer sitting out in a 1940 Plymouth," he says. "We had a bass tied on top in a 9-foot cotton sack. When I walked in I guess Marion (the receptionist) could tell I was a hungry picker.

"She said, 'If you came to audition, I'm sorry. Mr. Phillips isn't listening to anyone. We've got this boy called Elvis and he's real hot.'

"I said, 'I know.'

"I looked around. There was a life-size cardboard likeness of him. I said, 'Is that Elvis?'

"She said it was.

"I said, 'God, he's pretty.' And he was. He was a handsome dude."

Perkins is soft-spoken in conversation, but when the picks up his guitar and sings, the language of his music has a raw energy to it that is anything but soft. He sang two songs. The second, "Birth of Rock and Roll," utilized the same hot guitar licks that mesmerized ex-Beatle George

Johnny Cash and Jerry Lee Lewis in Sun Records studio
Photo courtesy of Gary Earhart

Harrison two decades earlier. Of the four artists, Perkins was still the consummate rocker. The rough had never been cured off his hide.

Eventually, Orbison showed up at the studio, several hours late, looking pale and nervous. He sang the first few bars of a song he had co-written, "Coming Home," then he left for the hotel after spending less than fifteen minutes at the studio, complaining of a sore throat.

JOHNNY CASH RETURNED TO MEMPHIS on Wednesday after his mysterious absence. He arrived at the studio early, dressed in black. He ambled into the room, engaging in playful banter with the musicians and technicians. He picked up an acoustic guitar and sang a song in which producer Jack Clement, Sam Phillips' right-hand man in the old days, was mentioned. Like everyone else, Clement had moved from Memphis to Nashville, where he had enjoyed a very successful career as a producer and song publisher. At the precise moment Clement's name was uttered in the song, Clement himself walked into the studio. He had come to play rhythm guitar on Cash's session. Everyone started grinning. Seeing the grins, Cash turned around and stood face to face with Clement. He burst into laughter. Jack had caught him talking about him.

With his sleeves rolled up to his elbows, Cash hammered out the lyrics to a song he had written called "Home of the Blues." Beneath the music, the drumbeat shuffled, a night train without a whistle. As Cash sang, a distant look came over his eyes. It was as if he were singing the song to himself. Perhaps he was. When he felt he had the song nailed down, he stepped up to the microphone. The tape rolled. Suddenly, the room was quiet but for the unamplified licks of the pickers, and the steady rolling beat of the drummer.

When the song was finished, Chips' voice boomed from a speaker: "That sounds good, John."

"Well, let's put it on the radio," joked Cash.

Cash left the studio, which by that time had become unbearably hot from the camera lights, and walked outside to the truck. He shook hands with everyone inside the cramped space. In the dim light, the interior of the truck resembled a control center for NASA. There were enough blinking lights, dials and levers to put a rocket into orbit. Chips played the song back for Cash. It was a take on the first try, but just to be certain the film crew had enough angles for the television special, he asked Cash to go through it once more. Cash returned to the studio and again sang the song without making a single mistake.

Later, Perkins came into the studio to sing a duet with Cash. The song, "Waymore's Blues," had been written out by Waylon Jennings in longhand on a sheet of notebook paper. Cash and Perkins tried to read the handwriting, but kept stumbling over the words. Finally, Gene Weed volunteered to type the song so it would be easier for them to read. He put a typewriter on a cardboard box and pecked at the keyboard while the band stood around and waited impatiently in the hot studio.

Using the typewritten lyric sheet, Cash and Perkins went through the song again. At the end of the song, Moman's voice broke the silence: "That could use a little more fire in it. It seems to lack energy."

"We'll try it," Cash says.

With his guitar slung high up under his arm, Cash arched his back, then twisted at the waist and spun his face down to the microphone, his voice rumbling like a distant train on the tracks, sparks flying.

"Early one morning it was drizzling rain," he sings. "Around the curve came a Memphis train."

Perkins, hands on hips, twisted and swayed as he sang on background. Occasionally during the song, their eyes met and they smiled. Beneath their voices, Gene Chrisman's drum shuffled, steady and unrelenting. Chips got his fire and then some.

Later, Chips told Cash "Home of the Blues" would not be included on the album. I don't know what excuse he gave Cash, but I imagine it had something to do with the title "Home of the Blues" and the fact that Waylon Jennings had written "Waymore's Blues" especially for the session. One of the reasons Chips left Memphis was in protest to the city's music being marketed as "soul" or rhythm and blues. Releasing an album that contained two songs with references to the blues was probably more than he could stand.

"Wish you'd play the songs for Jim, to see what he thinks" Cash said, indicating me.

Chips played the song again.

"I like 'Home of the Blues' better," I said. "The vocal is sound and the music has better energy than most of the songs I've heard so far."

"I just don't think it works," snapped Chips, his eyes not shielding his rising anger.

Cash looked at me, his eyes saying, thanks for trying.

Orbison and Lewis stayed away from the studio the entire day. Moman concentrated his efforts on Cash and Perkins. For most of the day, Cash was surprisingly low keyed and kept to himself, no doubt because Chips had chosen Waylon's song over his. By the time the session that day was completed, everyone was exhausted, mentally and physically.

Later that night, sitting in the Gridiron Restaurant across the street from The Peabody, Chips and his studio musicians talked about the session over scrambled eggs and grits. Bacon sizzled in the background. At a nearby table, a man wearing a set of plastic eyes attached to 10-inch springs stared at Chips.

"This album is an extremely important part of history," said Chips, ignoring the man with the plastic eyes. "Sun Studio is a monument to music. It's not just history. It's a monument. It's important to me personally because I looked up to these guys for years. Our lives ran parallel but we never got involved. Then down at the crossroads we met."

The man with the plastic eyes dashed from the restaurant and returned moments later brandishing a blackjack. Chips' bodyguard, a decorated Vietnam veteran named Frank, was already on edge after a full day of keeping the peace at the studio. When he spotted the man with the blackjack, he watched his every move, ready to pounce into action.

At the end of a full course of eggs and grits, Chips and the band rose to leave the restaurant. As they approached the cash register, the man with the plastic eyes leaped from his chair and hurried over to Chips' plate. There was a moment of uncertainty as everyone watched to see what would happen next. Was he going to attack someone with the blackjack? With his eyes still glued to Chips, the man with the plastic eyes scooped up the food left on his plate, packing his face with the leftovers.

ON THURSDAY THE SESSION MOVED to American Sound Studio. Dreary and in disrepair, though it housed a Memphis music museum, the windowless studio looked old and tired, like the carpets in a cheap hotel. Nonetheless it brought back warm memories to Chips and the band.

"There's something magic about it," says guitarist Reggie Young.

After listening to a practice session from the truck, Chips entered the studio. He was excited. "That old sound is still here," he said, smiling broadly.

For the four artists it was a new experience.

**827 Thomas Street Band: From left: Bobby Emmons, J.R. Cobb,
Reggie Young, Bobby Wood, Mike Leech, and Gene Chrisman
(Note: Chrisman is not a "little person"-he is standing in a hole)
Photo by James l. Dickerson**

"I've never recorded here, but I think I'm going to like it," said Cash. "It has a mood more than anything else."

Perkins, never late for a session, was first to sing that day. The song was "Class of '55," a ballad written by Chips and keyboardist Bobby Emmons. Two nights before Chips had played it for the first time for Perkins in the privacy of his bus. "He's very shy," Perkins says about Chips. "He won't push his own material. Carl Perkins is a million miles from having a hit single but there is a feel on that song that is convincing. It seems like something I wrote myself."

Seated on a stool, wearing jeans and white sneakers, Perkins twisted a pencil in his hand as he sang the song.

"That sure is good," said Chips when Perkins finished. "It makes me feel good just hearing music of mine again in this old building."

For the first time since Monday, all four artists were in the studio together. As Cash sang his part on "We Remember the King," Perkins sat on the floor near the piano, his legs folded beneath him. More than once he gave Cash the high sign, indicating his approval of the way he was

244

doing the song. Later they all would join in on the chorus. Cash, perhaps responding to Orbison's obvious discomfort, put his arm around his shoulder as they sang, holding him close the way you would a brother.

When the song ended, Johnny Cash, Jerry Lee Lewis, Roy Orbison and Carl Perkins filed into the cramped trailer outside American Sound Studio with the solemnity of pallbearers and the pent-up energy of racehorses being led from the paddock to the starting gate.

Waiting for them at the sound board with the quiet patience of a schoolmaster was producer Chips Moman. As was usually the case when he was happy about something, he displayed a small, twisted smile beneath eyes that sparkled. In the dimly lit room, the four music legends stood behind him with their backs to the wall as engineer David Cherry pushed the start button.

"We remember the King," goes the song, an awkward gospel-blues ballad that celebrates Jesus—or Elvis Presley, depending on your point of reference. As it played, the four stood in stony silence. It had been thirty years since any of them had recorded in Memphis. When the song ended, they stood stock-still. Finally, Perkins spoke.

"Well, fellows, it has taken thirty years for me to look all three of you in the eyes and say this, but I've got to get it out of my soul," says Perkins, his voice low and resonant. "I love all three of you and you won't ever be without a true friend as long as I'm living."

All four men wept.

"If you outlive me," he continued, "I want you to sing a verse of this when I'm gone. If you do, I might just raise up out of the box and help you sing it."

The four men embraced, the tears flowing freely. The recording session had taken its toll, but, then, rock 'n' roll had taken its toll on all four men over the years. Each had his share of problems. Each somehow had survived. No one could have known then the clock was ticking for first Orbison and then Perkins and finally Cash.

"We've got to pull ourselves together," said Chips, his cheeks streaked with tears.

Like smooching teenagers caught in the sudden glare of a porch light, the men broke apart, awkwardly searching for the exits. Cash, the most aloof of the four, returned to the hotel. Orbison, the shy one, sought refuge in his bus. Lewis, the wild one, sat on the steps of the trailer with Perkins standing over him.

"Jerry, you know and I know how it hurts to lose someone you love," said Perkins. "I want you to remember these words: When you're running from God, He's crying just like you are now."

Jerry looked up at Perkins, his face expressionless.

"You really do love me, don't you?"

"You'd better believe it. I always have."[79]

By Thursday everyone but Orbison had recorded a single. Not until late that night did he venture from his bus into the studio. He was dressed in black and wore a Maltese cross around his neck, a medal that many people mistake as a Nazi emblem. It isn't. It is an emblem that originated in Malta in the 16th century and was later appropriated by the German military long before Nazi Germany came into being. Nonetheless, people often associated it with Nazi Germany because it was displayed on Nazi uniforms, a carryover from previous generations.

Roy Orbison was often criticized for wearing the Maltese cross, but he countered that he wore it because he was a Christian and he preferred that design in a cross. However, rumors still persisted that he and his German-born wife had leanings in that direction.

When Roy entered the studio, the room was cleared of all but essential personnel and the lights were dimmed. "Coming Home," the song he had co-written for the session, is a ballad that pulls at the heart. Whatever he was feeling that night, he poured himself into the song, living up to his reputation as one of the most durable vocalists in the history of rock 'n' roll.

Hardship was the common thread throughout the careers of all four artists. Orbison was never linked to drug abuse, but the tragedies in his life were the type that had driven lesser men over the edge. His wife, Claudette, was killed in a motorcycle accident. No sooner had he recovered from that than a fire at his Nashville home killed two of his three children. Somehow he survived.

For most of the Memphis sessions, Orbison looked shaky. His hands shook and his voice trembled. On the first takes of "Coming Home" his voice was embarrassingly tenuous. He was a pitiful sight sitting in that darkened studio with a roomful of musicians. After several takes, Orbison and Chips, who had stayed inside the studio to offer moral support, went out to the sound truck to listen. The technicians in the trucks were unanimous in their verdict. They told him it was a smash. Orbison leaned against the wall and listened to the playback. Once or twice he smiled.

"I think it's great," said Chips, though he seemed to squirm.

Orbison nodded, but said nothing. One can only guess at the emotions that flowed through him while he listened. He had come home to Memphis, but his wife and children, for whom the song seemed directed, had been tragically lost along the way.

BY FRIDAY EVERYONE WAS EXHAUSTED. For the final song of the session, Chips selected "Big Train (From Memphis)," written and previously recorded by John Fogerty. Shortly before they were to record the song, Fogerty himself walked into the studio and introduced himself to the four artists. He flew in that day from Los Angeles after Moman put out word that guests would be welcome to jam on the final song. When Fogerty arrived at the airport, he realized he didn't know where the studio was located. He phoned Duck Dunn, formerly of Booker T. & the MGs and more recently the bassist with Eric Clapton's touring band, to get directions.

Fogerty confessed he felt light-headed in the presence of his heroes. "I was trying to relate back to when I first heard the Sun sound," he says, talking about the genesis of "Big Train." "I was about ten and used to play on the tracks. You know the old game. You put pennies on the track and a freight train flattens them, all very innocent stuff. Yet that was the sound I loved, and I wanted to write a song about that, with my producer being Sam Phillips. Obviously, it is a tribute to Elvis, but it is more than that. It is a tribute to the whole era."

Also dropping in for the jam were Rick Nelson, who like Fogerty had made a special trip to Memphis, producer Dave Edmunds, saxophonist Ace Cannon and the Judds. Edmunds wandered about the studio speechless. "I'm just overwhelmed by the whole thing," says the Englishman. "Memphis is the home of rock 'n' roll. I'm a bit in shell shock."

Nelson, dressed in black, moved quietly about the room, watching—shyly it seemed—the legends from a distance. I tried to strike up a conversation with him. He politely confessed a loss of words and faded into the background. Later he did talk to me.

"I've always been such a big fan of all these guys," Nelson said, his eyes never leaving the center of the room where the legends were standing. "I wouldn't have missed it for anything."

The next morning, while taking off from the Memphis airport, Nelson's 45-year-old DC-3 developed engine trouble and the take-off was aborted. Nelson left the airplane in Memphis for repairs and returned to Los Angeles aboard a commercial flight.

Marty Stuart, on board the plane when it attempted to take off from Memphis, said it was ironic that he and Nelson were taking about a mutual hero, Buddy Holly, when the plane started down the runway. "We were talking about Buddy Holly's glasses, about how some farmer found his glasses after the plane crash," says Stuart. "Rick was laughing, and he was talking about how the plane used to belong to Jerry Lee Lewis. But I was thinking about how rickety I felt on it." Three months later, on New Year's Eve, Nelson and his band perished in the DC-3 when it crashed under mysterious circumstances in Texas.

On the night of the jam, tragedy was the furthest thing from anyone's' mind. The mood was jubilant. Bassist Mike Leech said he felt like an autograph hound. "I'm taking pictures and getting autographs like people off the street, and I've worked with all these guys at one time or another," he says. "I'll be sitting there talking to someone like Carl Perkins, then I'm thinking, 'Gosh, I'm talking to a legend.' Then the next thing you know I have my camera out taking pictures."

Sam Phillips, who you think would be used to such things by now, told me that he had never seen a group of artists gather under such circumstances. "Invariably, everyone here I have talked to feels the same way," he says. "You can feel it in the air. It's not just, 'Oh, boy, we have us a hit record.' They see a future in a city they know started it all, and believe me, this cycle is going to make itself known again."

The jam itself gave everyone in the room goose bumps. There were seven musicians, fourteen voices—all wailing the words to "Big Train." As the driving bass and guitar licks of the song walked the music downward, the spirits of the singers climbed upward, the collision creating a joyous harmony that filled the room. Even the sound and video technicians, who had kept their thoughts to themselves throughout the session, erupted into spontaneous applause when it ended.

In the early hours of Saturday morning, there was a sudden hush, as if people were thinking *you really can go home again*, then the studio cleared quickly, the four artists of apocalyptic vision running fastest of all. As everyone filed from the studio, Chips sat on a stool in the center of the room. Tears streaked down his cheeks.

Toni was standing maybe twenty feet away. I heard her call my name. I looked and she tilted her head in Chips' direction, a pleading look in her eyes. I walked over to talk to him.

"I can't believe this happened," he said, looking at me with eyes that were bursting with happiness. "I never thought I'd ever see anything like this."

"It was pretty impressive."

Chips looked directly at me, the previous anger in his eyes vacated.

"None of this would have happened without the stories you wrote," he said.

"I was just in the right place at the right time."

The room emptied, technicians turning out lights as they exited. Before leaving Cash, Perkins, and Rick Nelson posed for a photograph at the door going outside, Nelson and Perkins beaming, and Cash looking unhappy. Neither Cash nor Orbison had smiled much during the session. Cash had experienced a run-in with Chips over one of his songs and Orbison's manager had a difficult time with Chips. Whether it was those things or a lack of enthusiasm for the material being recorded may never be known. Everyone told them they had a hit album. Lewis and Perkins readily bought into that assessment. Cash and Orbison, who had enjoyed more experience with hit albums, seemed not so eager to celebrate.

On the doorframe next to Perkins, someone had written: "See you in heaven." As it turned out, Rick Nelson only had three months to live. Carl Perkins had thirteen years to live. And Johnny Cash had fifteen years to live. Heaven could wait longer for some than others.

We stood beneath the only light remaining in the vast room. I didn't know what else to say, so I said nothing. Chips was paralyzed by his emotions. Little did he—or I—know then, but storm clouds were forming over Memphis. Dark, ugly clouds that soon would rain on the *Class of 55* session and send Chips' high-flying career into a tailspin, shrouding Memphis music in a veil of darkness.[80]

EASILY THE MOST PROLIFIC producer in American history, Chips recorded another album with Willie Nelson for Rick Blackburn at CBS Records, only this one was a duet with Grand Ole Opry star Hank Snow. They recorded the album at Willie Nelson's Texas studio. Snow had never before recorded with Chips, so it was a new adventure for him to work with someone known as the Steve McQueen of American music. The entire album was done within a day or so.

Surprisingly, Snow had three songs on the album—"Golden Rocket," "I'm Moving On" and the title song, "Brand on My Heart"—with no songs contributed by Nelson, a rarity for him. Apparently, Chips chose the other songs with input from the artists. The album had a brief shelf life, for whatever reason, and never made the charts.

As *Class of '55* entered the musical pipeline to be prepped for a final wrap, I took Chips around town to hear various local bands I thought might interest him. One night we went to a warehouse to hear a group called Vienna. It was so named because the lead singer, Klaudia Kroboth had immigrated to Memphis from her native Austria in search of love and music (she found both).

"I want what everybody else here wants," she said. "The American Dream of finding a record company and doing an album."[81]

Chips listened to several songs and asked them to make a tape and drop it off for him so he would have a better idea of how the group sounded. Before leaving, Chips asked the band members about themselves. His ears perked up when drummer Trey Bruce called out his name. Trey was the son of country songwriter and singer Ed Bruce. He asked if Trey was Ed's son. Trey nodded yes. Chips smiled, perhaps thinking about his old friend Ed entering his Nashville apartment, seeing the naked stripper, then turning around and leaving. Chips complimented guitarist Chuck Jones on his playing and asked what he wanted to do in music. "Money doesn't mean everything," he responded. "But you want to reach the point where you can go to the grocery store and buy anything you want, or be able to have a regular checking account."

Chips never signed the group—Klaudia was an excellent songwriter, but her music fit more into the alternative category, with lyrics like "I like to show my legs from far away, but to touch them is like dying because they are made of broken glass," a style that was ill-suited for Chips—but Chuck Jones and Trey Bruce went on to become very successful songwriters. Unfortunately, that day Chips never asked them about their interest in songwriting. Bruce went on to write eight Number 1 singles and numerous Top 10 singles for artists such as Faith Hill, Reba McEntire, Carrie Underwood, Randy Travis, and others. Jones went on to write

Number 1 songs for Diamond Rio, John Berry and others.

AFTER THE SESSION WRAPPED, Chips decided to name the album after the song he had written, *Class of '55*. Before the recordings could be pitched to the major record labels, they had to be mixed, a process of adjusting the sound levels on each track and editing out any imperfections in the tape. Then they had to be mastered, the final stage in which a tape is finished to become the original from which all copies will be made. Then the album would be transferred to cassettes that could be sent to the major record labels. Sometimes responses take months, other times word comes back within days. After nearly three months of submissions, it was obvious that record executives could not figure out what to do with the album. It wasn't rock 'n' roll, despite some of the song references to rock 'n' roll, but it wasn't country, either, because there were no steel guitars, banjos, or fiddles. Neither would it fit into any pop category. The album was so special, it was a letter to nowhere. If it couldn't be placed into a specific marketing genre, then it couldn't be sold in retail outlets.

Class of '55 was pitched to every label in Nashville, New York and Los Angeles. Everyone turned it down, including Rick Blackburn of CBS Records, who was the primary record executive Chips worked with in Nashville. Only Steve Popovich, the recently appointed head of PolyGram's country division, showed an interest in taking on the retail distribution of the album. Of course, that was only half of the solution. There could be no retail distribution unless Chips created a record label to release and promote the album. The demise of Triad Records the previous year had left a bitter taste in his mouth, but Chips knew that the creation of a record label was the only solution left to him. He had recorded a record that was essentially worthless unless he could get it into the marketplace (remember, this was years before the Internet made self-publishing music possible).

When Rick Blackburn at CBS Records received the demos for *Class of '55*, he was shocked to see that Johnny Cash was on the album because

Cash was under contract to CBS and Chips had not asked for permission for him to do the *Class of '55* album. However, he didn't react right away. Like a crocodile basking in the sun, he kept his feelings about it inside. He would wait and see who released the album and then present them with a hefty bill for Cash's services.

Oblivious to Blackburn's unhappiness, Chips' stress levels mounted day to day. In years past, when faced with setbacks, he was accustomed to throwing one or two alcoholic binges a year that sometimes lasted for a couple of weeks, but he knew he could not afford to disappear at this critical point in his life. However, the stress was apparent as his face sometimes showed purple splotches caused by anxiety. Over the years, his bipolar mood swings had a predicable trajectory, but under the enormous stress he was feeling over the album's failure, the middle ground seemed to disappear. He was either up to the top or he was down to the bottom. The album's apparent failure had caused him to suffer an emotional amputation of his confidence.

It was during this time that someone he trusted told him he might want to try cocaine as a way to self-medicate out of his down periods. He had a longstanding policy that alcohol or drugs could not be used in his studio during a session. Neither he nor his house band members had ever broken that rule. But Chips was in freefall and felt he had to do something. He did drugs, but I have no reason to think he ever did so in the studio.

Chips went to several physicians seeking help for his mood-swing problems. Each diagnosed him as bipolar. Every time he heard that diagnosis he told the physician to go to hell, and each physician responded that they could give him medication to control the problems he was having. Each consultation ended with him angrily storming out of the office.

To Chips, with his eighth grade education, such a diagnosis meant that he was crazy. No one had ever educated him on the subtleties of mental illness. He knew he wasn't crazy. He just needed a way to control his mood swings which were clearly injurious to his personal relationships. It was during this period that he made the biggest mistake of his life. By trying to self-medicate his mood swings with cocaine, he created an alternate personality that sometimes took him to an ominous place "at the dark end of the street," as his legendary song goes.

IN THE MIDST OF THE DESPAIR over the lack of major record company interest in the *Class of '55*, Mayor Hackett announced that city lawyers finally had completed the long awaited agreement between Chips Moman and the City of Memphis. Chips was sent a copy of the proposed agreement and a date was set for the signing and a press conference.

In the months since Chips signed the letter of intent with Hackett, the proposed agreement had changed from a one dollar purchase agreement to a lease-purchase agreement that provided that the building would be leased, not sold, to Chips Moman for one dollar a year with an option to purchase the building at appraised value at the end of five years. To finance the remodeling necessary to convert the fire station to a recording studio, the Memphis Center City Commission arranged for a $750,000 loan with First Tennessee Bank of which Ron Terry was board chairman. Under the terms of the agreement, the loan would have to be repaid by Chips Moman.

Chips was shocked at the turnabout. Under the agreement, if he did not choose to purchase the studio, he would lose the money he spent remodeling it (it averages out to $12,500 a month he would have spent); if he agreed to purchase the building at the end of five years, the appraised value of a remodeled, two-story brick building could easily be $750,000. That could mean a total expenditure of $1.5 million. It was a wonderful deal for the city which would have paid nothing to Chips and collected five dollars in rent for a property that had been vacant for years. If he purchased the building at the end of five years, the city would make a profit of whatever the appraised value of the building would be. By any measure it was a terrible business deal that would leave him in a financial hole, whether he stayed and purchased the building or left without doing it..

Hackett blamed the change to the lease purchase agreement on city attorneys who informed him that the city could not sell the property without an appraisal. No doubt there was some truth to that, but there were other factors at work as well. After Hackett's April meeting with Chips, he was bombarded by complaints from existing studio owners who did not want Moman to return to Memphis. There also were dark forces at work behind the scenes, the same dark forces that had controlled Memphis since its days as a center for slavery. Different names, of course, but it was the same subterranean power structure that called the shots in the city.

"There's no way we can say we've given Chips a deal," said Mayor Hackett at the press conference. "He's given us a deal. He's brought more to the city than I ever thought possible. He's exceeded all my expectations."

With his back against the wall, Chips signed the agreement, looking weary from all the discussions and embarrassed by all the attention. He told a room full of reporters and television cameras that he was pleased to be returning to Memphis.

"Chips Moman is going to be the Fred Smith of the music industry," said Hackett, a reference to the founder of Federal Express. "Right now I don't think anyone realizes what the positive impact of his arrival may be. You are dealing not only with dollars but with an excitement."

What Hackett didn't address was the already growing resentment among those in the existing Memphis music community who were resentful that the city was doing something special for Chips Moman and not for them. The existing studio owners saw him as a competitor in their businesses of renting studio time for demo recording.

In truth, Chips had no intention of ever renting his studio out to anyone except hit-making producers. In 1985, the only hit-making producer left in Memphis was Willie Mitchell who had produced all the hits recorded by Al Green. He had not produced a hit in years, but he fell in the category of "once a hit, always a threat." In conversations with the author he said he was pleased Chips was returning to Memphis because it would bring more attention on the city's music-making potential. To those familiar with Chips' reasons for leaving Memphis in 1972, the petty, self-serving rumblings in the music community were an ominous sign. Before leaving for Memphis Chips admitted he wasn't sure exactly when they would be able to get the studio up to speed, but he promised to move as quickly as possible.

In retrospect, it was naïve for Chips and Toni to believe that Hackett would be allowed to live up to his initial agreement with the producer. Likewise it was probably naïve for myself and *The Commercial Appeal* to believe that the City of Memphis would ever be allowed to go out on a limb to revive and empower a business as racially charged as the music industry.

Bobby Womack, left, with Chips Moman in 3 Alarm Studio
Photo by James L. Dickerson

CHAPTER 8
Dream Busted
(1986-1987)

AT THE URGING OF DR. RICHARD RANTA, Memphis University dean of communications and fine arts, Toni Wine began teaching a songwriting course at the university in February 1986. Contrary to popular opinion, she explained, it is better to send producers and publishers rough tapes done on cheap cassettes instead of slick demos made in a studio. "A great song can't be hidden. You just carry a tune the best you can, get your chords down, and that's fine. Truthfully, a producer doesn't want to hear a twenty-piece demo. He wants to hear something simple that will give him the creativity to produce what he hears."[82]

The class was scheduled to begin February 12th.

The day before classes began, I called to ask Toni the location of the class so that I could write an article for the newspaper. She said she would just pick me up on the way and we could look for the class together. When we arrived all of the students had already found the classroom. She told the students that the class would meet one evening a week for six weeks. Anyone with songs would be expected to play their songs on the piano or guitar for the class.

"About 50 percent of songwriters are one way, either they write lyrics or music," she explained. "I was mainly a music writer, then I got into writing lyrics. But you don't have to be both. I know many a great lyricist who can't sing in the shower."

Toni's class went so well she signed up to do it again in the spring of 1988. Sitting in the class that day was the father of an aspiring songwriter named Mel Rutherford. He had called his son who was enrolled at Ole Miss and told him about the class, but since Mel had a test the following day, the father volunteered to attend the first class in his place and take

258

notes. Mel began the night classes the following week.

"The second time I went to the class, I played a song for the class," said Rutherford. "Toni said, 'There's something about that song. What else you got?' For some reason I decided to play her the only verse of a song I had written. She said, 'This is a smash.'"

In the third week of the class, Chips came to the class and spoke. With him, was Roger Sovine, vice president of BMI, one of the two major performance rights organizations in the United States. Sovine spoke as well to the students.

"When Chips came in I thought he was the janitor," said Rutherford. "He was fifty-two, the age I am now. But he had on blue jeans and a flannel shirt, and he smoked in the classroom, dropping the cigarette ashes into the rolled up cuff of his jeans. He was a piece of work. He suggested I stop by his studio."

After the class Toni said she would be happy to drop him off at the studio.

"I played Chips three songs. He said, 'You are a hit songwriter. You are probably going to make records yourself. You are going to play as a session player on the records of others. He called out my entire career. He had such a nose for those things."

Chips offered Rutherford $100 a week to write songs for him, but he made him promise he would go back to school and finish. Chips had learned the value of an education the hard way. He didn't want this young songwriter to make the same mistakes he had made.

Rutherford finished the semester at Ole Miss, but he did not enroll in summer school. Instead, he returned to Memphis so that he could hang out all summer at Chips' studio. Then that fall he returned to Ole Miss for his senior year. One day Chips called him and asked if he had heard a song named "Highwayman." Rutherford said he had not.

"Well, you've heard of the Highwaymen, Johnny, Waylon, Willie and Kristofferson, haven't you?"

Rutherford said he had.

"You really don't like country music do you?"

"No sir."

"I want you to go buy the single and write me the sequel. This will be a good exercise for you."

"I went and bought the cassette and stayed up all night and wrote what I considered to be the sequel to the 'Highwayman.' Of course, I was naïve. I called him and asked if I could come play it for him. He said, 'Sure.'"

Chips didn't specify a time or a day. That evening, Rutherford went directly to his house. It was already dark outside. He rang the keypad buzzer, but there was no response. He could see people moving around in the house in the distance, so he jumped over the fence. It never occurred to him that perhaps Chips didn't answer the buzzer because it was late at night and he didn't want visitors. He figured the buzzer was broken.

"About that time, a German Shephard named Maggie came tearing down the hill to get me. She was the sweetest thing in the world, but I didn't know that then. I climbed up a tree. Then the cops arrived and Chips came out and saw that it was me and sent the cops away."

Chips invited him into the house and listened to his song. Afterward, Chips took a drag on his cigarette, but said nothing for a while. Rivers was thinking maybe he should put his guitar back into its case and quietly leave, when Chips asked him if he would be free to go to Nashville on a certain date. Rivers said he would. That was just the beginning.

ALL ALONG ONE OF CHIPS' GOALS in going to Memphis was to start up a record label. However, his plan was to start the label using the success of a hit album. Now he was forced to start a record label out of desperation to sell an album that no one else wanted. With a Dick Clark Productions television special waiting in the wings to help promote the album, how was it possible for a major label to turn it down? Having an album turned down by record companies was not a new experience for him, but never had he had such a big album turned down. Just thinking about it, sent him into a deep depression.

After talking to Steve Popovich of PolyGram, Chips left with a laundry list of things he needed to do before he could launch *Class of '55*. *First,* he had to assemble a group of investors to finance the creation of a record label. Then he needed to create a marketing plan not only for the *Class of '55,* but also for whatever future albums would be released by the record label. In short, he needed a structured business plan, something he had never done as a record producer. He was used to going with his gut feelings. Mostly, he won those gambles. But sometimes he lost.

On February 11, 1986, Chips announced the formation of America Records. The name was associated with his recording studios in Memphis and Nashville, and it celebrated the contributions American musicians and artists had made to music the world over. Chips asked his socially connected friend of many years, Herbie O'Mell, to put together a group of investors. On paper the offering seemed attractive: a finished album with four music legends who had ties to Memphis, and a television special filmed by Dick Clark Productions waiting in the wings to promote the album. If that's not an attractive package, I don't know what would be.

In turn, O'Mell contacted Gary Belz, vice president of Belz Investment Company, which owned The Peabody Hotel. Gary acted as the general manager of the hotel. What the two men had in common were similar family histories: both were grandsons of European Jews who had immigrated to the United States to find a better life. Together, the two men organized a team of fifteen investors that included Belz Investment Company, Gary Belz, Frederick W. Smith, president and chairman of Federal Express, John B. Tigrett, a prominent entrepreneur and former newspaper reporter, whose son Isaac was the co-founder of the House of Blues and Hard Rock Café, Dan Alabaster, president of Alabaster Originals, and others.

Chips never revealed publicly the amount investors put into the company, but it is believed to be between $1.5-to-$2 million. "I asked for investors who were willing to work and help," said Chips. "I wanted people who were strong businesswise so we would have the use of these people's knowledge. People who would understand what it would mean to set up a new distribution system. "When I look at them I see more experience than any business I have ever looked at. It's an honor to sit at the table with these people who put together incredible businesses."

"We are not passive investors," said Gary Belz, who indicated he planned to participate in the operation of the label. "Right now we are in the process of learning to dance with one another."

Belz went on to explain that he envisioned "Great possibilities if things work out well. I see social and economic importance. My family's interest has to do with our faith in Chips. We're investing in the person as well as the idea. It seems like a safe investment."

Chips interjected, perhaps mindful of his previous record label failures, "There's no sure thing. No one should invest who cannot afford to lose."

Gary Belz apparently derived his interest in music from his grandfather, Philip, who had a passion for music and sang opera several times a week on local radio, focusing on arias and classical songs, singing in English and Yiddish. He also played flute in the Memphis Symphony Orchestra. Philip and his wife, Sarah, had a national reputation as benefactors of the Philip and Sarah Belz School of Music at Yeshiva University in New York City.

The Belz family had purchased and remodeled the Peabody Hotel only four years before Chips relocated to Memphis. To hear Gary talk, he relished a role in music more than he did his future as potential successor of his grandfather and father in the family's multi-million-dollar real estate business. Gary had two sisters and two brothers, but he was clearly the Golden Boy expected to propel the family business to even greater heights. However, one got the impression in talking to him that it was his grandfather's failed musical ambitions more so than his father's successful business ambitions that had captured his heart.

Describing his plans for the first year of operation, Chips said his goal was to market eight albums in 1986. He would be able to do that he explained by "looking at masters from other producers."

While embarrassed and disturbed by the rejection of the *Class of '55* album by all the major record labels, Chips was elated to have finally found investors for a record label. He was only forty-eight, but it had been a lifetime search. His most recent effort, Triad Records, had failed for two reasons: lack of investment and a first album that bombed because of lack of promotion. To remedy the latter failure, Chips planned to build America Records into a television media company that could break new artists and sell the records of established artists by using television advertisements to promote the albums. He did so without research, using his gut as a compass. Research would have indicated that television had never been a good sales tool for music, except those late-night packages that promised oldies but goodies at discount prices.

"When all the independent labels were bought out by the big corporations, you closed the door on innovative music," Chips said. "The only alternative to having anything fresh is to be independent again. That's the purpose of this company—to be independent so we can have new things that people haven't heard."

The *Class of '55* album was unique in that one of the most famous music production companies in the world, Dick Clark Productions, was allowed to film the session from start to finish for the purpose of selling it to a television network for a special. In return, Chips would be able to use snippets from the film to use for advertisements for the album. However, with future records from America Records the record label would film the session and the record label would profit from the sale instead of a third party.

"I have an album that I cut on Robert Duvall—he's really hot now," Chips told me. "This album I would like to put into the new record company. Johnny Cash and Willie Nelson and Waylon Jennings have all agreed to do a television special with Duvall. They all love him. I would like to sell that to a network. You do the special and you cut out your videos to help market the record. I think you can sell more records this way."

Not only did he have the Duvall album, he also had completed albums by the Atlanta Rhythm Section, Jessi Coulter, and others. Already, he had the basic ingredients of a catalog for the new label. All he needed from *Class of '55* was a hit record.

With a fully funded record label, Chips set the wheels in motion. First, he had to get all four artists signed to the new label. To do that, he offered each artist an advance on royalties of $250,000. It was a hefty paycheck for all four artists at this stage in their careers, much more than they ever would have received from a major, but Chips could not afford to have one or more to drop out of the project. All four artists happily agreed to the terms. In addition, Chips took an advance of the same amount as producer of the album. Depending upon the size of the original investment, that left only an estimated $250,000 to $750,000 with which to pay for album and cassette production, advertising and television time purchases.

The album cover was done in shocking pink, with a group photo of the four artists with a black background. In the photo, Lewis and Perkins were wearing reading glasses they needed to see the song lyrics. It was not a strong cover, especially when compared to the cover of Chips' most recent album, *Highwayman,* but Chips approved it for production, his first administrative decision as president of America Records.

Flip the album over and there were much better photos of the four artists, along with a shocker in the form of liner notes by Joe Sasfy, a freelance stringer for the *Washington Post*. That did not go over well at *The Commercial Appeal*, which considering the printing ink used to report on the making of the album, had expected their music critic (not me) to have been asked to do the liner notes. The attachment of *The Commercial Appeal*'s name to the album would have caught the attention of other newspaper writers around the country, especially the other newspapers in the Scripps- Howard chain. Outside of the Washington, D.C. area Joe

Sasfy was a total unknown. This mistake would prove to be fatal for the project.

Class of '55 was released in May 1986. Telemarketing sales of the album were tepid, despite a constant stream of television ads. Mail order sales for the album were a disappointment as were the retail sales under the direction of PolyGram Records. Locally, the album did well in record stores and several radio stations gave it airplay. FM-100 program director Robert John gave Jerry Lee Lewis' "Sixteen Candles" a lead-in and later said the station would play all the cuts on the album "The reaction has been phenomenal," he said. "There was not one negative call."[83]

However, nothing prepared Chips and his investors for the national reviews that followed. *USA Today* declared the album one of the five worst of the year. Especially devastating was the review from *People* magazine: "Anyone who has ever gone to a high school reunion and come away disappointed will recognize the likely reaction to this record. Maybe they should have left the memories well enough alone . . . this is one of those albums that beats nostalgia to death with a stick."

IN MARCH 1986, Chips formed an alliance with one of the largest song publishing companies in the world, Chappell and Intersong Music Group. Explained Irwin Robinson, president of Chappell and Intersong Music Group: "Our basic goal will be to match those of the city of Memphis, which is to again make Memphis an important music capital. We will try to seek out the best writing and recording talent we can—and we know there seems to be a lot coming from that area—and we want to exploit it to its fullest in the best sense of the word."

For Memphis songwriters the partnership offered a gateway to success. There had been song publishers in Memphis in past years, but none of this magnitude. The advantage to Chips was obvious. In addition to inspiring local songwriters, it would result in songwriters from other parts of the country relocating to Memphis. The lesson that Chips had learned over the years was that to record great music you had to have great songs.

Ira Jaffe, a senior vice president with Chappell in Los Angeles, said the agreement will give the company "considerable exposure in an area we believe has untapped talent."

Jaffe described Chips as a "winner," adding, "When I first discussed it with him, we both said the Otis Reddings, the Elvises, the Box Tops—they couldn't all have disappeared."[84]

IT WAS OBVIOUS by June 1986 the album needed help. Steve Popovich at PolyGram hired Arnold Levine to travel to Memphis to make a video for Carl Perkins' song, "Birth of Rock and Roll." Formerly an executive with CBS Records, Levine had been producing videos for the past four years. Among his clients: Neil Diamond, Billy Joel and Bruce Springsteen.

"Steve [Popovich] and I had worked together at CBS," explained Levine. "His first idea was for me to use the footage taken by Dick Clark at the session and to use that with older footage and make a nostalgia piece. After listening to the music and looking at the footage, I thought that was all wrong."[85]

Levine wanted new video footage. He wrote a treatment for the video and flew to Memphis alone. Once he arrived he hired a local film crew to shoot the project. "I wanted to do a 'now' project. Basically, what I did was to take a vintage car and use it as a time machine. I have two kids out on a joyride in the early morning. The two kids happen to be 50-year-olds doing what kids do. In the course of a number of antics they do while driving around, I use parts of the car as a screen for vintage footage. I needed a foil for Carl, so I decided to put Jerry Lee Lewis in the backseat. So what happens is Carl is performing and I shoot Jerry and he's playing the backseat like it was a piano."

At some point, Ron Wood of the Rolling Stones joins the group as they drive through Beale Street. The car they used for the shoot was a 1955

Carl Perkins, left with Ron Wood of the Rolling Stones and his wife, Jo
Photo by James L. Dickerson

blue Cadillac allegedly once owned by Roy Orbison. At one point Carl is driving and Jerry Lee and Ron are sitting in the backseat.

"This part of the music industry was always something someone else did," Carl told me. "To tell the truth, down inside, I was hoping I would someday be out front doing something. You don't want to be in the background all the time. There have been so many years since the 1950s there hasn't been that much going on for me. The Cinemax special, then this album, it's created something out there I never thought would happen to me."

Ron Wood had been a fan of Memphis music since he was a young boy. "I remember W.C. Handy's name being thrown around by my older brothers," he said. "They were into jazz. They weaned me on Louis Armstrong, Big Spider Benton, Robert Johnson and people like that." He said he was invited by Jerry Lee Lewis to be in the video. "I looked further into it and found it was Jerry and Carl's video. Hopefully I will meet Roy and Johnny, too. I'm a fan of them all."

A footnote to the video shoot is that I went to write about the event for my newly launched magazine, *Nine-O-One Network*. When the time came to shoot the scene of Jerry Lee playing piano on the back of the front seat with his feet, the Killer was nowhere to be found. He was supposedly on his way to the shoot, but Levine was working on a tight schedule and asked me if I would stand in for Jerry Lee.

After some initial hesitation I agreed. They brought me Jerry Lee's pants, shirt and shoes and took me to a makeshift dressing room. My job was to keep my feet pumping imaginary piano keys on the back of the front seat while Carl drove the car. They did the close ups of my feet while I sat on the top of the back seat, but for the long shots I had to lie down on the seat so that I would not be seen. When Jerry Lee finally arrived, he replaced me on the back seat. Once the car arrived on Beale Street, Ron Wood joined him in the back seat.

Two weeks later, while previewing the video with Carl, my scene came into view, prompting Carl to look at me and say, "You don't keep bad time for a writer."

SHORTLY AFTER THE CREATION of America Records, one of the prominent investors, Frederick Smith of Federal Express, decided he wanted out of the agreement and asked for his money back. The other investors considered his request, but declined to release him from his obligations because it would be unfair to everyone else who had invested in the venture.

By chance, I attended one of the board meetings that was held in Chips' Peabody Hotel office. Along with the board members, the meeting also was attended by several investors, including Frederick Smith's new representative, John Fry of Ardent Recording. Fry's presence at the meeting caught Chips by surprise. He protested, saying that Fry was a competitor whose studio would compete for attention and business with the studio he planned to build. Fry responded that he and Smith had been childhood friends and he had accepted Smith's request out of friendship.

Chips relented and the group started going over plans for the record company.

As the meeting progressed, Fry seemed less and less comfortable.

Finally, Fry looked at me and said he did not feel that a reporter for *The Commercial Appeal* should be present.

"Why?" Chips asked.

"He might tell people what we're doing," said Fry.

"We've got nothing to hide," Chips said. "It's an open meeting."

I remained at the meeting. It never occurred to me to leave.

Eventually, America Records moved from The Peabody hotel to a suite of offices with a view of the Mississippi River. The building, which was owned by Belz Investment Company, was downtown off Beale Street, within walking distance of 3 Alarm Studio. Chips Moman was elected president of America Records, with Herbie O'Mell vice president and head of operations. Chips was provided with an office, but he only visited once or twice because he didn't feel comfortable there. His studio was his office. Always had been. Always would be.

Not being a musician or an artist, this frustrated Gary Belz because he had been taught by his businessman father that putting in time at the office was a critical ingredient for success in business. Caught in the middle was Herbie O'Mell. Chips complained to O'Mell that he didn't like to talk about his work with Belz because he didn't understand how things worked in the music industry.

In between business and studio meetings, discussions and inspections regarding the renovation of 3 Alarm Studio, and a constant stream of telephone calls relating to all of the above, Chips somehow found time to record another album for Rick Blackburn with Willie Nelson. This time he travelled to Willie's Pedernales Studio in Texas, then on to his studio in Nashville to do strings and overdubs, finally ending up at 3 Alarm Studio for remixing.

Titled *Partners*, it was Willie Nelson's thirty-third studio album. Among the songs used on the album are two written by Chips and Bobby

3 Alarm Studio in Memphis
Photo: James L. Dickerson

Emmons—"Partners After All" and "So Much Like My Dad"-with two song written by Willie, "My Own Peculiar Way" and "Kathleen." Other songs included a cover of Neil Young's "Heart of Gold" and Johnny Rodriguez's "Hello Love, Goodbye."

When *Partners* was released in September, it peaked at Number 13 on the country album chart, but there were no hit singles.

IT WAS NOT UNTIL Johnny Cash's manager Lou Robin told Rick Blackburn at CBS Records about Johnny's contract with America Records and the large advance on royalties, that the record executive started asking questions about the record label. As it became clear that his Nashville competitor PolyGram was going to undertake retail distribution, it pissed off Blackburn who still had Cash on his roster. But he maintained his cool until Robin told him that Federal Express was funding the album. That really made him furious. [86]

It was an incorrect statement about Federal Express and I have no idea who would have told Robin that, but it would prove to be a very costly exaggeration. It was around that time that I had begun asking Blackburn to make a scouting trip to Memphis to check out the city's musical talent. Several times he said he would like to when he could clear the time to make the three-hour trip.

One day, I think it was late June or early July, I received a call from Blackburn. He asked when it would be convenient for me to show him around Memphis. It was during this same time period that I invited A&R executives from New York and Los Angles to Memphis to listen to the local talent. Chips' arrival in Memphis had created a buzz in New York and Los Angeles. No one wanted to be left out. The following is an excerpt from a letter sent to me by Michael Barackman, vice president of EMI America Records in New York:

> It's been a while, and I wanted to check in with you. I want to keep up to date on the Memphis music scene. My friend Dick Williams has been real aggressive in scooping up talent from there. I feel I need to do the same. Are there any new acts that you are high on right now? I'd love an update from you. If you think there is a new act that I should see, please tell me and I'll be on the next plane.

I called Michael Barrickman, and he flew to Memphis to sample the talent. I took him by Chips' studio and Chips played him the demos he had recorded on Reba and the Portables. I also invited him to listen to a group called Vienna. It featured a female singer, Klaudia Kroboth, who had immigrated to Memphis from Austria and married a Memphis building contractor. Barrickman passed on both groups. I took another A&R executive from Los Angeles by to hear another group. I still cringe when I think of his brutal, and, I think, incorrect, assessment of the female singer: "The last thing we need is another unattractive female singer."

But she has a perfect voice, I argued.

"Doesn't matter," he said.

When Rick Blackburn arrived in Memphis he checked into The Peabody Hotel. That evening I picked him up at the hotel. As we were leaving, he said he had a favor to ask.

"What's that?"

"Would you take me by Chips Moman's studio?"

"No problem—I planned to take you there anyway."

When we arrived at 3 Alarm Studio, Chips greeted us just inside the entrance and we followed him into the control room and sat. It was the only room in which he felt comfortable talking. Ever since he moved into the studio, he suspected there were hidden microphones in the building. He had the control room checked and it was certified clear of listening devices.

The three of us sat in the deeply padded chairs and exchanged pleasantries, after which Blackburn turned to me and said, "Jim, if you don't mind, I need to talk to Chips in private."

I looked at Chips.

"I've got nothing to hide. I don't mind if Jim stays."

Blackburn looked at me again and said, "Jim, I really need to talk to him in private."

Enough said. I left and waited in the entrance room while they talked.

Years later, I learned what went down.

Blackburn expressed anger that Chips had recorded an album with Johnny Cash without obtaining permission to do so. He told Chips he had two choices: he could delete Cash's voice from the recordings or he could pay a fee of $100,000.[87] Chips chose to pay up. By that point a payment that size would have been a big hit on America Records' bank account, unless Chips paid it himself.

When the two men entered the entrance room, where I was seated, their faces were expressionless. Just as Blackburn and I got into my car, a tremendous thunderstorm, complete with frenetic lightning bolts, swept across the studio. I started the engine and turned on the windshield wipers, only they were frozen in place. I flipped the switch back and forth and nothing happened.

"Don't worry," I told Blackburn. "There's more than one way to skin a cat."

When it comes to business, Nashville is a much more gentile city than Memphis. I could tell by the way Blackburn's face contorted that the Southern tradition of cat skinning was probably entirely new to him. Born in Cincinnati, Ohio, he was probably also a cat lover. My attempt at giving him confidence in our stormy-night journey fell flat.

I rolled down the driver's window and stuck my head out into the rain, looking ahead as I pulled away. Visibility was almost zero. I didn't know what else to do. Suddenly, through the pouring rain, I heard Blackburn's voice urgently asking me to stop. I turned and looked at him, water streaming down my face. He was ashen.

"Why don't you just call for another car?"

That made sense.

I ran back inside the studio. Chips was still in the area near the door. He pointed me in the direction of the nearest telephone. I called a young woman I recently had assigned two stories for an upcoming edition of my magazine. She gladly came to my rescue and picked us up at the studio and remained our chauffer for the remainder of the evening.

Our first stop was a hotel ballroom where Reba and the Portables were performing. He was impressed with Reba, but did not like the band. Apparently, Chips had played him the tapes he had on the group before we left the studio. His opinion must have been based on what he heard on the tapes because that night the band sounded good in performance mode.

We took Blackburn to a couple of nightspots to listen to bands, including the Willys, fronted by guitarist Shawn Lane; but he was not very impressed (Lane would later play on a Highwaymen album). Then we dropped by Ardent Recording Studio so that I could introduce him to John Fry. They were having some sort of party in the studio at the time and they told me Fry was too busy to meet Blackburn.

I was astonished. It was probably the first time a Nashville record head had ever travelled to Memphis to meet local people in the industry. Fry was a bright man, but that was an incredibly dumb decision. It was not until that point that I truly realized why the Memphis music community had failed after Chips left in 1972.

Then I took Blackburn by a recording studio named Sounds Unreel, owned by Jon Hornyak and Jack Holder. He talked to them in the privacy of the control room and emerged beaming. He leaned over and whispered to me, "You better keep your eye on these fellows."

"Why," I asked.

"Because they've got some good ideas and they know what they're doing. I may be able to do some business with them."

There was one country group I wanted Blackburn to hear because I felt he probably would have signed them. When we arrived at the venue, the door was locked. The band had moved to another venue, but I had no idea where. The evening was pleasant enough, but it ended in failure, if the goal was to introduce Blackburn to Memphis talent he would not be able to resist signing.

BORN WITH A GAMBLER'S disposition, Chips needed a sure bet to offset his recent loses. During the planning of what became *Class of '55,* he felt a good follow-up to that album would be to assemble four of the black stars of the rock era and record a reunion album with them. He mentioned Fats Domino and Little Richard to me, but subsequently discovered that would not work because Fats Domino was leery of recording an album of that type with him. Domino's manager probably saw that Chips' most recent hits were with Elvis Presley, Willie Nelson, and Waylon Jennings, not going deep enough to discover that Chips had written one of the best rhythm and blues songs ever recorded for a black artist, "At the Dark End of the Street," and had written songs for Aretha Franklin, and recorded Carla Thomas and Dionne Warwick.

The more he thought about it, the more convinced he became that

**Leon Redbone was an early visitor to the new studio.
Here Chips is giving him a tour of the facility
Photo by James L. Dickerson**

Bobby Womack would be the best candidate to become the first artist he recorded in 3 Alarm Studio. Chips had recorded hits with Womack in the past and the artist had enjoyed a successful career since their last session. Womack was currently under contract with MCA Records, so Chips contacted the label to see if Womack would be interested. He was very interested, despite warnings from his friends that he should stay in Los Angeles and not return to the Deep South to record. As a result, MCA Records, issued Chips a contract to record an album with Womack.

After eighteen years, Bobby told me he was nervous about returning to Memphis. Chips said he also was nervous about the session. "I'm nervous on the start of every session I do, but I was extraordinarily nervous with Bobby this time because I didn't know whether the studio was going to go up in smoke." He was referring to the fact this was to be the first session in his new studio. "But you know I couldn't think of anyone I would rather try to get a hit with than Bobby. He's got a distinct style. He's a great singer, writer and guitar player. That's about all you could ask for. He's also one of the best arranger of horns I've ever heard in my life."

"When I got here, I said, 'Chips if you don't want to do it just tell me,' Bobby said. "Then we got to jamming and all hell broke loose."

With the exception of the addition of J.R. Cobb of the Atlanta Rhythm Section, who had joined Chips' band in recent years, the players were the same musicians who played on Womack's earlier hits. On keyboard, Bobby Emmons and Bobby Wood; on bass, Mike Leech; on guitar, Reggie Young; and on drums, Gene Chrisman.

"I had all the people on my end saying, 'What do you want to go to Memphis for?' Bobby said. "I told them my music is what Memphis is all about. It's very peaceful, it's loving and caring, and the people there, the musicians, are like that. I'm surprised that nothing has been lost. Chips has been cutting country and western and has been away from rhythm and blues. He is one of the pioneers. He's the same laidback guy. It's a magical place."

Once the session began the music flowed effortlessly and Womack's

Bobby Womack in 3 Alarm Studio
Photo by James L. Dickerson

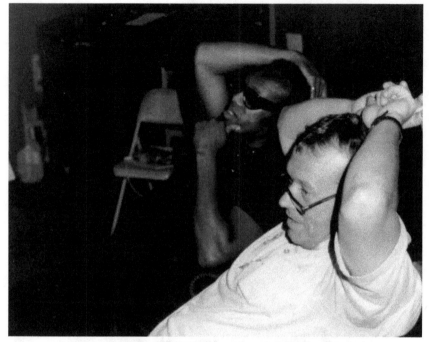

Chips and Bobby Womack pondering a song
Photo by James L. Dickerson

vocals often seemed inspired. At one point, while working on a song titled "More Than Love," written by Bobby Wood, Chips asked Bobby Womack to leave the vocal booth and play his guitar. Chips watched him, cat-like through the control room glass, calculating when he should pounce. Bobby was struggling to find himself.

"Bobby is singing right, but the music is not right for him," Chips said to me inside the control room. "That song has got to become Bobby's song."

After a short time on guitar, Bobby molded the song to a rhythm that better suited his voice. When he returned to the vocal booth, he belted out a vocal that left everyone smiling.

Chips watched through the glass, memory seizing his face. With an intense gaze he targeted Womack, a look of recognition in his eyes, simmering, as if he saw something for the first time. Suddenly, he sat in the chair, a look of shyness overtaking his face.

"If Chips had not been there, I might not have known what was missing," Bobby said later. "I was overwhelmed. I was so charged up when I walked out of there. That's what makes a great producer."

Womack feels Memphis is on the verge of another music revolution. One day at the hotel he ran into his friend Stevie Wonder, who was in town for a concert.

"He said, 'Bobby, why you cuttin' here?'"

"I said, 'Stevie, this is where it's happening.'"

"I called him the next night at the hotel," Bobby said, laughing, 'and they said Stevie had gone to a studio."

"I go where the soul people are, not just the people in the studio, but the people who walk the streets," Bobby explained. "That is where you get the raw soul. You can come here and go to work. You can get inside your soul. In L.A. you have to lock the door to get inside your soul, and even then you can get caught up in the electronic slickness of what everyone else is doing."

The album was titled *Womagic*. Chips only sent in nine songs to MCA Records, including three written by Womack—"When the Weekend Comes," "I Can't Stay Mad," and "Can'tcha Hear The Children Calling," with one written by Bobby Wood, "More Than Love," another written by Dean Pitchford and Tom Snow, "The Things We Do (When We're Lonely)", a Jerry Lynn Williams songs that had previously been recorded by Keith Richards, "(I Wanna) Make Love To You, " and others. MCA Records asked a Los Angeles engineer to re-work two tracks, "It Ain't Me" and "Can'tcha Hear The Children Calling." Chips was hopeful of another hit or two with the album, but it failed to chart and there was no mention of the album on *Billboard's* Year-End chart Top R&B singles.

CBS RECORDS HEAD Rick Blackburn dropped a bombshell in Nashville on July 15, 1986. He released Johnny Cash from the CBS

Records roster, after a twenty-six-year run with the country music legend. Cash had enjoyed an incredible string of Number 1 albums, including *Ring of Fire, I Walk the Line, At Folsom Prison* and *Man in Black*. There was a firestorm of protest by both fans and music insiders who just couldn't believe that a music legend would be treated that way.

Among the critics was Marty Stuart, who was under contract with CBS Records at the time. "When Blackburn dropped Cash, I went into his office, being the arrogant punk that I was," Stuart told me. "Then I went downstairs and the promotions man said, 'I don't know what you just did, but congratulations, you just killed your career around here.'" CBS was getting ready to release Stuart's second single, but they pulled it and gave the song to another artist.

Stuart knew his career at CBS was over, but he was philosophical about it, speaking in a Tennessee dialect sometimes known as "'famous last words: "There's always been a price to pay for speaking your mind, and a lot of time it's worth it."[88]

The backstory on the firing was rooted not just in Blackburn's disagreement with Chips Moman over the *Class of '55* album, but also with an "off the record" interview Blackburn had with *Tennessean* reporter Robert Oermann, a highly respected music writer. Blackburn had a habit of having off-the-record conversations with reporters so that he could freely discuss difficult decisions he needed to make. On July 14th Blackburn had such a conversation with Oermann in which he disclosed he was considering dropping Cash from the roster. When Oermann returned to the newsroom he realized that if CBS Records dropped Cash that would be huge news. He tried to get in touch with Blackburn to get permission to use the information, but the record executive had already left town for a business meeting and could not be reached.

Oermann called Cash's manager Lou Robin to inquire about the status of Cash's contract. He said the contract had run out. One of the most damning things a reporter can do is to betray a news source who has been guaranteed that his or her "off the record" comments will not be published.

Oermann obviously struggled with his decision to break that trust and run with the story anyway because of its important news value to the music community.[89]

After publication of the story, Blackburn was quoted as saying he had been "ambushed" by Oermann and Cash let it be known that he was upset that the decision had been made public without letting him know in advance. Oermann ended up writing a column a week later apologizing to both Blackburn and Cash for not handling the story differently. He said he should have held the story until he had comments from both parties.

Blackburn was not finished with Johnny Cash, however. He approved a second *Highwayman* album that, of course, included Cash (how could he do otherwise?). Luckily for Cash and Chips, Steve Popovich at PolyGram signed Cash to its Mercury label and offered Chips a contract to produce an album with Kris Kristofferson. It would be Kristofferson's first solo album since 1981. His inclusion in the hit album *Highwayman* almost certainly influenced PolyGram's decision to release a solo album produced by Chips.

Titled *Repossessed*, the album was influenced by Kristofferson's political activism. All of the songs on the ten-track album were written by Kristofferson. Some of the songs included on the album were "Mean Old Man," "Shipwrecked in the Eighties," "Anthem '84," "They Killed Him," (which was covered by Bob Dylan) and "Love is the Way." Interestingly, Chips broke his cardinal rule of recording only with the 827 Thomas Street Band instead of an artist's performance band. This time the musicians on the tracks were Kristofferson and his band, The Borderlords, which included Muscle Shoals veteran Donnie Fritts on keyboards and recording artist Billy Swan, whose "I Can Help" was a smash hit in 1974. None of his fellow Highwaymen offered to record a duet with him. Released in October 1986, *Repossessed* was tirelessly promoted on the road by Kristofferson and his band, but it was not embraced by country radio because of the political nature of the songs. Thirty-one was the album's highest ranking on the country albums chart.

In reviewing the album for AllMusic William Ruhlmann wrote: "The tracks had a true country-rock band feel . . . such songs as 'Shipwrecked in the Eighties,' 'They Killed Him,' and 'Anthem '84' reflected on various aspects of politics and war. But there were no real insights to be found in the more philosophical (songs) such as 'The Heart' and 'Love is the Way.'" Offering a different opinion was Linda Timms' review in *Nine-O-One:* "Once heard, *Repossessed* is not an easy album to forget. There's nothing cute about it. Nothing flippant. Its themes are pain and suffering and loneliness, and the songs raise questions about truth and honor and the price of both . . . It's not so much a theme album as it is a unified work of art."

CHIPS MOMAN AND I were sitting around 3 Alarm Studio one morning in February 1987, drinking hot chocolate. Otherwise the building was vacant and the studio as quiet as a church on Saturday night. He and Toni had vacationed in December in the Bahamas, where they had run into ex-Beatle Ringo Starr. Chips was in the process of telling me about that encounter when the studio telephone rang (cellphones were not quite in vogue).

Chips grimaced as the spoke on the phone. His responses were brief. Suddenly, he hung up the telephone and hurried out of the room. I followed him into the kitchen area, where he was pouring himself more hot chocolate. His hands were shaking so badly he could not bring the cup to this lips.

"What's wrong?" I asked.

"My first wife is in the hospital," he said, his eyes glistening. He looked devastated. "She's dying. I need to go to the hospital."

You don't need to drive," I said. "I'll take you."

As we were getting into the car, Gary Belz came rushing up from nowhere.

"I came over to visit with you," said Belz.

Chips brushed him off, saying he couldn't talk. Then, seeing that he'd hurt Belz's feelings, he quickly added, "My ex-wife's dying and we're headed to the hospital." Belz was speechless, a look of horror on his face. As Chips was getting into my car, Belz reached out to hand me a set of photos, saying "If you ever want to use these." I put the envelope on the dash and got behind the wheel. With his cup of hot chocolate still in his hand, I drove Chips to the hospital, which was located just past the Sun Records' studio location.

When we arrived in the waiting room, Chips' daughter Monique was in the intensive care waiting room with other family members. Soon Toni arrived as well. The waiting room was small and every seat was filled with family members. After speaking to everyone, Chips left to visit Lorrie. Toni comforted the others in his absence. Lorrie's condition was grave. She had experienced several heart attacks, the most recent requiring resuscitation.

Chips was ashen when he returned to the waiting room. He sat with Monique and spoke to her. After a couple of hours, he and I left.

On the drive back to the studio, he said, "She told me she wanted to be cremated and wants me to scatter her ashes along the river."[1]

He was clearly shaken by the experience. At times he could be the toughest talker in the room, sometimes to exaggeration; but in reality he was one of the softest-hearted men I had ever met. He wore his emotions on his tattoos. I dropped him off at the studio and watched him shuffle inside with a slightly dejected gait.

On the drive home, I opened the envelope that Gary Belz had handed me. Inside were several photographs that were taken during our visit to Jerry Lee Lewis's penthouse overlooking the Mississippi River. In the photographs, which I took with Belz's camera, were Chips, Jerry Lee,

---

[1] Years later I asked Monique if her mother had, in fact, been cremated, with her ashes scattered along the river. She confirmed that she had been cremated and that the ashes had been scattered, but she's didn't know if Chips had scattered the ashes himself. She was too upset at the time to participate in the ceremony.

Gary Belz and Jason D. Williams. Looking over the photographs, I recalled that Jason was too nervous to sit in a chair and kept circling about the room like a cat that knew it might be skinned.

WITH THE *CLASS OF '55* AND *WOMAGIC* on the rocks, Chips Moman decided to return to his pop music roots. That was one area in which American Sound Studio had been unrivaled in the late 1960s. Ironically, for salvation he turned to a former member of the very group that had brought about the demise of the Memphis sound—the Beatles. He and Toni had run into Ringo while vacationing in the Bahamas. He had recorded nine solo albums prior to 1987, but only two, *Ringo* and *Goodnight Vienna* had charted in the Top 10. His most recent album was 1983's *Old Wave*, co-produced by former Eagle Joe Walsh, and it had failed to chart.

Chips talked to him about his second album, *Beaucoups of Blues*, which had been recorded in Nashville with Peter Drake as producer and Scotty Moore as the engineer. Charting at Number 65, it was his fourth bestselling solo album of all time. Chips liked the album and suggested to Ringo that he should return to the South to record another one. He reminded Ringo of what a pleasant experience that had been.

When the Beatles performed in Memphis at the Mid-South Coliseum in August 1966, they were picketed by the KKK (Imperial Wizard Robert Shelton attacked the Beatles for being communists and supporting civil rights) and cherry bombs were thrown on stage during the performance. Each time an explosion went off onstage the Beatles looked at each other to see who had been shot. Visiting Memphis was a terrifying experience for them. They vowed never to return.

Chips was well aware of Ringo's concerns about Memphis as a city, so he naturally played up the support Chips had from the city and the morning newspaper. The more the two men talked, the more interested Ringo became. Chips offered to record up to three albums on spec and pay the costs himself. All that sounded fine to Ringo, who was eager to record

Ringo Starr with Chips Moman in 3 Alarm Studio
Photo by James L. Dickerson

again after a three-year drought. In Chips' mind, this could fulfill his commitment to offer six to eight America Record albums during the first year of operation. If he added *Class of '55* to the total, along with already existing albums on Robert Duvall, the Atlanta Rhythm Section and Jessi Colter, that would give him a total of seven albums.

When Ringo Starr arrived in Memphis in February 1987 to record at both the Sun Records Studio and 3 Alarm Studio, Memphis assumed all the characteristics of a giddy teenager. There was a buzz on the streets wherever people gathered in small groups. TV newscasts contained news of "Ringo sightings." It had been twenty years since a Beatle had been in Memphis. This time there were no Ku Klux Klan protests, as there were for the last visit. No cherry bombs were thrown at the ex-Beatle, as had happened at the last visit.

The Beatles had always been my favorite group, so I was delighted when Chips invited me to drop in on the sessions. I knew everyone there except Ringo and his beautiful wife, Barbara Bach. When we were introduced by Chips, Ringo was cordial and offered a hearty handshake.

Barbara smiled so radiantly with a movie star glow that it nearly made my knees buckle. The sessions lasted throughout March and into April, with Ringo and Barbara going back and forth during that time to Los Angeles for brief visits to take care of business there.

Three things impressed me most about the Ringo sessions. First, I was surprised at how strong his voice was in its natural state. I had been lead to believe over the years that Ringo's voice required extensive rehabilitation in the studio. Not so. Between takes, Toni Wine spent time with him at the piano, coaching him on specific lines, but his voice was remarkably resonant. Second, I was surprised Chips did not have his A-list band in place, the 827 Thomas Street Band. Two members of the band, Mike Leech on bass and Gene Chrisman on drums, played on some tracks, but on guitar it was Chips and J.R. Cobb of the Atlanta Rhythm Section; Sam Shoup, currently Director of Commercial Music for the University of Memphis, played bass on most of the tracks and alternated with Jimmy Whitehead on keyboards.

What surprised me most was that Ringo was recorded live with the band, a departure for Chips who preferred to have the instrumental tracks perfectly aligned in advance. Third, I was surprised at how cozy he was with Barbara. Throughout the session, he was extraordinarily relaxed and playful, snuggling during the playbacks with Barbara, who often sat on his lap with her arms around his neck. Never once did I see any indication Ringo was drinking or using drugs.

The session was going well until Ringo and Barbara left town for a few days. While they were gone a columnist for *The Commercial Appeal*, wrote a piece about the session, describing Ringo as an "aging Beatle" who was yesterday's news. Not only did she write that she felt sorry for him, she depicted him as "the ugly stepsister of the Fab Four." I read the column, but thought nothing about it. The columnist was entitled to her opinion, however misguided, but her lack of knowledge about Ringo's contributions to music (Jim Keltner, considered by many to be America's top session drummer, once said Ringo was "the guy that we all tried to

Chips Moman and Toni Wine Moman
protesting in front of the newspaper
Photo by James L. Dickerson

play like in the studio), and her lack of research on Ringo's past experiences with the KKK in Memphis were disturbing and not typical of her usual work.

Later that day, I stopped by 3 Alarm. Chips was livid. He was afraid the column would sabotage the session. Ringo had suggested that the session should be moved to Los Angeles. Chips' voice was raised. He paced. He called people on the phone, one right after the other. The one thing that he told everyone was, "We've got to do something."

He envisioned the entire session going up in flames—and with good reason. After discussing the situation for most of the afternoon, he decided to picket the newspaper. I tried to talk him out of it. I reminded him that *The Commercial Appeal* had encouraged him to relocate to Memphis and had given unprecedented news coverage of the making of *Class of '55*. All he said in response was, "They've turned against me."

I explained to him that the columnist did not represent the newspaper's opinion. He didn't buy that. It must be the newspaper's opinion, he reasoned, or the newspaper would not have printed it. I explained that newspapers print all sorts of opinions that editors disagree with. For the first time since meeting Chips, I was totally unable to reason with him. He called for a picket line the following day on the sidewalk in front of *The Commercial Appeal*.

Chips pulled me away from the others in the studio.

"You with me or against me?" he asked.

What could I say? People do silly things for their friends. Besides, he was at the upper end of his bipolar disorder and appeared to be self-medicating. After I left, he called a press conference at the studio.

However, before it began, he ordered two reporters and a photographer from *The Commercial Appeal* out of his studio. When one of the ousted reporters, John Branston, held out a tape recorder and asked him a question, Chips forcefully slapped it out of his hand.

.The next morning I showed up outside the newspaper and walked the picket line with Chips, Toni, and about two dozen placard-carrying marchers. I looked up at the massive glass wall of the third-floor newsroom and saw former colleagues peering out at me, eyes bulging. Chips was wrong to picket the newspaper, but it did offer relief to a tense situation. Chips really did believe the column would sabotage everything he had worked so hard to build. If carrying a picket sign made him feel better, so be it. Sometimes you do things you know are wrong, but you do them for reasons that you think are right.

Ringo returned for the session. A reporter asked him about the controversy. He said he hadn't read the column. "Why would I?" Why, indeed, would he admit to such a thing?

Toward the end of the session, Ringo and Barbara gave a party aboard the riverboat Island Queen to show they had no hard feelings toward Memphis. I attended the party, along with Charlie Rich, David Porter and 251 other invited guests, including Chips dentist Gary Earhart, a sometimes movie extra, who took a number of photographs. No one was quite sure what to expect when the Island Queen churned out into the Mississippi River. It was like any other Memphis party. Lots of barbecue.

Chips Moman, playing guitar, Ringo Starr in rear
Photo by Gary Earhart

Lots to drink. Reba and The Portables provided the music.

The highlight of the party occurred later in the evening. With the river lapping lazily at the bow of the Island Queen, Ringo sat in with the band. The hot, smoke-filled room must have taken him back to the day when the Beatles were playing tiny, people-infested pubs throughout Europe. With a cigarette dangling from his lips, he demonstrated why he is the most celebrated drummer in the world. Within minutes, he had the guests mesmerized.

"I can't believe it," said a young woman standing next to me. "I'm really seeing him play."

The woman's amazement was justified. Except for a handful of studio personnel, who actually had ever heard the ex-Beatle play a live set? Not the hundreds of thousands of fans who packed the stadium when the Beatles toured, for they would have been too overwhelmed by the hysteria of the moment to actually hear the music.

A couple of days after the party, I saw Ringo again in the studio and asked him about it. "That was the first time I ever played a riverboat," he said, laughing. He said he was afraid to sample the barbecue. "It's my stomach," he said plaintively, referring to an incident several years ago that almost cost him his life. "Most of the things I eat now have to be broiled. I can't eat spicy food."

Work on the album was drawing to a close. They had more than a dozen completed songs. Bob Dylan had flown in to sing and play harmony on one of the songs. Chips played me all the songs and I thought it was the best I had ever heard Ringo sing. I especially liked "Whisky and Soda," because it expressed the cavalier attitude that had been his trademark in the early years. Other standouts included Billy Swan's "I Can Help" and "Stormy Weather."

Earlier, I had presented Chips with a gift copy of his production of Tommy Burk and the Counts' recording of "Stormy Weather" that I had purchased while a student at Ole Miss. Chips' eyes brightened and he smiled as he placed it on a turntable. Hearing the music, Toni, walked up and grimaced. "That's terrible," she said, and then walked away.

Over his shoulder, Chips said, "You've got to consider when it was made."

Toni kept walking. It wasn't her cup of tea.

For his part, Chips couldn't believe the record turned out as well as it did, considering his likely state of mind when it was recorded. He didn't bother to explain to Toni. He just shook his head from side to side, the way a man does when his fishing companion tosses his line into the creek with the wrong bait. In a marriage, some things are just better left unsaid.

Chips mixed the album after Ringo left and sent a cassette to his home in Los Angeles. Later, Ringo telephoned him and told him he had rented a limo so that he and a couple of friends could listen to the tape in style. Unfortunately, there was a problem.

"Wouldn't you know I'd get the only fucking limo in town without a tape deck," he said.

Perhaps it was an omen.

During the next few months the project fell apart. Ringo wanted to overdub some of the drum parts that had been done by Gene Chrisman so it would have his style of playing on the tracks. Incredibly, Chips said he was opposed to doing that.

John Hartman, a spokesman for Ringo, told reporters Ringo also wanted to record tracks with another producer (he tossed out Elton John's name) and wanted to combine the two sessions into one album. The disaster that Chips feared was becoming a reality. He was losing control.

The Highwaymen: Johnny Cash, Willie Nelson, Kristofferson, Waylon Jennings
Liberty Records-Photofest

CHAPTER 9
Against the Wall
(1988-1994)

CHIPS HAD HIS BACK AGAINST THE WALL at this point. He had an album that had been done on spec in the sense that he had not offered Ringo a contract and royalty advance to participate in the project. For him to sell it he would have to have Ringo's consent. For now, Ringo had decided not to discuss the project with Chips. Patience was not Chips' strong suit, but there was little he could do until Ringo either discussed it with him or notified him of a problem. Chips was left hanging uncomfortably in the wind.

Running parallel to his problems with Ringo were increased problems with America Records of which Chips was still president. The failure of *Class of '55* most likely depleted the company's bank account. Since they had no product to sell, the only way they could release another album would be if the investors put more money into the company.

The Ringo album must have been suggested by someone as an album that American Records could release. I say that because I was at Chips house one day listening to the album when one of the investors dropped by to also listen to the album. He had with him a pad on which he took notes. He asked Chips numerous questions and he asked me questions as a journalist and magazine owner. I told him I was a huge Beatles' fan and especially liked Ringo.

I'm not sure what happened with the Ringo album as far as America Records was concerned, but in retrospect I can see how that prospect put Chips in a predicament. For America Records to acquire the album, Ringo would have to agree to sign with the company. That would involve an appropriate royalty advance to Ringo. It would also involve Chips agreeing to allow Ringo to overdub his drum parts on the album. Frankly, he should have agreed to that in the beginning. But that left Ringo's desire to record more tracks for the album with a different producer in Los Angeles. It is unlikely Chips ever would have agreed to that condition, and if he did, it would have escalated the production costs of the album considerably. In brief, there did not seem to be a way in which the Ringo album could be released by America Records.

Perhaps the only person on the board of directors who would have understood those economics was John Fry, Frederick's Smith's representative on the board. As a studio owner, he had undertaken numerous failed attempts over the years to launch independent labels. He knew it was a risky business. America Records investors probably would have stepped away from the company if it were not for Gary Belz, who was passionate about entering the music business. There was nothing wrong with Gary's ambition to get into the music business, but his life experience had been with his father's businesses and he had no experience in the music business.

That put him at loggerheads with Chips, who had considerable experience in the music business and little business experience in other areas. Unfortunately, Chips was also an artist and had an artist's temperament. Chips once told me that he always entered a music-related meeting with strangers trying to figure out who the one honest person in the group might be.

By the time the Ringo album was completed, Chips had produced records with Willie Nelson, Bobby Womack, and Kris Kristofferson. America Records investors did not understand why Chips had not given those recordings to America Records. Of course, the reason was because they all had been contracted with major record labels. Chips was a paid producer and did not have ownership of the albums.

The investors incorrectly figured that if you worked for a company you worked for that company only. That's not the case if you also are an independent producer. Chips, the president of America Records, and Chips the record producer were two separate economic entities. Because Chips had borrowed $750,000 from First Tennessee Bank as Chips the Producer with which to make the empty firehouse into a recording studio, it was imperative he continue to work independently of the record label.

Meanwhile, Gary Belz was becoming more and more impatient with Chips taking jobs as an independent producer to meet his expenses while the record label was on hold. Eventually, Belz appealed to the board and investors, many of whom were family friends, to replace Chips' right-hand-man Herbie O'Mell as the label's general manager and put Gary in that position.

Herbie was fired from the record label, but Chips told him he could operate the studio; it was not so much a job as it was a title because the studio did not rent out the facility for demos or other recordings. In other words, the studio had no income. Herbie assumed he was still on the company health insurance, but when his wife, Laura, went into labor with their first child and he took her to the hospital, they informed him he would have to pay fourteen hundred dollars for his wife to be admitted. Fortunately, Herbie was able to raise the money from family members and admit her to the hospital, but he was stung by the injustice of having his health insurance cancelled without notification.[90]

Herbie and Laura were a rarity in the music business. Married in 1980, they raised two sons and sustained their marriage for over three decades. With his frizzy hair, Herbie was not what you would call a handsome man, but he had an oversized personality that compensated for that. By comparison, Laura was a striking blonde, who would not have looked out of place in a fashion magazine.

Herbie and Chips often were seen in public together. Because he possessed a higher level of social skills, Herbie often ran interference for Chips and kept him out of trouble. It was when Herbie was not around that Chips sometimes stepped into the deep end of the pool.

In dealing with Chips, timing was everything. One night Chips was sitting in his den when he got a telephone call from Gary Belz. He apparently was at Ardent trying to organize a session for America Records, but he had done so without talking to Chips. One thing led to another during their conversation and Belz called Chips a "motherfucker," according to Chips. He calmly hung up the phone, got in his car and drove to Ardent, where Belz was waiting.

"I'll be back in a few minutes," he said to me as he walked out the door.

Chips strode into the studio and went from room to room looking for Belz. When he found him, he walked up to him and slapped him hard across the face, without explanation.

"You call me a name, you do it to my face," he said, and left.

Belz was stunned.

With that gesture, more symbolic than anything else, Memphis music entered a new era. All-out war erupted in the Memphis music community—and the dark side of Memphis, always alluded to by record producer Jim Dickinson in such graphic terms as "the center of all evil in the known universe," rose from the ashes to bay at the moon.[91]

CHIPS DEALT WITH THE FALLOUT of the Ringo album for most of 1987, particularly the problems associated with recording it. So far, at least, the man was unstoppable. Most people who had been through what he had encountered upon his return to Memphis would be cowering in a corner somewhere. Not Chips. At his 300-plus acre farm near Nashville, he had a bulldozer that he drove whenever he felt frustrated. Anything that got in the way was demolished. Too bad he didn't take the bulldozer to Memphis with him. He clearly had need of it.

Somehow Chips kept making music. In late summer 1987, while the Ringo Starr situation festered, he went to Texas to record an album with Willie Nelson. It was yet another album for Rick Blackburn at CBS Records. Chips liked working with Willie. It was usually quick, relatively painless (Willie's ego didn't need massaging) and usually profitable for everyone involved. I fantasized about him letting out a rebel yell and driving his bulldozer into the lobby of the Peabody, demolishing everything in sight

Chips brought the album back to Memphis and mixed it at 3 Alarm. One day I got a call from Chips. He was at a house he had purchased on Horseshoe Lake across the river in Arkansas. It was summer and he and Toni were having a cook-out for a few friends. A free meal sounded good to me. It was hot that day, pushing 100 degrees, and we spent much of the day on the lake in Chips' boat. Toni and Chips bickered constantly, which, for them, was an indication they were still close. If they ever stopped bickering, and withdrew unto themselves, that would be an indication the relationship was over.

After the other friends left, Chips played me the Willie Nelson album he had just recorded. In a moment of supreme irony, it had been titled *What A Wonderful World*. The album consisted of old standards such as "Spanish Eyes," a duet with Julio Iglesias, "Blue Moon," "Some Enchanted Evening," "The Song From Moulin Rouge (Where Is Your Heart)" and, of course, the title song. The album had a healing quality about it. Had he recorded it with an unconscious wish to remake the world around him?

When "What a Wonderful World" came up, Toni abruptly got up and went into the kitchen (was the irony too painful for her to bear?). Chips and I sat in silence and listened as Willie, as only Willie can, extolled the colors of the rainbow and the cries of newborn babies. The last song on the album was "Ac-cent-tchu-ate The Positive." When the album was over, there was not a dry eye in the house. [92]

When the album was released in March 1988, it quickly moved up the country album charts, finally peaking at Number 6. It was yet another hit from a producer who had few, if any, peers. When Chips returned to Memphis in 1985, there were only five Memphians who had ever recorded hit records—Sam Phillips at Sun Records, Willie Mitchell at Royal Studios, Jim Stewart and Estelle Axton of Stax Records, and Bobby Manuel at the Daily Planet—but none of those individuals had voiced opposition to Chips' return to Memphis. Phillips participated in Chips *Class of '55* venture. Willie Mitchell telephoned me to let me know about his approval. Manuel, who was the most recent producer in Memphis to have a Number 1 record (with 1976's "Disco Duck") was supportive of Chips' return, hoping it would help everyone. Jim Stewart and Estelle Axton didn't approve of Chips' return, but they didn't publicly oppose it either. They kept their thoughts to themselves.

Despite all the craziness of the last four years, there were plenty of good times. Early one evening I got a call from Chips. Did I want to go on a boat ride?

"Tonight?" I asked, looking at my watch.

Well, why not? I drove over to Chips' house and we hooked up a massive pontoon boat to his Blazer. Going with us were songwriter David Porter, whose hits "Soul Man," "Hold On, I'm Coming" and "When Something Is Wrong with My Baby," had influenced an entire generation of music lovers and another black gentleman, whose name I don't recall. The history of white men asking black men to go on a midnight boat ride in a swampy southern lake was not a good one. Not certain what Chips was up to, but not wanting to turn down the opportunity, Porter had asked a close friend to go with us. He was an athletic looking black man who owned several of the local Wendy's franchises.

By the time we reached the lake, it was past midnight. It was a small lake located just across the state line in Mississippi. Populated with cypress trees, it was just the sort of lake usually featured in horror movies. The boat ramp was deserted when we arrived, but between the four of us we were able to lower the pontoon boat into the lake and get underway.

For several hours we churned up and down the lake, talking about nothing in particular. There were no lights on the boat, but there was a partial moon and we could at least see where we were going. Every once in a while Chips would light a cigarette, the brief flicker of the lighter illuminating the faces of his perplexed passengers.

Things were going great until I decided to tell my snake story. In retrospect I should have known better, but a good story is a good story, regardless of its repercussions. When I was growing up in Mississippi, I went fishing every week with my grandfather during the summer months. This lake we went to was famous for its bluegill bream and for its plentiful supply of poisonous cottonmouth snakes. One day this girl was water skiing on the lake when the boat hit a massive bed of cottonmouths. The boat stalled in the water and the girl, screaming for help, sank into a swarm of snakes. She was pulled from the water by nervous rescuers, but she died before she reached the hospital.

After I told the story, no one said a word.

The water lapped ominously at the pontoons.

"Speaking of the devil," says Chips, pointing out across the water.

Ahead of the boat in the moonlight was the black triangular head of a cottonmouth slithering across the surface of the water with great deliberation. Suddenly, a bushy tree of lightning illuminated the sky.

"That's it," says David, shaking his head. "I want to go home."

So did everyone else.[93]

EARLY IN 1989, after spending a half day bemoaning what appeared to be a hopeless situation for Memphis music, Don Nix and I decided to start a record label. It would be named Pulsebeat Records, a spinoff from a radio syndication I co-owned. "The vast majority of the music heard on radio today can trace its roots back to Memphis," I told a newspaper reporter, then brashly added: "That makes Memphis an ideal place for an independent label. Simply put: We're going to pick up where Stax Records left off." Yeah, right.

Don's enthusiasm equaled my own. "When someone sees a record label with the word Pulsebeat on it, I want them to know they have a quality product."

For our first artist, we chose a talented Beale Street bluesman named Don McMinn. He had become a fixture on the street, where his four-piece group appeared nightly as the house band at the Rum Boogie Cafe, a popular restaurant and bar. Over the years he had recorded with an impressive assortment of artists, including John Mayall, Memphis Slim and Jerry Lee Lewis. In 1989 there was a "roots" mentality in country music. We asked him what he would think about recording a country album. He said he had always wanted to do a country album.

I asked Herbie O'Mell if we could have spec time at 3 Alarm Studio to record an album. He asked Chips, who graciously allowed us to become the first—at that point—individuals outside of himself to ever record in the studio.

For the session, we put together a solid group of local musicians, including Tommy McClure, then playing bass with Kris Kristofferson's band, drummer Greg Morrow, who played on the road with Amy Grant, keyboardist Doyle Newmyer, who played with the Memphis Symphony, and an unknown steel guitarist named Robby Turner whose mother and father had performed in Hank Williams' band back in the 1950s.. For background singers we had Chips' daughter Monique, and Becky Russell of Reba & the Portables.

Nix and I assembled a solid list of songs, including, "Black Like Me," written by Mack Gayden, Ken M. Smith, and Gary Talley, formerly of the Box Tops, "Pick a Dream," written by Larry Raspberry, formerly of the Gentrys, "If Only Your eyes Could Lie," written by Bob McDill and John Jarrad, and others. We titled the album *Pick a Dream*.

I was so impressed with Robby Turner's performance that I called Chips and suggested he drop by the studio to hear him. He did and ended up hiring him to play on an upcoming Highwaymen album. That opened other doors for Robby. He moved to Nashville and became known as one of the best steel guitar players in country music.

Chips became a frequent visitor to our sessions. He didn't say much. Mostly he sat in the rear of the control room and watched and listened. Sometimes he seemed depressed. Other times his speech was slow and somewhat distorted, indicating he was self-medicating again. Never once

300

did the manic side of his personality surface. Mostly, he sat Buddha-like.

Unfortunately, Nashville record executives didn't agree with us about the timeliness of *Pick a Dream*. There was something that grated on them about a 40-something bluesman singing country music. I met with executives from all the labels. None would pick the album up for distribution. One record executive, upon listening to the song, "Quittin' Time," frowned and asked, "What's that I hear?"

When I told him it was a saxophone, he growled, "You can't use saxophones on country music. It's just not done." Another executive bristled at "Black Like Me," a song about a young boy's struggle to understand racial discrimination: "You can't talk about things like that in country music! That's not our base!"

Pick a Dream was not released for another 25 years.

AS CHIPS WAS GETTING READY to go to Nashville in late February 1989 to record *Highwayman 2,* the second in what would be a series of three Highwaymen albums with Johnny Cash, Willie Nelson, Waylon Jennings, and Kris Kristofferson, I told him that I had received a tip from a source that a new weekly alternative newspaper, *Memphis Flyer*, was doing an article on him that my source within the newspaper staff told me was probably not going to be favorable. Because I could clearly see that he was in his manic phase, I suggested he might not want to do any interviews for a while. I could see he was not in good emotional shape. Who would be after what he had been through? He asked who I thought was being interviewed. I told him I had no idea. He responded, "I think I know who their sources are."

Going with him to the Nashville Highwaymen session was his new prized songwriter Rivers Rutherford and his "new" discovery on steel guitar Robby Turner. Also included on the session were the 827 Thomas Street Band, Mickey Raphael, Willie Nelson's harp player, with Reggie Young, Chips, Johnny Christopher, and Shawn Lane playing guitar. Lane was a highly regarded hard rock and jazz fusion guitarist from Memphis.

Chips took Rivers with him to Nashville because the song he had climbed a fence to play for him was one Chips wanted to use on the next Highwaymen album. They all met at Emerald Sound Studio on 16th Avenue South.

"Everyone got quiet when I got there," Rivers told me. "Chips told them I was a new writer of his. Glenn Campbell played two or three Jimmy Webb songs and then I played my song, 'American Remains.'"

When he finished, Kris Kristofferson said, "Well, hell, that's right up my alley."

"That was it," said Rivers. "They recorded my song with me singing the scratch vocal."

When the song ended, Johnny walked out into the studio and said he wanted to sing his part. He entered the vocal booth and began singing, but then he stopped and said he was having problems with the melody. He asked Chips to turn up the volume of Rivers' vocal on the speaker.

"The control room was packed and I was in the back behind a tree, peering through the leaves," said Rivers. "When Johnny said my name, I stood up and he saw me. Everyone grinned. Then he said, 'Why don't you just come out here and show me how to sing your song.' I got into that little booth with him. It was just Johnny and me. Johnny Cash had a way of making you feel super special. I was a kid. I didn't know my butt from a hole in the found. I didn't know how to behave. Did he really want me to help him learn the song? Or was he just being nice? He was so accommodating, a real gentleman. I was twenty-one at the time."

Rivers wasn't surprised to see all the Highwaymen present at the studio, but he was taken aback to find Glen Campbell in the studio, guitar in hand. Campbell ended up singing and playing guitar on several of the tracks. At that time, Glen Campbell and Reggie Young were considered two of the most accomplished guitar players in the country.

There were only six songs on the album by the artists themselves: "Two Stories Wide" and "Texas" by Willie; "Anthem '84" and "Living Legend" by Kris Kristofferson;" Angels Love Bad Men" by Waylon

Jennings; and "Songs that Make a Difference" by Johnny Cash. Other songs included "Silver Stallion" by Lee Clayton and "We're All in Your Corner" by Buddy Emmons and Troy Seals. Although the album was recorded in the first week of March in 1989, it was not released until February 1990. One reason for a delayed release may have been because Columbia Records had been purchased by Sony Music and the new ownership replaced Rick Blackburn, who then formed his own production company for a year or so before being hired by Atlantic Records to manage their Nashville office. Another reason could have been to give marketing enough time to organize a Highwaymen tour to promote the album.

Shortly after Chips returned to Memphis after recording the Highwaymen, he was greeted by a *Memphis Flyer* cover story with the headline "Goodbye, Mr. Chips: The City fathers brought him back to save Memphis music. But will Chips Moman just take the money and run?" *The Memphis Flyer*, which had been in business for less than eight weeks, was an alternative weekly that was owned by MM Corporation which also owned *Memphis* magazine. Principle stockholders were Jack Belz, who had by that time lost the money he had invested in America Records, and Ward Archer, whose son Ward Archer, Jr., was co-owner of Cottonwood Recording Studio, one of several recording studios in Memphis that sold studio time to hopeful musicians.

The gist of the article was that Chips had received public money from the city and was going to leave town without fulfilling his obligations under his agreement with the city. "So why did we spend our money on Chips Moman?" asked the newspaper. "And what did we get for it? The answer, some say, is 'not much.'" That was a false representation. He borrowed money from First Tennessee Bank to remodel the fire station into a recording studio. If, at the end of five years if he did not purchase the studio, he would lose that investment. Leaving with money was not an option. His options were to either repay the loan or file for bankruptcy protection. Referring to America Records, the newspaper said "the money went fast." Interviewed was one of the investors Marty Grusin, who told the newspaper the record company was "not a good deal. Some are and some aren't. But we were businessmen. We just took out losses." Incredibly, the newspaper did not disclose that there was overlap with their parent company's investors and America Records investors. Legitimate journalists call it a conflict of interest.

Finally, the newspaper stated that the "interview" done with Chips before he came to Memphis was a "plant." So, they libeled not only Chips but me as well. There was only one "interview" and that was the one I did for *The Commercial Appeal* editorial page; the truth was that I scheduled a joint interview with three Nashville producers. One producer had been the drummer in my college band. Another was a producer who had been in the news of late. Before I chose a third producer, the layout editor for the editorial pages suggested I contact Chips Moman. Not being a recording studio groupie, I had never heard of Chips Moman.

However, by the time I arrived for the interview I had thoroughly researched Moman and learned that he was a legend within the industry. The other two producers failed to meet me at Moman's studio, so he ended up being the only one interviewed; of course, the writer of the *Memphis Flyer* article David Lyons, never contacted me to find out the truth. The article was pretty much a hatchet job, written and edited by individuals who apparently had little or no knowledge of libel law.

Surprisingly, the *Memphis Flyer* made no mention of the elaborate ruse to lure Chips to Memphis, the promises made but not kept. In retrospect, the city's offer to Chips appears to have been an elaborate flim-flam scheme to set him up for a fall. At best the newspaper's story was terrible reporting; at worst the newspaper was complicit in the conspiracy.

Chips filed a lawsuit on June 2, 1989 alleging libel and defamation. He asked me if I would testify regarding my knowledge that the article was in the works. I told him I could not do that without revealing the identity of my source within the organization and that was something as a journalist I had never done and would not do in this instance. Two things have characterized my work over the years: first, I was among the first journalists to record all of my interviews, thus making it difficult for anyone to falsely claim I had misquoted them, and second, I have always protected my sources. Besides, I explained to him, the issue is not what I knew they were doing, but what they actually wrote.

I told him, in my opinion, they had violated libel law. In retrospect, I should have encouraged him to pursue a criminal conspiracy investigation into possible behind-the-scenes activities by America Records investors with M. M. Corporation. In the South, the most common instigators of libel-with-malice news stories are the owners and publishers of the newspapers or magazines whose motivation may be to settle a score, or advance a social or political agenda, not individual editors and reporters who usually are hyper-sensitive to libel. As a noted *Washington Post* reporter once sagely advised, "just follow the money." Usually, it will take you to the source of the problem.

THERE WAS NO DENYING that the *Memphis Flyer* article was damaging to Chips' Memphis efforts. But just as he had done when the column about Ringo Starr ran in *The Commercial Appeal,* he interpreted it as a sign that Memphis itself had turned against him. For that reason, that ill-thought-out and poorly researched article, was enough to turn him against Memphis. From that point on, it was just a matter of time before he left town. Indeed, why would he want to stay?

Chips and Toni separated in 1989, with her being the first to leave their Memphis home. She returned to their Nashville farm. The Memphis Dream was now officially dead, lynched by a deep well of Dark Money (just as there is a Dark Web, there are sources of Dark Money in Memphis) and a mob of failed music wannabes who had grown comfortable over the years in the button-down-collar quietness of their musical hobbies.

Experienced producers such as Bobby Manuel weren't happy about losing Memphis' newfound scrutiny from New York and Los Angeles music executives, which would all disappear when Chips left town, but at least Bobby would still hold the distinction of producing the last Number

1 record out of Memphis before the lights were turned out. That wouldn't put dinner on the table, but it would be something of which to be proud.

In the 1950s and 1960s, Chips Moman was as instrumental as Sam Phillips and Jim Stewart and Estelle Axton in making Memphis into a music city with a worldwide reputation. He returned to polish the city's image and breathe new life into the music industry—and all he got in return was a public media lynching.

As the months went by, it became obvious Ringo had no interest in furthering his relationship with Memphis—or Chips Moman. In the fall of 1989 Ringo's attorneys filed a lawsuit in Atlanta in an effort to stop Chips from releasing the album on a record label he had established in Atlanta, CRS Records. In the complaint, Ringo said he had recorded the album while on alcohol and drugs and considered it an embarrassment.

Before going to the trial in November, Chips went by to see his dentist, Dr. Gary Earhart, to have his teeth worked on, perhaps anticipating extensive media interest in the case. At the trial, Ringo testified he had not signed a formal agreement with Moman. In response, Moman's attorney said Chips would never have agreed to work with Ringo without an agreement. In one light moment, Ringo took the stand and said into the microphone: "Is it on? Are we rolling, Bob?"

There was laughter in the courtroom.

During the trial, Toni called me and asked if I would come to Atlanta to testify. I had never seen Ringo drink or use drugs in the studio, so I told her I would be happy to testify about what I had seen. Unfortunately, I could not get a taxi to the airport because of a sudden thunder storm and I missed my flight to Atlanta. I phoned Toni and told her I had rescheduled, but she said they had obtained a continuance and it would not be necessary.

In January 1990, the judge rendered his verdict. Chips was permanently barred from releasing the album and Ringo was ordered to pay Chips $74,000 for his time in recording the session. Chips had asked for $146.239. "This amount is right in line with what the expenses were and what we were ready to pay," said Starr's attorney Robert Fleming, Jr.

"The judge must have agreed that the agreement was what we said it was and enforced it accordingly."[94]

That old Memphis curse was again working its black magic.

FIRST TENNESSEE BANK filed a foreclosure lawsuit against Chips Moman in March 1990, alleging he had defaulted on more than $2 million in loans. Included were the $750,000 loan for the remodeling of the fire station, a result of the Center City Commission issuing bonds which were purchased by First Tennessee; a $425, 000 loan for his house on Waring; a $100,000 loan for Toni Wine Moman; and assorted loans for additional work at the fire station.

Chips counter sued, alleging First Tennessee had misled him about the interest rates on his loans. In a deposition for that case, Chips stated that he refused to sell his interest in the record company to Belz: "He [Belz] became quite angry. He said, 'You don't understand . . . Money is bigger than any man, and I'll break you." Chips further stated in the deposition: "As a rule, if one of the Belz family is mad at you, they all are. And basically I think that's what happened to me here in Memphis."[95] Gary Belz told a newspaper reporter that Chips' account was fiction. "I think he's giving dad more power than he has. I wouldn't waste time on vengeance, and Dad wouldn't, either."[96]

The same month that First Tennessee foreclosed on Chip's Memphis home, *Highwayman 2* was released by Columbia Records, now under the ownership of the Japanese-owned Sony Music group. Reviews were tepid, but the Highwaymen fan base was solid and kept the album in the money. The album stayed on the charts for almost a year, peaking at Number 4. Not every Highwayman was happy with it. "As an album, it could have used a little more time spent on it," said Waylon. "We ran in and out too quick, and we didn't have that one great song."[97]

Typically, Chips would put in the time necessary to find that one special, Number 1 song, but that wasn't the case in this instance. With his emotions racing up and down over his troubles in Memphis, he was preoccupied and didn't have the patience or focus to write, encourage or find a smash hit song. At the end of the recording session Chips put his arm around Robby and said, "You need to do the tour." Both Robby and Rivers were invited to join what would become a legendary tour. Chips would go along as the musical director and producer of the live recordings they planned to make.

A few weeks before they hit the road, Chips approached Robby, who played steel guitar, bass and dobro, and asked if he played mandolin.

"I've never touched one."

"Johnny Cash asked if you played mandolin because he liked the way Marty Stuart played the mandolin, and I told him you did."

"I don't have one."

"Well, you can take mine. You need to start practicing."

"I started because I had to. He told Cash, 'Yeah, he plays mandolin.'"

I thought back to the night I called Chips to hear Robby play during the recording session I co-produced with Don Nix. "Isn't he great?" I said.

Chips snapped his head around, smiling, and said, "He's a professional musician. He can play anything." I didn't know until much later that Chips had crossed paths with Robby when he played steel guitar with Ace Cannon as a teenager. Chips didn't put two and two together until later. All things considered, the world of music is a small universe.

Soon they headed out to Phoenix, Arizona, to rehearse for the tour. It was supposed to be a six-week tour, but it ended up lasting five years. As Chips and Robby entered the rehearsal facility, Chips turned to Robby and said, "You are like a son to me."

"That meant a lot," said Robby. "One of my greatest achievements is to work with Chips. What talent this man had. To me, 'Dark End of the Street' should be the dictionary definition for rhythm and blues. There was no one ever more creative than Chips. No one who could inspire you the way he does."

During the rehearsal, Johnny Cash said he wanted to do "Ragged Old Flag," a song he had recorded in 1974. "When we learned of that, I went up to Reggie Young and said, "You played banjo on a Dobie Gray song, didn't you?"

Chips chimed in with, "Robby plays banjo."

Waylon overheard that exchange and left for a few minutes and then returned with a beautiful Gibson banjo. He handed it to Robby, saying "Here's your banjo to play."

Robby ended up playing steel guitar, Dobro, mandolin, and banjo on the tour.

Of course, all of the Highwaymen had their own tour buses (Chips had a smaller Blue Bird bus), so that when you added trucks for the equipment and buses for the musicians there was a quite a caravan involved with the tour. Each of the artists' buses was a world unto itself. There was a Baptist preacher named Will Campbell that Waylon and Jessi were crazy about. Campbell was an award-winning Mississippi writer whose book *Brother to a Dragonfly* was nominated for a National Book Award. He was also a graduate of the Yale Divinity School and formerly served as the Religion-in-Life Director at the University of Mississippi. He died in 2013 at the age of eighty-eight, after providing a lifetime of guidance on the subject of race relations.

One time, right before the Highwaymen headed out on a tour date, Waylon and Jessi learned that Brother Will, as he was called, was having financial difficulties.

"If you want work," Waylon told him, "come over to the house tonight. The bus rolls at midnight."[98]

Brother Will had an undefined job title while out on tour with Waylon. He ended up taking several trips with the outlaw and the lady. When people asked Jessi why he was there, she told them he was Waylon's spiritual advisor. It was her deepest hope that Brother Will would inspire Waylon to someday stand tall for Jesus.

On one of their trips Waylon wrote a song, "I Do Believe," for the Highwaymen's third and final album. He sat Jessi and Brother Will down together and sang the song to them. The song spoke of not talking too much about one's beliefs, but being a believer in his "own way" in a "loving father" that never has to be "feared."

Jessi was thrilled by the heartfelt confessional, something she had waited a long time for, and Brother Will . . . well, he put another notch on his Bible and called it a job well done.

For Rivers Rutherford the tour offered the sort of education he could not have obtained on a college campus. "I rode on the bus with Chips for a while, then I rode with Willie for a while. I was supposed to write songs with him, but we never did. I got to see the big tour and how it worked and all the people behind it. I realized you didn't have to be a star to make a good living in the music business."

What went on behind the scenes of the tour was just as entertaining as what took place on stage in front of the audience. The 827 Thomas Street Band was the core of the touring band. Because each artist on the tour brought along his own tour manager and a musician he wanted to be part of the band, it created problems for Chips because that often put him in the position of negotiating non-negotiable decisions about sound levels. He would get a sound level that was balanced and then someone's tour manager would come along and demand that his client's guitar be turned up louder than the others, or a tour manager would demand changes in his client's microphone level.

"Each time those things were starting to pile up," recalls Robby Turner. "Chips doesn't work well under pressure. With people trying to tell him how to do his job, he'd get to a boiling point where he was ready to kill somebody or something, because usually the other person is dead wrong."

Sometimes the competitive nature of the artists themselves would take center stage. Kristofferson showed up with something that was new to the others—wireless transmitters that allowed him to roam the stage, playing and singing, while the others were glued to their microphones. Two weeks into the tour Johnny Cash got a wireless, so that soon he was spinning around the stage with Kris, like a dog chasing a cat, while Waylon and Willie looked like sticks in the mud.

"I asked Willie why he didn't go wireless," said Robby, "and he laughingly said, because the cord was the only thing that kept him on stage. Willie was one of the cleverest guys in the world. Willie and Johnny had the same sense of humor, while Kris and Waylon were total opposites."

Sometimes politics entered the equation. The most liberal member of the group, Kris had an Iraq flag hanging over his guitar when he performed. Waylon assumed it was a rag to wipe the sweat off his hands. Chips hears about this—and things start bubbling.

When he's at the microphone Kris sometimes mentioned the innocent children that were being killed in the war in Iraq. From the other end of the stage, Waylon looked at him like, what the fuck is he talking about. Kris said it again and Waylon stepped up to the microphone and blurted out, "Because we should be."

At one point, someone tells Waylon that Kris is sporting an Iraq flag in protest of the war.

"Waylon says, 'What?—what are you talking about?' said Robby. "So now the fucking war is on. Cash thinks it is funny. He supports everyone. Willie and Cash had not worked together as much. But they are egging it on. Chips knows what is happening, but he is having so many other issues he decides not to get involved. He knows Cash is having a good laugh over the whole thing. He let it go because they were all smiling. He tried to be neutral."

Finally, Waylon confronted Kris about the flag.

All of a sudden Chips was caught up in the middle of it all. Robby saw Waylon and Chips square off against one another. Waylon had his finger in Chips' face. Chips had his finger in Waylon's face. Robby was convinced they were about to get into a fist fight.

"I knew Waylon was set in his ways, but he and Chips were like brothers," said Robby.

Guitarist Reggie Young could not see them where he was seated, but he heard the commotion. He asked Robby what was going on. Robby told him they had their fingers in each other's face.

"Yeah, I know."

At one point, Chips shouts, "I'll just take my band and go home."

"I've worked with those guys for as long as you have."

"Hell, no you haven't."

Before the show began that night, Chips disappeared into the Blue Bird and sent the driver scrambling out the door. Then he drove off, leaving his engineer, David Cherry, behind to deal with the problems on the final day of the tour.

Chips cruised down the highway in the Blue Bird, no doubt chain-smoking Camel cigarettes. The "Steve McQueen of the music business" was on the road again, headed straight for Nashville in the Blue Bird equivalent of McQueen's fire-breathing Mustang in *Bullitt*.

DURING A BREAK in the Highwaymen tour in 1990, Chips returned to Memphis to deal with the rapidly accelerating demise of his Memphis dream. By then he had filed for Chapter 11 bankruptcy, lost his home to foreclosure (it was sold at auction on the steps of the county courthouse and purchased by First Tennessee Bank), and sold a majority interest in 3 Alarm Studio to a used car dealer, Will Johns. Under the terms of the sale Johns would be the studio president and Chips would be a staff producer. The studio would be operated much as the other studios in town operated in that 3 Alarm would rent the studio out to wannabe artists and producers, or record labels for the production of an album already under contract with an artist. With complete digital capability, it would be the most technologically advanced vanity recording studio in Memphis.

In the course of a lawsuit between Chips and Johns over whether Johns fully paid him for the studio and over whether Chips had removed equipment from the studio that Johns claimed he owned, Chips was ordered to return the equipment. He did not return the equipment, and when he subsequently appeared in court, the judge, Chancellor D.J. Alissandratos, held him in criminal contempt for not returning the equipment and for jumping to his feet in an outburst of emotion over the contempt citation. He was sentenced to seventy-two hours in the county jail. Moman was handcuffed and taken off to jail by a sheriff's deputy. He later complained about his accommodations, saying he was given a bloody mattress and a toilet that did not have a seat.

Chips was brought back to the courtroom the following day in handcuffs, but he not agree to return the equipment. Instead, he addressed the court: "I had a bad day. I've been involved in quite a few lawsuits lately and I'm trying to learn. I do admit I sometimes lose my temper and I apologize."

Johns' lawyers told the judge that Moman had previously grabbed Johns by the throat outside the courtroom. The judge told the lawyers to put it in writing and that could land Moman another contempt citation. Meanwhile, the judge sent him back to jail, but not before saying: "Since we're talking rock music, Mr. Moman, I might borrow from the song to remind you as you go to jail to think, 'I fought the law and the law won.'"[99] It was a reference to the hit song, "I Fought the Law," written by Sonny Curtis of the late Buddy Holly's band, the Crickets.

"Dad was in such a state of mind, I was afraid he was going to have a heart attack," said his daughter, Monique. "He was so stressed out. Him having to go to court, he was about to go over the edge. It was very serious."

Chips felt that Gary Belz was behind the attacks against him and that might have been part of it, I don't know. I accepted that view for a long while. Then I realized that Gary's problem was that he was a novice to the music industry. He believed what the local vanity studio owners told him. They convinced him that Chips should be doing what they had done for years—that is, sell studio time and "discover" new Memphis talent. The fact that they had never discovered any new talent was beside the point. Gary wanted Chips to do what they had done so that America Records could have records to release, whether they sold or not. The problem with that logic was that Chips had never rented out his studio and had seldom discovered new talent since the early days of the Gentrys. He was a "name" producer who worked with "name" artists, for the most part.

Gary Belz had a consuming blind ambition to get into the music business. He ended up leaving the family's multi-million dollar business to pursue that blind ambition, surely a decision that disappointed his father. Gary opened a recording studio named Kiva and rented it out for recording projects, including Steve Ray Vaughan's last album. After a year or so of that, he learned what Chips already knew—renting out studio time, whether to record labels or to wannabe recording artists, was not a good investment of time if the goal was to be profitable.

Belz changed the name of his studio to House of Blues and then sold it and moved to Nashville to build a House of Blues studio there. After building a couple of successful studios in Nashville he sold them and moved to California where he built studios with a partner. In time he realized he would never make hit records, but could rent out his studios to individuals who did make hit records, thus vicariously scratching the music itch for which he paid such a high price.

Chips was soon out of jail and returned to the extremely successful Highwaymen tour, Johns relinquished his interest in the studio, and the former studio ended up in foreclosure. Today the building is home to the Memphis Music Initiative, an optimistic, although probably doomed, nonprofit dedicated to using music to improve prospects for young Memphians. Music is a hard sell in Memphis, despite its glorious history.

AFTER A TIME, Rivers Rutherford left the Highwaymen tour and packed up his wife of one year and moved to Nashville in 1993. He had been signed with Chips for five years and had only one of his songs recorded, "American Remains" for the *Highwaymen 2* album.

"My song was a single, but it didn't hit," said Rivers. "With royalties and everything I think I made about $12,000 to $15,000. It wasn't life changing in that respect. It was eight years before I had another song recorded. The only thing that kept me going was, if the Highwaymen thought enough of one of my songs to record it, surely others will, too. Chips was charming but mercurial. He could cock an eyebrow and grin at you and make you feel like a million bucks. He believed in me, too. He was unique."

Early in 1993, Chips obtained a record deal for Rivers with Giant Records (an imprint of Warner). Acclaimed producer James Stroud headed up the label that was begun in 1992 as a subsidiary of Warner Records. Stroud had formerly headed up Capitol Records. Rivers was among the label's second year signees. "It started out gangbusters," said Rivers. "But Chips and Toni were having really bad problems and the whole process imploded. It was a mess. We didn't have much to play for them."

The recordings were made at Chips' studio at his farm in Nolensville, just outside Nashville. Toni wrote some of the songs, Chips and Rivers wrote others. It began guns blazing with Reggie Young on guitar, Bobby Emmons on keyboards. Robby Turner on bass and steel guitar. It was the first new artist Chips had worked with in a while.

Unfortunately, the building of the album coincided with the dissolution of Chips' marriage to Toni Wine. What had a good beginning in the studio soon descended into foot-dragging lethargy as Chips devoted more and more time to depositions and court hearings in a divorce that ultimately lasted four years. There came a point when the recording session came to a complete halt. Days went by with nothing happening, creating more and more distress for Rivers.

Finally, he pleaded with Robby, who had producers' credits of his own, to book time in Chips' studio to produce new tracks. The goal was not to subvert Chips' efforts, but to get him back in the saddle again.

"I went along with it because I really wanted to see Chips get back working again," explained Robby. "He was going through craziness with the divorce and was in a non-creative dark place in his life. He'd call me to come out or I would just show up to hang out with him, hoping to see that twinkle in his eyes he always got while he was working on an album."

The ploy worked. After watching Robby and Rivers working on

several tracks, Chips sprang back to life and resumed work on the project. Robby returned to work as a musician on the project. In no time, Chips' magical eyes were again twinkling.

Finally, the album was completed and Chips invited Stroud out to the farm to listen to the tracks. Unknown to Chips, Stroud was feeling the heat from Warner Brothers. Although Giant's first country release by artist Dennis Robbins did well and Stroud had experienced success with a self-titled album with Clay Walker, there were corporate doubts about the future of the country music division of Giant Records.

Stroud respectfully listened to Rivers' album, and then delivered the bad news: He rejected the album and explained that River's cancellation was only one of almost a dozen that he was going to have to cut loose. Within a year, Stroud himself would be cut by Warner. He would quickly land on his feet as president of Dreamworks' Nashville record label. Giant would continue without Stroud at the helm and find success with Clay Walker and newcomer Blake Shelton, but by 2001 Giant ceased to exist when its roster was absorbed by Warner Records.

By that point, Chips was devastated by his run of bad luck. Nothing was going right for him. Not in his personal life or his professional life. He doubted he would ever record another album.

"He called me out to his house and said, 'I don't know how much more I can help you as an artist,'" said Rivers. "He didn't offer me any explanation. I don't know if he lost interest or what. I said, 'Well, I would like out of my publishing deal, the one we signed in 1988.'"

Rivers took Chips comments as a rejection of his potential as an artist. I don't think Chips meant it that way at all. I think his comments were an admission that he felt he was washed up, unable to help anyone. Like most bipolar individuals, Chips obsessed over things he couldn't control—like letting people down. He constantly worried that people would think he had let them down. I can't tell you how many times he asked me in 1985, before he returned to Memphis, "What if I let everyone down?" It was something he often obsessed about.

No one knows what was going through Chips' mind over the Giant Records' rejection. He and Toni were not really on speaking terms during that period, and if he was seeing Jane at that time, it is unlikely he asked her opinion about his business affairs. He did not easily share his feelings. He probably thought that with all his experience he should have seen that Giant records was in trouble. He likely blamed himself for not seeing it coming. After almost forty years of record deals, this would prove to be Chips' next-to-last recording of his career for a record label.

Chips no doubt saw the disappointment in Rivers' eyes when they spoke. Chips had built his career on having a top-notch studio band and on building a stable of hit-making songwriters. In Rivers, Chips saw another Mark James—one of his most successful songwriters—which was why after telling Rivers he could do nothing more for him as an artist, he did not immediately offer to release Rivers from his songwriting contract. He always felt there would be another big deal just around the corner. There always had been.

All that Rivers knew was that he had a wife and two children and he felt desperate. "I was going under and I called him and left a message that I needed to hear from him," Rivers said. "I explained I was helping my sister move to Florida and I was in a motel in Florida. He called me the next morning. We finally came to an agreement and I later met Toni at a Nashville restaurant and she gave me a piece of paper saying they were releasing me from the publishing agreement. Chips was brilliant, but he was volatile and had his own demons."

By that time, no doubt Chips was eager to release Rivers from the contract. He had enough stress in his life. He was hemorrhaging relationships like a gored matador.

The next day Rivers signed with Universal Publishing. In 2019 Rivers was inducted in the Nashville Songwriter's Hall of Fame, thus confirming Chips' initial assessment of his writing ability. Cited were hits such as "Shut Up And Drive" by Chely Wright, "If You Ever Stop Loving Me" by Montgomery Gentry, "Ladies Love Country Boys" by Trace Adkins,

"Living In Fast Forward" by Kenny Chesney, "Real Good Man" by Tim McGraw, and "When I Get Where I'm Going" by Brad Paisley with Dolly Parton. His co-written song "Ain't Nothing 'Bout You" by Brooks & Dunn was named the 2002 ASCAP Country Song of the Year. Rivers was named 2006 ASCAP Country Songwriter of the Year. By then he had exceeded the hit song output of his mentor, Chips Moman, and shown himself to be, along with Robby Turner, one of the two biggest successes Chips took away from his disastrous return to Memphis in 1985.

Suddenly, Chips found himself staring into an end-of-life abyss.

Sadly the worst was yet to come.

Chips with his father back on the farm in Georgia
Photo courtesy of Monique Moman

CHAPTER 10
The Final Years
(1995-2016)

AS SO MANY HAD DONE BEFORE ME, I loaded a truck in 1994 with my possessions and headed east to Nashville to freelance for magazines. I left behind a handful of friends and a pair of burned-out dreams. Looking in my rear-view mirror, I surveyed the Memphis skyline one last time. I hoped the last one to leave would remember to turn out the lights. *A woman clothed with the sun, the moon under her feet.*[100] Yes, I now understood.

Once I got settled in Nashville, I gave Chips a call. We talked about getting together, but it was a year before I actually made it out to his farm. I called in the spring of 1995. Toni answered the phone and said Chips didn't live at the house anymore. They were getting a divorce. He had built a studio out on the farm and was living at the studio. She gave me his number. I called and Chips told me to come on out. He'd like to see me.

He wasn't there when I arrived, but Monique and her boyfriend, Kim, were at the studio, along with Rivers Rutherford, the talented singer/songwriter Chips had discovered in Memphis. Chips had been working with Rivers. I had only been there a few minutes when Chips drove up. It was good to see him again. Though I had talked to him several times over the years, I had only seen him once since he left Memphis. He looked older, somewhat tired, but he still had the old Moman magic about him. It is said actor Robert Duvall, with whom Chips once worked on an album, used Chips as a model for characters he subsequently portrayed in movies. I believe that because I see many of Chips' mannerisms in the character of Gus McCrae that Duvall depicted in *Lonesome Dove* and in Mac Sledge in *Tender Mercies*, for which he asked for Chips' approval.

Chips played me the material he had been recording on Rivers, plus some things he had recorded with Monique. Other than working with family and friends, he didn't want to make any more records. Music just wasn't fun anymore like it used to be.

Monique went to the store and came back with a mess of ground beef. We cooked out on the grill, talked about the weather and some of the good times we had in Memphis, but we danced around the nightmare part of it.

"I took everything they threw at me," Chips said finally, shaking his head in a way that let me know his self-respect had not been pounded out of him. Chips was as surely a victim of the Memphis Curse, as Elvis and Stax had been—and Lord knows how many innocent passersby who may have first entered Memphis on country roads—but he was just as much a victim of his own fierce attraction to the musical cauldron that had simmered in Memphis for nearly a century. It was that particular witch's brew that has made Memphis unique. A man is not just what he carries inside himself, he is what others project onto him or steal from him or cajole from him with praise or money or cocaine or illicit sex.

While I was at the farm, Casey came in from school. He had grown into a handsome young man. He has his mother's face and his father's walk. He wants a career in music, but Memphis is a subject he won't discuss. He tossed his school books into a chair, ready for his dad to crank up the studio. What are we waiting for, his impatient glances asked?

Before I left, Chips and I went for a drive in my Miata, with the top down. Chips had owned a Triumph in the early days in Memphis. He wanted to see if the Miata drove like his Triumph. We sped up and down the hilly countryside with Chips at the wheel, him pushing the car to the max, zipping past the farms and dirt roads, making the gearbox whine, skating around the curves, me clinging to the door latch. The sun slanted across the highway, distorting the shadows that danced over the potholes in the road. The cool, spring wind whipped against our faces. The sun shone brightly. Time stood still. It was a good way to end a day. Back at the farm, Chips got out of the car and I never saw him again.

Chips' divorce would take four years to complete, with Chips clawing and scratching every step of the way. Finally, the divorce was finalized in 1999, much to the relief of the judge hearing the case, prompting Chips to pack up and leave for LaGrange, Georgia, with a one-way ticket in his back pocket. He took his studio equipment with him and Casey tagged along to help his father set up yet another working studio.

CHIPS' ELEVEN-YEAR LIBEL LAWSUIT against the *Memphis Flyer* finally was resolved in 2000 when the newspaper offered Chips a settlement, prompting the presiding judge in Memphis to dismiss the case with prejudice, meaning Chips could not file another lawsuit on the same issue. In his order, the judge noted that the parties had compromised and settled.[101] M.M. Corporation, doing business as the *Memphis Flyer* never publicly admitted it had libeled Chips, but under the non-disclosure terms of the settlement the conclusion of the case was held "within the bosom of the client," meaning Chips and the *Memphis Flyer* agreed to never disclose details of the settlement. And Chips honored that agreement, taking details of his victory to his grave.

Whether by political influence, payoffs, or bureaucratic inertia, the case files were buried in the archives vault of the courthouse, hidden away from the public. What the litigants didn't figure on was an investigative reporter, who also had been libeled by the weekly newspaper, who was dedicated to resurrecting the truth.

In sending the original case back to Shelby County, the Tennessee Appeals Court highlighted the following exchange between H. David Lyons, the writer of the *Memphis Flyer* article, and Chips' attorney, as a reason for finding in Chips Moman's favor and remanding the case back to Shelby County for resolution:

Q: Well, how much of it that you published did you receive or you think was true and how much did you think was not true?

A: I don't try to make a judgment on that.

Q: Anything in that article that you wrote that you thought when you wrote it was not true?

A: It is not my prerogative to determine what is true and what isn't.

Q: Would the truth or falsity of the information enter into whether or not it is newsworthy?

A: If I understand the question correctly, I don't think that the truth or falsity of an item affects its newsworthiness. It would be newsworthy either way.

Q: Are you saying that an item is newsworthy, in your opinion, in accordance with your definition, if it is false?

A: It would certainly be raised.

Q: A fact known to you to be false, do you consider that newsworthy?

A: Yes.

"I seems obvious that Lyons did not care whether the statements he published were true or false," responded the Appeals Court. "We believe that this shows reckless disregard of whether the article was true or false."

M.M. Corporation was assessed the costs of the appeal.[102]

Bruce W. Sanford, an authority on media law, has written: "Generally speaking, truth is a complete defense—it will totally bar the plaintiff from recovery. Therefore, the best safeguard against a libel suit is to make certain before publication that any potentially libelous statement is true and, even more importantly, can be proven true."[103]

Truth very much matters in journalism.

Shortly after the dismissal of the case, M.M. Corporation was dissolved. A new corporation, Contemporary Media, Inc., was created to continue the publication of both *Memphis* magazine and the *Memphis Flyer*, hopefully with the intent of pursuing honest journalism. The issues I have seen in recent years have been impressive for their heightened level of professionalism. Clearly, editors learned a lesson from the experience.

However, in all my years as a journalist, this libel case represents one of the most egregious violations of journalist ethics I have ever witnessed. When the newspaper presented a headline on the front page that asked the question, "Will Chips Moman just take the money and run?" it was incumbent upon the publication to answer the question in a definitive manner. Instead it offered a "he said, he said" story that left the reader

Chips with his daughter Monique on the occasion of her marriage in 2006
Photo courtesy Monique Moman

concluding that wrongdoing must have been involved, *wink, wink*. Left to defend the libel in court the newspaper was unable to muster the only defense there is for a charge of libel—the truth. Furthermore, their defense was destroyed by a writer who did not, upon questioning, display an appreciation of the importance of the truth.

Newspapers and magazines that do not value truth above all else are unacceptable guardians of the First Amendment. In this instance, not only did the newspaper cripple the career of one of America's greatest record producers, it doomed any possibility of a music revival in the City of Memphis. When you beat the life out of a person or idea, it is more likely than not to remain dead, at least until the Second Coming.

IN 2000 CHIPS MARRIED a local LaGrange woman named Jane he had been seeing for several years, using the name Lincoln Moman. He moved in with Jane for a while, then they bought a house on West Point Lake close to the Moman farm. Shortly after they were married, the man formerly known as Chips and the woman named Jane went to Memphis to have lunch with his old friend Herbie O'Mell and introduce him to Jane. Ironically, Herbie died on Chips' birthday, June 12, 2019, thus ensuring that the two would be linked for all eternity. Herbie was eighty-two.

Interestingly, Jane didn't know about her husband's music background until later. However, when she learned of his many accomplishments, she was unimpressed because she was a British Invasion fan (the Beatles, Rolling Stones, etc.) and never listened to the influential artists with whom Chips had worked. As a matter of fact, by all accounts, music never became a part of their marriage. They seldom turned on the radio or listened to the stereo. I doubt he ever took her dancing. She allowed him to be the person he wanted to be. She had a daughter and grandchildren from a previous marriage, but they were never told of Chips' fame as a record producer. They accepted him for what he was—a friendly man with an engaging smile who often wore farmers' overalls at home and around town.

It must have come as a shock to Jane in 2007, when Chips notified her that he was going to Nashville to record an album with B.J. Thomas and the 827 Thomas Street Band. He didn't have a contract from a record label to do the album—sadly, those days were over—but he enticed Thomas and the band by agreeing that the royalties should be shared equally. They would each invest time in the project and hope it would be picked up by a major label. Of all the people that Chips recorded with over the years, it was Thomas with whom he had the most ups and downs, but also the most success. When the two men were in sync they were an unbeatable duo.

For this session, Chips made an arrangement with a studio owner he had worked with before to allow them to come in every day to work like they used to in Memphis when they cut all the hits.

"We cut every day with the guys," said Thomas. "Everyone was committed to doing it—and we had some great stuff."

Chips and Bobby Emmons worked on songs, as did other members of the band. The only song Thomas wrote that they recorded was a re-take on his "Hands on Me Again." In all they recorded about a dozen songs. Unfortunately, before the session could be wrapped, the studio owner booked time for Kenny Chesney to come in and record vocals. Chips and friends were unceremoniously booted out.

"Chips and the studio owner had a serious falling out," said Thomas. "Chips was upset. He just wasn't right. Everything just seemed to be off."

Chips was in one of his manic phases, and self-medicating as usual.

"That led me and Chips to sit down and talk," said Thomas. "We had had problems before. It wasn't like a relationship ending thing, but we needed a break."

The session ended abruptly, with everyone heading out in different directions. The album apparently was never pitched to a record label because of misunderstandings over percentages and ended up in Chips' tape vault with many other unfinished projects.

Thomas, the boys in the band, all had their individual thoughts on what was wrong with Chips. They never labelled those problems. They only recognized and acknowledged the behaviors that made him impossible to be around. In the early days, Chips was either depressed or he was extremely talkative or excitable. When he wrote songs he was usually in a depressed or exhausted state. He once told me he couldn't write a decent song unless he was too tired to do anything else. However, when he wore his producer's hat he couldn't afford to be down or tired. In the studio, dealing with a band and a vocalist, he needed to be at the top of his game. People who had known him a long time said it was in Memphis that he first turned to cocaine to maintain his manic phase.

Not long after the studio blowup, he contacted B.J. Thomas and the 827 Thomas Street Band and asked if they would come to LaGrange to put on a benefit concert to raise money for the local sheriff. They all agreed. The show went well. They performed a lot of Elvis Presley material and songs Thomas had recorded with the band, but when Chips got on stage to participate in a segment that featured songwriters, he was unable to remember the lyrics of the songs he had written.

It must have come as a second shock to Jane, following the B. J. Thomas session, when Chips told her that he was going to bring Willie Nelson, George Jones, Hank Williams, Jr. and Merle Haggard to Georgia to record another Highwaymen-type album for Lost Highway Records. The commission for the album, issued by legendary label head Luke Lewis, a free spirit who was known for riding about Nashville on an Indian motorcycle, would prove to be Chips' final record deal with a major label. The deal was put together by Willie's manager, Mark Rothbaum, and financed by the late billionaire film producer Steve Bing of California. Bing showed up for at least one of the sessions and impressed everyone as an engaging person who was greatly interested in the music. Sadly, by 2020 it became clear that he was suffering from depression. That year he ended his life by leaping from a high-rise residential building.

Chips recorded numerous songs with Willie, but when it came George Jones's time, he had a difficult time learning the melody and he just couldn't get the notes out because of his deteriorating voice. Chips spent several hours trying to get vocals from him, but to no avail. He got nothing usable from George. Subsequently, Jerry Lee Lewis showed up for one track and then he was gone. By that time Chips was falling asleep at inappropriate times while holding a burning cigarette. Everyone was fearful he would end up burning the studio down. Formerly luminous with self-confidence, he was now a faded portrait of himself. Someone had to watch him at all times so they could slip the burning cigarette from his fingers, lest it burn his flesh. His musical wisdom was invisible not just to himself but also to those around him who believed in him and his legend.

After about two weeks, Chips' dream of another Number 1 Highwaymen-type album ended with two songs that the record label included with others on Willie's compilation album titled *Lost Highway*. Chips' songs were "Superman" and "Both ends of Goodbye." It proved to be Chips' last hurrah.

It was at around that time Chips' health began to seriously fail. He had a stroke in 2008. He entered a rehabilitation center and they were able to bring him along to where he could do things for himself such as making his own sandwich. What the rehab professionals could not do was restore his ability to play his guitar. That he could not do that took a mental toll on him. By then he was confined to a wheelchair and dependent upon others for the basics of life.

In the summer of 2014, Chips Moman and the 827 Thomas Street Band went to Memphis for the unveiling of a Shelby County historical marker near the site of the former American Sound Recording Studio. The building that had housed the studio was torn down in the late 1980s while Chips was going through his legal difficulties in Memphis.

Chips attended the ceremony in a wheelchair. Seated next to him were members of his band: Reggie Young, Gene Chrisman, Bobby Wood, and Bobby Emmons. Mike Leech was not in attendance. In recent years Leach had created a stir, not to mention headlines, when his wife turned him in to police for possessing child pornography on his computer. He was convicted and spent some time in prison. When he was released, he found it difficult to resume his career as a musician.

The smile on Chips' face indicated that the marker had provided him with a measure of closure on Memphis. Chips returned to the tranquility of LaGrange, Georgia, only to have his life shattered a year later when he received news that his friend and songwriting partner of nearly fifty years, Bobby Emmons, had passed away. That was probably the last thing Chips expected. He was close to all the members of the 827 Thomas Street Band, with the exception of one, but his relationship with Bobby was particularly close because of the songwriting they did together, an intensely personal process that involved considerable sharing of emotions.

A distraught Chips Moman was driven to Nashville for the funeral service at the Williamson Memorial Funeral Home. When he arrived his wheelchair was placed at the end of a row. He looked around the room and saw Toni and Casey, his daughter Monique, Reggie Young, Bobby Wood, Gene Chrisman. Robby Turner and others he recognized. He had only been there a few minutes—the service was about to begin—when Mike Leech walked in and approached Chips with his hand out, prompting Chips to angrily struggle to get to his feet.

"Don't you fucking touch me," screamed Chips, struggling to maintain his balance. "I'm going to knock your head off."

Mike was stunned. Everyone was looking in their direction. Attracting attention in public is the last thing a convicted pedophile wants to do. He stepped back and faded out of sight as someone hurriedly took control of Chips' wheelchair and pushed him outside to his vehicle and helped him get inside. Moments later Monique and Casey hurried out to the vehicle to see about him. Chips told his children he was fine, but wanted to be left alone.

Chips' emotional reaction to coming face-to-face with Leech should have surprised no one. There could be no greater betrayal of Chips' musical "family" values than an attraction to children. Like the flickering points of light inside a movie projection room of his youth, memory bursts must have rushed through his brain. *Did I ever leave Casey alone with him? Did he ever say anything inappropriate to Casey when I was not around?* No one would fault Chips for asking himself, *How did this, too, become my failure?* He was in his Seventies now. Everything around him seemed to be collapsing like weather-worn planking in a barn, leaving him with a dusty taste in his mouth.

After a while Robby Turner walked out to the vehicle and got inside to talk to Chips. He told him that Mike had left the funeral home.

"We are all hurting," said Robby, referring to Bobby Emmons' death. "Don't you feel like a part of you is gone?"

"Yes, a big part is gone."

"Let's focus on healing."

They talked for a while, mostly about the old times they shared. Then Robby asked Chips if he wanted him to help him inside. Chips said yes. Robby got out of the vehicle, reached in, and lifted Chips into his arms and carried him to the door of the funeral home. He helped him stand and then walked him over to the table where Reggie, Toni and others were seated.

Later, he carried him back to the vehicle and helped him get inside. At that point, Chips put his arm around his neck and said "thank you . . . I have a lot of peace now that I didn't have."

Robby cried, later explaining, "I loved him."

The following year, Chips developed serious respiratory problems, the result of a lifetime of smoking unfiltered Camels. Once the situation became hopeless he was placed first in a nursing home and then in a hospice in LaGrange. A broken man at the end, he dreaded the inevitable. Sometimes he was fearful of the unknown. Other times he was willing to turn loose of the past and just let it be. In the end, he played the hand he was dealt.

Throughout his life he struggled with his relationships with his children, always welcoming them, loving them, and including them in his work, but sometimes he was uncertain of the relevance of their lives to his.

By the time the music had left his body and his weary heart had ceased beating, it had come down to two of his three wives and both children, moving in and out of his life like floating shadows. Among his recurring last words were plaintive requests that he not be left alone.

The last few weeks of his life he was in and out of consciousness. There were no music legends in attendance on June 13, the day after his birthday, when Chips passed over to wherever Elvis Presley, John Lennon and Jimi Hendrix reside. There were only the four people most important to him: his wife Jane, his ex-wife Toni Wine and their son, Casey; and his daughter, Monique, from his first marriage.

If Chips was depressed at the end of his life, it should not come as a startling revelation. A sense of melancholy was the driving force in his music and it enabled him to communicate with people in a way he was unable to do conversationally, touching their hearts through his music with his understanding of their innermost feelings about love lost and found.

Clearly, the time has come for Chips Moman to be inducted in both the Rock 'n' Roll Hall of Fame and the Country Music Hall of Fame. Already inducted into the Rock 'n' Roll Hall of Fame are Phil Spector, Quincy Jones, Jerry Wexler, and Jim Stewart. In the Country Music Hall of Fame are Jack Clement, Sam Phillips, Billy Sherrill, Chet Atkins, and Owen Bradley.

One of the most famous movie lines in history occurred at the end of the film *King Kong*, when machinegun-firing airplanes toppled the giant gorilla from the Empire State Building:

"It wasn't airplanes . . . it was beauty that killed the beast."

In Chips Moman's case, it wasn't the famed producer "taking the money and running," as the *Memphis Flyer* falsely editorialized in a headline that asked a question that was tantamount to a declaration, that had the effect of killing Memphis music; it was the jealousy among his wannabe peers in Memphis that slandered and media-lynched a great man and destroyed any chance Memphis music could ever again rise from the ashes of its self-destruction.

Chips Moman gave the world a new way of recording music that opened the door to pop artists and rock bands throughout the 1960s, 1970s, and 1980s to discover innovative ways of layering and recording music and expanding the possibilities for new expressions of their creativity. By applying what he had learned in Memphis he transformed country music by opening the door for greater success for country artists, especially female artists.

What he did in the studio in the 1960s with Sandy Posey made it possible for female artists such as Shania Twain and Faith Hill, then later Taylor Swift, to achieve great success as crossover artists. No one in country music ever even dreamed about recording platinum albums with solo country artists until Chips proved it could be done. America has produced a number of great record producers, but only one who can be considered an authentic genius in most musical genres. His name is Chips Moman and he lived the American Dream for sixty-five years, even when it occasionally dragged him kicking and screaming into a raging nightmare.

The chaos of his personal life ended with his death, but the beauty of his musical creations, baptized in a fiery cauldron of emotional surrender, will endure past the point of no return, and will live on forever.

THE END

Acknowledgments

The author would like to thank his extraordinary mother, Juanita Dickerson Caldwell, who passed away during the writing of this book at the age of 98 years. No one ever had a finer, more loving mother. Not until two years ago did he realize it was her lifelong dream to become a writer. He helped edit her first and only book, *Miss Juanita's Delta Cuisine.* The author also would like to thank photographer Dave Darnell, who did not accompany the author on his first interview with Chips Moman, but did so on several subsequent interviews; his editor at *The Commercial Appeal*, the late Michael Grehl, Don Nix for is long friendship, Scotty Moore for his support and friendship, the late Jack Clement for sharing his memories, Petula Clark for her stimulating and funny conversation, Dionne Warwick for her engaging memories, B.J. Thomas for his insight and memories, Johnny Cash for is friendship and support of *Nine-O-One* Magazine, Toni Wine for her friendship and coconut macaroons, Monique Moman for sharing her memories and photos, the late Rick Blackburn for his open door policy at CBS Records, Carl Perkins for being so damn entertaining, Bobby Manuel for his insights and studio experience, the late Estelle Axton for her frank honesty and lively lunch conversation, Robby Turner, Rivers Rutherford, Reggie Young, the members of the James L. Dickerson Literary Trust, and perhaps most of all, Chips Moman for his friendship and insight into the music industry.

SOURCE NOTES

INTERVIEWS

Chips Moman (1984-1989, 1995; 2001: studio sessions, home visits, dinners, outings, etc.), Toni Wine Moman (1984-1989), Monique Moman, Abraham Lincoln Moman and Mildred Moman, Johnny Cash, June Carter Cash, Waylon Jennings, Jessi Colter, Willie Nelson, Petula Clark, Dionne Warwick, B.J. Thomas, Sandy Posey, Gary Walker, Jack Clement, Reggie Young. Gene Chrisman, Bobby Wood, Bobby Emmons, Mike Leach, Phillip Rauls, Don Nix, Scotty Moore, Rick Blackburn, Estelle Axton, Bobby Manuel, Rivers Rutherford, Robby Turner, Carl Perkins, Jerry Lee Lewis, Sam Phillips, Carla Thomas, Rufus Thomas, David Porter, Sam Shoup, Dick Hackett, Ron Terry, John Evans, Bobby Womack, Ringo Starr, and the incomparable Herbie O'Mell and his wife Laura.

BOOKS

Barlett, Karen. *Dusty: An Intimate Portrait of a Musical Legen*d, Lesser Gods Books, 2017.

Bronson, Fred. *The Billboard Book of Number One Hits*, Billboard, 1985.

Brown, Mick. *Tearing Down the Wall of Sound: The Rise and Fall of Phil Spector*, Vintage, 2007.

Burnette, Billy. *Crazy Like Me*, self-published, 2013.

Colter, Jessi. *An Outlaw and a Lady: A Memoir of Music, Life with Waylon, and the Faith that Brought Me Home*, Nelson Books, 2017.

Dickerson, James L. *Goin' Back to Memphis: A Century of Blues, Rock 'n' Roll and Glorious Soul,* Simon & Schuster/Schirmer, 1996. (Subsequently republished as *Memphis Going Down*, Sartoris Literary,

2013).

--------------- *Coming Home: 21 Conversations about Memphis Music*, The Commercial Appeal-Scripps Howard, 1985.

Fletcher, Tony. *In the Midnight Hour: The Life and Soul of Wilson Pickett*, Oxford University Press, 2017.

Grossman, Alan, Bill Truman and Roy Oki Yamanka. *Diamond: A Biography*, Contemporary Books, 1987.

Guralnick, Peter. *Sweet Soul Music: Rhythm and Blues and the Southern Dream of Freedom*, 1986.

Harkins, John E. *Metropolis of the American Nile*, Guild Bindery Press, 1991.

Hill, Robert. *Johnny Cash: The Life*, Little, Brown and Company, 2013.

Howard, David N. *Sonic Alchemy: Visionary Music Producers and Their Maverick Recordings*, Hal-Leonard, 2014.

Jennings, Waylon with Lenny Kaye. *Waylon: An Autobiography*, Chicago Review Press, 1996.

Jones, Booker T. *Time is Tight: My Life, Note By Note*, Little Brown, 2019.

Jones, Roben. "Memphis Boys: The Story of American Studios," University Press of Mississippi, 2010.

Kon, Andrea. *This is My Song: A Biography of Petula Clark*, W.H. Allen, 1983.

Mansfield, Brian and Gary Graff, editors. *Country: The Essential Album Guide*, Visible Ink, 1997.Ivis

Moore, Scotty as told to James L. Dickerson. *That's Alright Elvis: The Untold Story of Elvis's First Guitarist and Manager, Scotty Moore*, Simon & Schuster/Schirmer, 1997.

Nix, Don. *Memphis Man: Living High, Laying Low*, Sartoris Literary, 2015

Stambler, Irwin and Grelun Landon. *Country Music: The*

Encyclopedia, St. Martins's Griffin, 1969-19997.

Thomas, B.J. with Jerry B. Jenkins. *Home Where I Belong*, Word Press, 1978.

McDonough, Jimmy. *Tammy Wynette: Tragic Country Queen*, Viking, 2010.

McAleer, Dave. *Hit Singles: Top Twenty Charts from 1954 to the Present Day*, Miller Freeman, 1994.

Nelson, Willie with David Fritz. *It's a Long Story: My Life,* Little, Brown and Company, 2015.

Vanhecke, Susan. *Race with the Devil: Gene Vincent's Life in the Fast Lane*, St. Martins's Press, 1968.

Warwick, Dionne with David Freeman Wooley. *My Life as I See It: An Autobiography*, Atria Books, 2010.
Wexler, Jerry and David Ritz. *A Life in Rhythm & the Blues*, St. Martin's Press, 1993.
Womack, Bobby. *Bobby Womack: My Story,* John Blake, 2006.
Zanes, Warren. Dusty in Memphis, Bloomsbury Academic, 2007.

ARTICLES

Beifuss, John. "Mar chers Criticize Column, Reporting on Memphis Music," *The Commercial Appeal*, March 11, 1987.
Burch, Barbara A. "Record Producer Bringing His Music Home to Memphis," *The Commercial Appeal*, April 6, 1985.
Burk, Bill. "Memphis Music Forecasts," *Memphis Press-Scimitar* , April 14, 1979.
Buser, Lawrence. "Bank Sues Moman, Alleges Loan Default," The Commercial Appeal, March 30, 1990.
--------------- "Moman Sent to Jail for Contempt in Dispute over Studio Property," *The Commercial Appeal*, November 27, 1990.

Cortese, James. "Sandy Finds a Song: 'It Sounds like Me,'" *The Commercial Appeal*, November 26, 1967.

Darnell, Tim. "Atlanta Crackers, *New Georgia Encyclopedia.*

Dickerson, James L. Dickerson, James L. "Hackett Alters Proposal for Producers of Records, The Commercial Appeal, November 29, 1985.
---------------"Top Publisher Follows Moman's Piper's Song, *The Commercial Appeal.*
--------------- "Class of '55 Goes Out to Play," *The Commercial Appeal.*
--------------- "Investors Expect 'New Beginning' for City's Music," The Commercial Appeal, February 20, 1986.
--------------- 'Aspiring Musicians Beat a Hopeful Path to Publishing Office as Moman Moves In," The Commercial Appeal, August 26, 1985.
--------------- "Lyrical Line from Judge Puts Moman Back in Jail," *The Commercial Appeal*, December 5, 1990.
--------------- "901 Interview: Ron Wood," *Nine-O-One-Network*, September-October 1986.
--------------- "Perkins & Friends," *Nine-O-One Network*, September-October 1986.
--------------- "Together Again," *Nine-O-One Network*, November-December 1986.
--------------- "Willie Nelson: Going After the Album That's Always on His Mind," *Nine-O-One Network*, April 1988.
--------------- "The Music Man," *Mid-South Magazine*, May 5, 1985.
--------------- "Memphis is Getting Groovier," The Commercial Appeal, December 28, 1985.
--------------- "Waylon at Ease," *The Commercial Appeal*, July 19, 1986.
--------------- "901 Interview: Rick Blackburn," *Nine-O-One Network*, January-February 1987.
--------------- "An Interview with Chips Moman," NineO-One Network,
--------------- "Sun Records reunion: Together Again in Memphis," *Nine-O-One Network*, first edition 1986.
Dries, Bill. "Lease on Former Three Alarm Studio in Foreclosure Again," *Daily News*, September 16, 2011.

Flans, Robyn. "Gene Chrisman," Modern Drummer.
Flynn, Brown Alan. "Petula Says Working here Is 'Like Having a Party,' Memphis Press-Scimitar, February 25, 1970.

Grimes, William. "Chips Moman, Hit-Making Producer and Songwriter, Dies at 79," *The New York Times*, June 14, 2016.

Hudak, Joseph. "The Highwaymen Live," Rolling Stone, May 5, 2010.
Hurt, Edd. "Chips Moman: The Cream Interview," *Nashville Scene*, August 17, 2012.

Johnson, Robert, "Memphis Recording Studios Are Turning Out Hits," *The Commercial Appeal*, April, 8, 1967.
--------------- "The Story Behind the Memphis Sound," *Memphis Press-Scimitar,* September 29, 1967.
--------------- "Petula Likes Memphis Sound—Hopes to Record Second Album," *Memphis Press-Scimitar,* May 20, 1970.

Kaye, Elizabeth. *Rolling Stone,* 1985.

Lee, Mary Anne. "Dionne Warwick to Headquarter Here," *Memphis Press-Scimitar,* September 8, 1972.

Lewis, Dr. Selma. "Baron Hirsch Synagogue to Honor Philip Belz," Southern Jewish Heritage, Winter 1993.
Lollar, Michael. "Moman: Memphis Firms Let Him Down," *The Commercial Appeal,* December 10, 1990.
Lyons, David. "Goodbye Mr. Chips, " *Memphis Flyer*, April 6-12, 1989.

Maxey, Ron. "Momans Lose Home, Say Goodbye to Memphis," *The Commercial Appeal*, May 23, 1990.
Morgan, Kay. "A New Memphis Sound," Memphis Press-Simitar, January 5, 1968.

Reese, Dan. "Chips Moman Lets Songwriters Go, Files Countersuits," *Memphis Business Journal*, September 1987.
Risher, Wayne. "New Life for 3 Alarm Studio," *The Commercial*

Appeal, July 19, 2017.

Roberts, Jeremy. "Back When Memphis Was Electric," (publicatlion unknown), January 2, 2017.

Stuart, Bill. "Heroes" (a review), *Nine-O-One Network*, September-October 1986.

Timms, Linda. "Repossessed" (a review), *Nine-O-One Network*, March-April 1987.

Washington, Pearl. "Video Memphis," *The Commercial Appeal*, June 12, 1986.

DOCUMENTS

Lincoln W. (Chips) Moman
v.
MM Corporation, d/b/a The Memphis Flyer
No. 29502-6T.D.
Circuit Court of Tennessee for the Thirtieth Judicial District at Memphis

Lilncoln W. (Chips) Moman
Vs.
M.M. Corporation, d/b/a The Memphis Flyer
The Court of Appeals of Tennessee, Western Section at Jackson
C.A. No. 02A01-9608-CV 00182

ENDNOTES

NOTE: Quotations without attribution are from interviews conducted by the author. He has used the phrase "told to me" on occasion.

[1] Tim Darnell, "Atlanta Crackers, *New Georgia Encyclopedia.*
[2] LaGrange, Georgia. Wikipedia.org.
[3] Lewis, Dr. Selma. "Baron Hirsch Synagogue to Honor Philip Belz," *Southern Jewish Heritage,* Winter 1993.
[4] Scotty Moore, *That's Alright, Elvis.*
[5] Fanelli, Damian. *Guitar World*, August 2, 2015
[6] Don Nix, *Memphis Man.*
[7] Linda Seida, allmusic.com
[8] Peter Guralnick, *Sweet Soul Music.*
[9] Booker T. Jones, *Time is Tight: My Life, Note By Note*
[10] ibid
[11] James L. Dickerson, "Coming Home: 21 Conversations About Memphis Music" (Scripps Howard).
[12] Jerry Wexler, *A Life in Rhythm & Blues.*
[13] Peter Guralnick, *Sweet Soul Music.*
[14] Peter Guralnick, S*weet Soul Music.*
[15] Roben Jones, Memphis Boys (University Press of Mississippi), 2010.
[16] Larry Raspberry interview.
[17] Famousinterview.com
[18] Barney Hoskyns, *Say It One More Time for the Broken Hearted (*Bloomsbury Publishing), 1998.
[19] Roben jones, Memphis Boys (University Press of Mississippi), 2010.
[20] Guralnick, Sweet Soul Music.
[21] Tony Fletcher, In the Midnight Hour: The Life & Soul of Wilson Pickett (Oxford University Press), 2017.
[22] Jerry Wexler, A Life in Rhythm & Blues.
[23] Peter Doggett, RPM Records, a division of Cherry Red Records, United Kingdom.
[24] Bob Mehr, "Chips Moman: The Missing Man of Memphis Music," The Commercial Appeal (July 13, 2008.
[25] James L. Dickerson, Memphis Going Down
[26] Nancy Randall, *Nine-O-One Network,*(October 1987).
[27] No byline, the Memphis Press-Scimitar, July 1, 1967.
[28] Kay Morgan, "A New Memphis Sound Amid the Pop Explosion," Memphis Press-Scimitar, (January 5, 1968).

[29] Robert Johnson, "Memphis Recording Studios are Turning Out Hits," *Memphis Press-Simitar* (April 8, 1967).
[30] Redkelly2.blog-spot.com.
[31] Wikipedia.com, creative commons attribution.
[32] "The Life and Times of Wilson Pickett," BBC 6 Music.
[33] James L. Dickerson, *Dixie's Dirty Secret*.
[34] Don Nix, *Memphis Man*.
[35] James L Dickerson, *Memphis Going Down*.
[36] Don Nix, *Memphis Man*.
[37] Booker T. Jones, *Time is Tight*.
[38] James L. Dickerson, *Dixie's Dirty Secret*.
[39] B.J. Thomas, *Home Where I Belong*.
[40] Warren Zanes, *Dusty in Memphis*.
[41] Jerry Wexler, *Rhythm and the Blues*.
[42] Roben Jones, *Memphis Boys*.
[43] Ibid.
[44] Karen Bartlett, *Dusty: An Intimate Portrait of a Musical Legend*.
[45] Jerry Wexler, *Rhythm and Soul*.
[46] Karen Bartlett, *Dusty in Memphis*.
[47] Dionne Warwick and David Freeman Wooley, *My Life As I See It*.
[48] Scotty Moore and James L. Dickerson, "That's Alright, Elvis."
[49] Liner notes, the two-record set of *The Memphis Record*.
[50] Scotty Moore and James L. Dickerson, "That's Alright, Elvis."
[51] Good Morning American, 1980 interview.
[52] Alan Grossman, Bill Truman, and Roy Oki Yamahaka, *Diamond: A Biography*.
[53] Roben Jones, *Memphis Boys*.
[54] Andrea Kon, *This is My Song: A Biography of Petula Clark*.
[55] Good Evening, "Petula Likes Memphis Sound," May 29, 1979, *Memphis Press-Simitar*.
[56] Billy Burnette, *Crazy Like Me*
[57] Bill Burk, "Memphis Music Forecasts," *Memphis Press-Simitar* (April 14, 1979)
[58] Robyn Flans, *Modern Drummer*.
[59] Billy Burnette, *Crazy Lie Me*.
[60] B.J. Thomas, *Home Where I Belong*.
[61] Ibid.
[62] Waylon Jennings, Lenny Kaye, *Waylon: An Autobiography*.
[63] EDD Hurt, "Chips Moman: The Cream Interview."
[64] Willie Nelson, *It's a Long Story*.
[65] Interview with Toni Wine Moman.
[66] Waylon Jennings, *Waylon: An Autobiography*.
[67] EDD Hurt, "Chips Moman: The Cream Interview," *Nashville Scene*.

[68] Jimmy McDonough, *Tammy Wynette: Tragic Country Queen.*
[69] Willie Nelson, *It's A Long Story.*
[70] Jessi Colter, with David Ritz, *An Outlaw and a Lady.*
[71] Ibid.
[72] Robert Hilburn, *Johnny Cash: The Life.*
[73] Jim Dickerson, *Coming Home.*
[74] Jim Dickerson, *Coming Home: 21 Conversations About Memphis Music, The Commercial Appeal.*
[75] Jim Dickerson, *Coming Home: 21 Conversations About Memphis Music, The Commercial Appeal.*
[76] Jim Dickerson, *Coming Home: 21 Conversations About Memphis Music, The Commercial Appeal.*
[77] Ibid.
[78] Elizabeth Kaye, *Rolling Stone*, 1985.
[79] James L. Dickerson, reprinted from Going back to Memphis, *Nine-O-One Network* magazine *The Commercial Appeal*, used with permission.
[80] Portions of the *Class of '55* section were previously published in *Nine-O-One* magazine and *The Commercial Appeal* with permission.
[81] James Dickerson, *The Commercial Appeal*, December 1985.
[82] James Dickerson, "Teacher Has A Proven Record," The Commercial Appeal, December 28, 1985.
[83] James Dickerson," Class of '55 goes out to play," *The Commercial Appeal.*
[84] Jim Dickerson, *The Commercial Appeal*, March 1986.
[85] James Dickerson, "Perkins & Friends, *Nine-O-One Network*, September 1986.
[86] Robert Hilburn, *Johnny Cash: The Life.*
[87] Ibid
[88] Ibid
[89] Ibid, Robert K. Oermann, "Man in Black Without a Label," Nashville *Tennessean*, July 16, 1986.
[90] Interview with Herbie O'Mell.
[91] James L. Dickerson, *Memphis Going Down.*
[92] Ibid
[93] Ibid
[94] Desert News, January 8, 1990.
[95] Michael Lollar, "Moman: Memphis firms let him down," *The Commercial Appeal,* December 10, 1990.
[96] Ibid.
[97] Waylon Jennings, with Lenny Kaye, *Waylon: An Autobiography.*
[98] Jessi Colter, with David Ritz, *An Outlaw and a Lady.*
[99] Michael Lollar, "Lyrical line from judge puts Moman back in jail," *The Commercial Appeal*, December 5, 1990.
[99] Sanford, Bruce W. *Synopsis of the Law of libel and the Right of Privacy,* Scripps-Howard, World Almanac Publications, 1981.

100 Revelations 12: 1.
101 Lincoln W. (Chips) Moman, Plaintiff, v. M.M. Corporation, d/b/a The Memphis Flyer, H. David Lyons, Kenneth Neill, and Gregg Cravens. Consent Order of Dismissal with Prejudice, The Circuit Court of Shelby County, The Honorable George H. Brown, Jr. Shelby Circuit No. 29502 T.D.lby
102 Lincoln W. (Chips) Moman, Appellant, Vs. M.M. Corporation, d/b/a The Memphis Flyer, H. David Lyons, Kenneth Neill, and Gregg Cravens, Appellees. In the Court of Appeals of Tennessee Western Section at Jackson. W. Frank Crawford, Presiding Judge, W.S.
103 Sanford, Bruce W. *Synopsis of the Law of libel and the Right of Privacy,* Scripps-Howard, World Almanac Publications, 1981.

About the Author

After a career as a journalist for three Pulitzer Prize winning dailies, *The Commercial Appeal* of Memphis, the *Clarion Ledger-Jackson Daily News*, and the *Delta Democrat-Times* of Greenville (MS), James L. Dickerson began a career as a full-time author.

His book *Colonel Tom Parker: The Curious Life of Elvis Presley's Eccentric Manager* was purchased by Warner Bros. for its upcoming Elvis movie starring Tom Hanks as Colonel Parker. His book *Mojo Triangle: Birthplace of Country, Blues, Jazz and Rock 'n' Roll* earned a first place award from the Independent Publishers Association, and two music-related books, *Goin' Back to Memphis* (since republished as *Memphis Going Down*) and *That's Alright, Elvis*, co-written with Elvis Presley's first guitarist, Scotty Moore, were finalists for the prestigious Gleason Award (formerly presented by Rolling Stone, BMI, and New York University). He co-wrote a second book with Scotty Moore titled *Scotty & Elvis.* He is the author of the first comprehensive book about women in music, *Women on Top: The Quiet Revolution That's Rocking the American Music Industry*, published in 1998 by Billboard Books.

Dickerson was the editor and publisher of *Nine-O-One Network*, at one time the third largest circulation music magazine in the United States, behind *Rolling Stone* and *Spin*. The magazine was the first magazine published in the South to obtain newsstand distribution in all 50 states. The magazine also had distribution in most European countries. In Russia it was read by underground radio announcers who worked to overthrow Communist Party domination.

Dickerson is the editor and publisher of Sartoris Literary Group, one of the most successful non-academic trade book publishers in the South. Sartoris has been licensed to publish the works of William Faulkner, Eudora Welty, Tennessee Williams, Richard Wright, Shelby Foote, and others.

As a freelance writer and book critic he has worked for the *Toronto Star*, *Baltimore Sun*, BookPage, *Good Housekeeping, Playboy, Penthouse, Omni*, the *Tennessean*, and others.

A longtime resident of Memphis and Nashville, Dickerson now lives in the Metro Jackson, Mississippi, area.